Crocheting

The FOR FUN & PROFIT™ SERIES

Craft Sewing For Fun & Profit

Crocheting For Fun & Profit

Decorative Painting For Fun & Profit

Holiday Decorations For Fun & Profit

Knitting For Fun & Profit

Quilting For Fun & Profit

Rubberstamping For Fun & Profit

Soapmaking For Fun & Profit

Woodworking For Fun & Profit

Crocheting

For Fun & Profit™

Darla Sims

PRIMA HOME
An Imprint of Prima Publishing
3000 Lava Ridge Court • Roseville, California 95661
(800) 632-8676 • www.primalifestyles.com

Library of Congress Cataloging-in-Publication Data

Sims, Darla.
   Crocheting for fun & profit /Darla Sims.
      p.   cm.
   Includes index.
      ISBN 0-7615-2161-5
   1. Crocheting. 2. Handicraft—Marketing. 3. Selling—Handicraft. I. Title: Crocheting for fun and profit. II. Title.

TT820.S5274 2000   00-35649
746.43'4'0688—dc21   CIP
00 01 02 03 04 II 10 9 8 7 6 5 4 3 2 1
Printed in the United States of America

How to Order

Single copies may be ordered from Prima Publishing, 3000 Lava Ridge Court, Roseville, CA 95661; telephone (800) 632-8676 ext. 4444. Quantity discounts are also available. On your letterhead, include information concerning the intended use of the books and the number of books you wish to purchase.

Visit us online at www.primalifestyles.com

Contents

Introduction

IF YOU DON'T KNOW HOW to crochet, this book is for you. Part I gives you expert advice on the tools and materials that will bring you the best results. I'll get you started with the simple basic chain that is the foundation of all crochet stitches. Before long you'll be ready to tackle any of the four crochet designs I have created for this book. Though the four projects may appear difficult, each one is surprisingly easy to make. Have you peeked at the projects in this book yet? Bet you're thinking that you could *never* make a sweater for your first project. Believe it or not, making that sweater is no different from making your practice swatch, because all the pieces (front, back, and sleeves) are simple rectangles and require no shaping.

If you are already a crocheter, maybe you dream about crocheting to your heart's content in some faraway and perfect world. Perhaps in the wildest of those dreams, you imagine actually getting paid for doing what you love best. This book shows you how to turn those dreams into reality. My career in crochet began with dreams, too—dreams that became my reality. If you want to learn how to profit from crochet, you'll find tons of ideas in Part II of this book.

How I Turned Crochet into a Career

You know the old saying, "The devil made me do it." Well, the truth is, the devil didn't really make me do it—my kids made me do it. They literally forced me into it!

By the time my three girls were in their teens, I was hooked not only on crochet—I was hooked on designing sweaters. I loved every aspect of design, from getting ideas to working out each stitch and every detail. My daughters' trunks and closets overflowed with sweaters. Those poor girls had sweaters bursting from every corner of their rooms, and after a few years they were pleading for relief.

I realized I had two choices: quit crocheting (though I couldn't imagine doing such a thing), or channel my enthusiasm and talent in another direction. I decided to find a way to make money with my sweaters. It didn't take long to figure out how to profit from crochet! That was more than twenty years ago and I'm still earning money with crochet today.

Crocheting, like knitting, is labor intensive. It takes time and effort to produce crochet products, whether it's a baby afghan, curtains for the kitchen, an edging for a special dress, or a cardigan sweater. I knew others who were making money selling their craft projects at bazaars, trunk shows, holiday open houses, and by traveling the craft-show circuits. But when I put pencil to paper, I realized I couldn't expect to make the same kind of profit as my crafter friends, because of the time it took to crochet my sweaters, hats, and scarves.

One day, while leafing through a magazine that featured patterns for sweaters, I noticed (along the side of each photo in very tiny print) the credits given for each designer. That was all I needed to be off and running in what turned out to be the right direction. Magazines might want my sweater designs, I told myself, and if magazines needed sweater designers, yarn companies probably needed them too. I simply wrote and sent out a dozen query letters, and within a couple of months I had my first check in hand and the thrill of seeing the fruits of my effort—my first sweater design published in *Woman's World* magazine.

Today I'm still designing sweaters for national magazines, publishers, and yarn companies. I also publish my own line of crochet and knit patterns, Darla's Designs, which are sold in yarn shops around the country.

Making money from your love of crochet really isn't that difficult and there are lots of ways to do it. I think you'll be surprised at some of the creative ways other crocheters featured in this book make money through their love of crochet. This book reveals how they do it and provides tips on how you can, too.

History of Crochet

Did you ever wonder where and when this "hooking" thing began? It is generally accepted that crochet began far back in history. A great many sources state that crochet can be traced back to the 1500s in Italy, where it was known as "nun's lace" or "nun's work" and was used to create lace vestments and other religious textiles. Other experts credit nuns in France with using the first hooks for lace making. Some say that crocheting originated in Arabia; others insist that the earliest evidence of crocheting came from South America where a primitive tribe is said to have used crocheted adornments in rites of puberty. Yet there are those who believe the roots of crochet began in China.

Some believe that *tambouring,* an ancient form of embroidery, is the true predecessor to crochet. Tambour is thought to have developed into what the French called "crochet in the air," a technique in which the background fabric for embroidery was discarded and stitches were worked on their own. Whoever figured that one out must have had a most creative and inventive mind.

Archaeological evidence has established that knitting, weaving, and other handicrafts date back to before the nineteenth century. However, despite myths and legends to the contrary, there is little firm evidence of crochet prior to the 1800s.

The earliest published crochet patterns appeared in European magazines and books in the early 1800s. Most patterns were for lace work: collars, cuffs, insertions, and hats for both women and children. However, color work was also included for purses, men's slippers, and caps. If you don't appreciate today's clear, concise pattern instructions, be thankful you don't have to wade through those early patterns, because they were often vague and unclear.

The work in these early publications was far more complicated than today's crochet and utilized a variety of techniques, combining knitting and embroidery with crochet. Recommended materials ranged from wool yarns of varying thicknesses to silk and linen threads, as well as hemp, mohair, chenille, novelty mixtures, metal threads, and string. Initially, the needlecraft magazines carried no advertisements, but it didn't take long for thread and yarn manufacturers to realize they could promote their goods by publishing their own magazines.

Over the years, much of the art of crochet has been handed down from friend to friend and generation to generation without written patterns. Small samplings of various patterns, stitches, edgings, and motifs were copied and assembled in a variety of ways. Sometimes the samples were sewn onto cardboard or paper; others were sewn or crocheted in long bands and became known as *samplers*.

Fortunately the instructions published today are much easier to follow than those of the past. For example, early instructions imply that tension and gauge were adjusted by working stitches either tighter or looser, indicating that the crocheter had to work with only one size hook. Today, crochet stitches remain much the same as they were in those earlier publications, but techniques and execution have changed so the stitches are easier to master.

Crochet Today

Crochet is currently undergoing a huge resurgence, thanks to the fashion industry. Movie stars, supermodels, and celebrities have eagerly donned crocheted garments, handbags, hats, stoles, and other adornments, creating fashion statements that are quickly copied by those who are handy with the crochet hook.

In many instances, the art of crochet seems to have skipped a generation when an increasing number of women began to work full-time in the '60s. Industry experts know that 29% of all women 55 and older crochet, but the real news is that the interest among today's younger women, and teenagers in particular, is at an all-time high.

How to Use This Book

Crochet is a fairly easy needle art to learn. In fact, children often learn how to "finger crochet" in pre-school or kindergarten. There are only a few basic stitches to master; most crochet techniques are simple and you only need some yarn and one tool, a hook, to crochet. It doesn't get much easier than that! If you aren't already an enthusiast, you'll be happy to know that crocheting takes approximately a third less time than knitting to produce the same amount of fabric.

Whether you want to learn how to crochet for pleasure, to improve your basic skills, or to discover new and exciting ways to make your dreams come true, this book is the place to begin your new and exciting adventures into the world of crochet.

You'll not only learn how to crochet, you'll also learn how to make money doing what you enjoy.

Basic Tools for Crocheting

1 Tapestry or yarn needle
2 Pins
3 Pincushion
4 Stitch checker
5 Tape measure
6 Crochet hooks
  (various sizes)
7 Scissors
8 Saftey pins
9 Blocking pins

Part One

For Fun

The Joy
of Crocheting

▼▼▼

THERE ARE SO MANY fun things to share with you about crochet, I hardly know where to begin! Considering that an estimated
34 million people in the United States crochet, many others clearly
agree with me about the enjoyment of this needle art.

Crochet traditionally was considered to be an art form, but in
more recent times it is more likely to be referred to as a craft. Crochet is a technique in which a hooked needle is used to draw thread
or yarn through loops to create fabric. Over the last century crochet
techniques, terminology, and patterns have changed dramatically,
but the basic stitches remain the same.

While it is believed that crochet began much earlier, the oldest
written record about crochet only dates back to the sixteenth century. Many legends abound about the beginnings of this needle art.
One account reports that the followers of Jesus crocheted socks and
other clothing, for example.

In the cold northern regions of Europe, practical articles of
clothing such as socks and mittens were crocheted with homespun yarns and homemade tools. A technique known as "shep-
herd's knitting" (crochet) was practiced by shepherds in Scotland
and, according to oral traditions, began thousands of years ago.

Specimens of threadwork that were excavated from an Egyptian tomb dated between A.D. 900 and 1100 reveal stitches remarkably similar to the crochet of today. Those artifacts are now on display at the Benaki National Museum in Athens. Similar items are housed in the National Museum in Berlin. Whether crochet originated first in China, Arabia, South America, France or other parts of the world still remains a mystery.

Crochet goes fast, enabling you to whip up wonderful creations for yourself or to give as gifts in a remarkably short time. The widely varied, richly textured and colored creations you can produce with crochet range from lacy curtains to cuddly afghans. It's a great fabric-making procedure for home décor as well as for garments, personal accessories, and novelty items, such as stuffed toys. The possibilities are endless, limited only by your imagination.

Just the process of mastering new stitches and patterns seems to get your creative juices flowing. Before you know it, you're envisioning all kinds of ways to use those stitches with different yarns or threads to make other splendid creations. While following a crochet pattern for a sweet, little baby sweater, for example, you might imagine the same stitch in gold metallic thread in a beautiful set of Christmas stockings hanging on your mantel. That's how it works! A new stitch, yarn, pattern, or project always seems to spark other ideas and new ways of doing things.

Though many crocheters claim not to have a creative bone in their bodies, I truly believe a bit of the innovative designer lives in everyone. Did you make the last craft project you saw in a magazine *exactly* the same as the original? Did you add your own special touch or change colors? Have you ever added silk flowers or dramatic tassels to a curtain tie-back? Maybe you've used leftover fabric to make matching lampshades or pillows for your family room. Being creative, being a designer, simply means seeing the possibilities and finding new ways to apply your craft. It's fun and satisfying to create unique garments to wear or items to decorate your home.

You will undoubtedly receive compliments from others about crocheting something with your own hands, which adds to your sense of satisfaction and accomplishment. Such compliments let you know that you and your work are appreciated, and they inspire you to crochet more or to do an even better job next time. Receiving compliments also, quite simply, makes you feel good inside. I think of it as the snowball effect. Once you get started, the desire to crochet—and the fun and fulfillment it brings—just keeps growing and growing. If it didn't, I wouldn't still be hooked on it after all these years!

Not only is crocheting fun, it is also relaxing—to many, therapeutically so. There is something almost magical about the rhythmic feeling of the yarn or thread passing through your fingers. When I crochet, the stresses of the day simply fall aside. I find the movement of my hands and the flow of the yarn to be both soothing and exciting at the same time. How can I explain it to you if you have yet to experience it!

While I am designing and crocheting a sweater for someone else, I'm thinking of that person. So, it is true what they say about handmade gifts: love *does* go into every stitch! The lucky recipients of handmade items feel the crafter's love every time they look at, wear, or use the treasured gifts—whether a lovely afghan for a newlywed couple or a darling sweater set for a precious new baby.

Because most crochet projects are portable, you can take your work with you. You can crochet on a plane, a train, or at the beach; when riding in the car or commuting on the bus; or while watching television or sitting on the sidelines at a soccer game. You can crochet just about anywhere!

Hooked on Hooking

The ability and affinity for needlework runs in my family. My maternal grandmother and, in turn, my mother were fabulous seamstresses. They both did meticulous work for other women in their communities who didn't sew. I'll always remember my mother bent over late at night, patiently sewing beautiful beadwork for someone's evening gown or hemming a voluminous taffeta skirt.

Neither was my paternal grandmother known to have idle hands. At the end of a day's work, she could always be found sitting in her favorite rocking chair, making beautiful crocheted lace, which more often than not ended up as a gorgeous white lace tablecloth gracing someone's dining table. She made exquisite pastel bedspreads, antimacassars, dresser scarves, and doilies. Like my grandmothers, my mother kept her hands busy with needlework in the evenings. She loved to needlepoint, and one year spent many long nights working on seats for eight mahogany dining room chairs, each featuring a different, beautifully appointed fruit: pears, plums, apples, and the like.

I have fond childhood memories of driving with my mother and sister over the mountains from eastern Washington to Seattle in search of needlepoint canvases and supplies. All the colors and textures of yarns on display in the shops completely enraptured my sister and me. I recall tentatively reaching out to touch the various yarns and trying to inhale the colors, thinking that if I breathed deeply enough, they would stay with me forever. And they have.

Although Mother also knit, my memories of her crocheting stand out the most. In particular, I recall that she liked crocheting ripple afghans as gifts for family and friends. When the grandchildren arrived, she crocheted a special afghan for each one, in favorite colors and styles that complemented the décor of each child's room.

It seems only natural, then, that I picked up needles and hook. Needlework is, after all, part of my heritage, and I began at an early age. At age four I was cutting out pieces of fabric and hand sewing dresses for my dolls. I must have been five when my mother taught me to knit and crochet. I don't remember which I learned to do first, but I do recall the little gold blanket I made for my favorite doll. I didn't become really enamored of the needle arts, however, until I was expecting my first baby. Once I saw the beautiful little hats, sweaters, booties, and blankets I could make all by myself, I was hooked on hooking!

Throughout my three daughters' childhoods, I designed and sewed clothes for them. But the really special outfits were the ones I crocheted for holiday occasions like Easter, Thanksgiving, and Christmas. For instance, I remember crocheting two-piece Easter dresses for each of my girls one spring, alike, but in three different pastel colors. I so enjoyed making them that I also crocheted and gave dresses to their friends. Years after the girls had grown, the mother of one of those little girls told me how much she treasured the pale blue dress I'd given her daughter. The mother had carefully wrapped it in tissue paper and tucked it away for safekeeping. Realizing that someone cherished my handiwork brought tears to my eyes. Knowing that my crocheting has created memories, as well as appreciated items, brings me great joy.

Going Pro

Faced with choosing between giving up my passion of crochet or going pro, in the late 1970s I made the plunge into professional design. It was thrilling to be doing what I loved most, and receiving paychecks for my efforts was especially satisfying. But before long, strange things began to happen.

LESTER'S STORY

If there is anyone who enjoys crocheting as much as I do, it is Lester Vaughn. An active member of our local crochet guild, Lester, at age 79, is constantly involved in passing along the joys of crocheting to others and is a constant source of inspiration to me. This amazing, tiny bit of a woman, all five feet and 90 pounds of her, maintains a full schedule, driving all over the greater Seattle area to teach and share her love of crochet with both adults and children.

Her blue eyes sparkle with pride when she gets out the photo albums filled with pictures of beaming schoolchildren hooking away. The time she spends teaching crochet to these children is donated, but well invested, according to Lester. The children's enthusiasm, reflected by the smiles on their faces, is contagious!

To the kids, taking crocheting lessons with Lester means engaging in something new, exciting, and fun. They don't realize that this diminutive dynamo is teaching them many other skills too, such as eye-hand coordi-

Many of my neighbors started referring to me as "the lady who crochets." The implication of this comment, as I read it, was that they thought I didn't really work and just idled away my time. I felt somewhat hurt that they didn't recognize me as a successful businesswoman and that they didn't take my work seriously.

Then one day I heard an author interviewed on the radio. (Unfortunately, I don't remember his name, but I do recall he was a well-known, bestselling author.) He related how his mother never really understood what he did for a living; she told her friends and neighbors that he "typed" for a living. That author's anecdote put

nation, manual dexterity, and color theory. They don't realize they're also absorbing a wealth of information about textiles, the various kinds and types of yarn and threads, not to mention valuable problem-solving skills. Under Lester's gentle tutelage, they learn that mistakes don't mean the end of the world, that they do get second chances, and that they can usually remedy a mistake or start over again. They learn to see a pro-

ject through to the end and to experience the thrill and satisfaction of completing what they started out to do. Best of all, the children learn to extend a helping hand to those sitting next to them when Lester is busy with another student.

I wish for you, too, a teacher like Lester!

things into a new perspective for me! What I do is different from what most other people do, and I can't expect others to understand.

After that, what friends or neighbors thought of my work no longer annoyed or distressed me. Besides, at that time, I knew of no other person who was as passionate about what she did for a living or who gained as much satisfaction from her work as I did. On top of that, I was lucky enough to get paid for having fun! I decided I truly had the best job in the world.

Well, one other little thing bothered me. After several of my designs had been published, the phone calls began. Phone calls poured in from family and friends who—fearing I would soon

A Cache of Crocheted Creations

Once you have mastered the basic crochet stitches, what can you make with crochet? Just about anything you can imagine. Here are just a few ideas:

- Afghans
- Appliance covers
- Baby buntings
- Baby layettes
- Baby rompers
- Baskets
- Bathroom sets
- Bedspreads
- Bibs
- Book covers
- Bowls
- Chair pads
- Christmas ornaments
- Christmas stockings
- Christmas tree skirts
- Coasters
- Coats
- Cover-ups
- Dishcloths
- Dog and cat sweaters
- Doilies
- Doll clothes
- Dolls
- Edgings
- Evening wear
- Flowers
- Hair scrunchies (ties)

run out of design ideas—told me to "hurry quick and turn on the television" to see the sweater a movie star was wearing. They'd suggest I look at the sweaters at such and such department store to get design ideas. They mailed magazine clippings, drew sketches, and passed along their ideas for what they were sure was exactly what editors were looking for, when they didn't have a clue what editors were seeking. But I didn't tell them that.

For some reason, they didn't realize the depth of my creative well. I kept trying to reassure them that generating design ideas was the easy part for me. Even after twenty years, the ideas still come freely. I never run out of ideas, and I'll never live long enough to execute everything I see in my mind's eye. So, I didn't turn on the television, run to the department store, or implement any ideas of

- Hats
- Headwarmers
- Insertions
- Jackets
- Jewelry
- Mantel scarves
- Mittens
- Pants
- Pet beds

- Pillows
- Placemats
- Purses
- Rugs
- Scarves
- Shorts
- Skirts
- Slippers
- Socks

- Stoles
- Sweaters
- Swimsuits
- T-Shirts
- Table runners
- Tablecloths
- Tea cozies
- Toys
- Vases

And this is just a beginning list. I'm sure you can think of many more items to add.

others. Instead, I learned to listen and trust that which came from deep within myself.

Oh, the Things You'll Crochet

Once you master any basic crochet stitch, which usually takes only a few minutes, you can begin to make a variety of wonderful things for yourself, your home, your family, and your friends.

When I teach beginning crocheting classes, I always design a garment for the first project. Every teacher has his or her own approach for teaching beginning classes and chooses a first project accordingly. I prefer that my students make a sweater, hat, or purse, rather than just a swatch, sampler, or dishcloth. As always, there is a method to my madness. My intention is to get students excited about crocheting. I want their enthusiasm to extend beyond their first projects, so they'll want to continue to crochet after the classes end.

In my experience, when beginning crocheters receive compliments about a crocheted item they are wearing, they are thrilled to know that others have noticed and appreciate their handiwork. For the sake of argument, however, let's say I start them off doing dishcloths instead. Dishcloths are quick and easy to make, and many people like to crochet them, because they are small and take little time. But how many times have you gone into a friend's home and raved over her dishcloths? It just doesn't happen.

When the beginner wears a pretty sweater and matching hat or carries a stunning handbag, she's likely to receive compliments: "You made that yourself? It's wonderful!" "I'm such a klutz, I could never make anything so beautiful." "How long did it take you to do that?"

When someone receives such accolades for her creations, several things generally happen:

The crocheter feels good about herself and her work.
She shares her love of crochet with her friends.
She explains how much fun it is to do, that crocheting isn't
    really difficult at all, and that they, too, can quickly learn
    the basic stitches.
Maybe she takes the time to show her friends how easy it is.

When I first tell students they are going to make a basic pullover sweater, they think they can't possibly take on such a task.

"Oh, my! That looks much too difficult," they say. "I couldn't do that all by myself."

But when I show them that the basic components of the sweater are simple rectangles, they begin to relax. By the time they've worked a third of the back, their excitement level has escalated, because they realize that they are actually making a sweater! They can see the sweater growing before their eyes, and they can't wait to finish the back and start on the front.

Inevitably, as students crochet the simple, basic short-sleeve pullover, they think of different skirts and pants that will go with it. They imagine various places they will wear their first sweaters. By the time they start working on the sleeves, they are full of confidence and planning to make a second sweater for someone else.

I'm always thrilled when students reach this stage in making a first sweater. They talk eagerly among themselves, saying things like: "I think I'll do my next one in stripes for a different look." "My sister's birthday is coming up—I'm going to make this same sweater for her in lavender, her favorite color." "My teenage daughter wants one in red for the homecoming game."

Remember what I said about being a designer? It's all about seeing possibilities. It doesn't take long before my students see all kinds of possibilities, and they can't wait to finish the first sweater and go on to another. They're enjoying themselves and feeling good about their efforts, and I'm happy knowing they're likely to continue to crochet, maybe for the rest of their lives.

Now you know why the first crochet project in this book is a pullover sweater. I want you to have fun, to feel excited about your creation, and to get hooked on crocheting!

chapter 2

Getting Started

▼▼▼

ACCORDING TO INDEPENDENT STUDIES conducted for the Hobby Industry Association (HIA), crocheting is the second most popular hobby/craft today, with only embroidery ranking higher in popularity. Many people crochet and for many different reasons. It is fun, relaxing, resourceful, and enjoyable. You can make wonderful things for yourself and others, and you can create lovely things for your home. Once you've mastered the basics, you can customize the colors, textures, and often the patterns to create one-of-a-kind items. Some of us even make money with crochet.

It doesn't take much to get started; all you really need is a crochet hook and some yarn.

Crochet Hooks

Let's talk first about crochet hooks. Hooks are made of steel, plastic, aluminum, and wood. You may want to experiment with several different types to decide which you like best. Wood tends to grip, or to hang onto stitches, which makes working with slippery yarns easier. Metal and plastic hooks allow stitches to slide more smoothly than wood. Because metal hooks can put a strain on hands, some manufacturers enclose the metal shaft with a padded handle.

Aluminum, plastic, and wood are the most commonly used hooks. They are used primarily with the more popular weights of yarn, such as sport weight and worsted weight. Steel hooks are most often used with lightweight yarns and threads to create finer and lacier work.

The size of a crochet hook always refers to the diameter of the hook. Sizes are designated by number, letter, and metric measurement; however, in the United States all hooks are commonly referred to by number (steel hooks) or by letter (hooks made of materials other than steel). In Europe, hooks are referred to by metric diameters.

Most manufacturers make hooks from size 16, the smallest, to size K. But, a few manufacturers make crochet hooks as large as size S. You'll find that crochet hook sizes are identified by a letter or number that is usually imprinted on the hook. Crochet hooks made of steel are an individualized category of hooks ranging in size from 16, the smallest, to 00, the largest. This size range is *only* made in steel. The smaller the number on the hook, the larger the diameter of the hook. Because a size 16 is so small and is seldom used, many yarn shops do not carry this particular size. Generally, steel hooks are used for working with threads instead of yarn.

Other crochet hooks are made of a wide variety of materials: plastic, aluminum, rosewood, other woods, and some are treated with various coatings that reduce wear and tear. These crochet hooks are generally used for yarn and are sized on a reverse scale

▼▼▼▼▼▼▼▼▼▼▼▼▼▼▼▼▼▼▼▼▼▼▼▼▼▼

Did you know???

The numbers on crochet hooks correspond to the same metric sizes used for knitting needles. This makes it easy for you to know what size crochet hook to use when, for example, you want to add a crocheted edging to a knitted sweater.

▲▲▲▲▲▲▲▲▲▲▲▲▲▲▲▲▲▲▲▲▲▲▲▲▲▲

from the steel hooks, with size A being the smallest size, and size S being the largest.

When looking at the materials list for a crochet project worked with yarn, you'll notice that the size of hook required is designated by a letter. In other countries, both crochet hooks and knitting needles are designated only by metric sizing and do not include either a letter or a number. Thus a size 4.50 millimeter knitting needle and 4.50 millimeter crochet hook have the same diameter. In the United States, knitting needles are sized by number only, while crochet hooks are referred to by letter when they appear in the materials list of a pattern. However, crochet hooks also have metric sizes (as shown in the chart below) so knitters know which size hook to use to add crocheted edgings and trims to knitting projects.

Common Crochet Hook Sizes

U.S.	Metric
14 steel	.60 mm
12 steel	.75 mm
10 steel	1.00 mm
6 steel	1.50 mm
5 steel	1.75 mm
B/1	2.00 mm
C/2	2.50 mm
D/3	3.00 mm
E/4	3.50 mm
F/5	4.00 mm
G/6	4.50 mm
H/8	5.00 mm
I/9	5.50 mm
J/10	6.00 or 6.50 mm depending on manufacturer
K/10½	7.00 mm

Regular crochet hooks range in length from 4¾ inches to 6¾ inches. There are also Tunisian, or Afghan, hooks. Tunisian/Afghan hooks are extra long and look much like knitting needles with a hook on one end. They are used for Tunisian/Afghan crochet, a technique in which, as stitches are formed, loops remain on the hook to the end of a row, then the loops are worked off on the next row. With this type of crochet, the work is never turned, and the right side always faces you as you crochet. Tunisian/Afghan crocheting is used to make many items, but is mainly used to create long strips that are later connected to make afghans.

In some areas, you can still find *cro* hooks. A cro hook is long, like the Tunisian/Afghan hook, but it has a hook on both ends. The technique of crocheting with a cro hook is sometimes called "cro-knitting," or "cro-hooking" because the fabric produced looks knitted. Cro-knitting is worked in much the same way as Tunisian/Afghan crochet, but is turned every second row and is most often used for color work. The instruction terminology for both Tunisian/Afghan crochet and cro-hooking differs from that of other crochet. For example, a "row" in cro-hooking actually consists of two rows that are called steps.

Yarns

One of the pleasures of crocheting comes from working with beautiful yarn colors and textures. All crochet patterns specify the particular yarns or threads to use in creating an item, and most list yarns by the manufacturer's name.

Yarn labels provide various information that you need to know, such as the yarn type, fiber content, yardage, care instructions, and recommended gauge. Time and again, while I've been in the aisles checking out new yarns, I've overheard one shopper tell another, "There really is no difference in yarn. Just buy what's on sale." I never say anything then, but now, I am here to tell you that there *are* differences in yarn, big differences! Let me explain . . .

Yarn Weights

There are five basic types of yarn, which are differentiated by weight or thickness. These five types of yarn, listed from the lightest weight to the heaviest with the suggested crochet hook sizes, are:

Type of Yarn and Suggested Hook Size

Baby, fingering, sock	E/4 (3.50 mm)—F/5 (4.00 mm)
Sport	G/6 (4.50 mm)
DK	G/6 (4.50 mm)
Worsted	H/8 (5.00 mm)—I/9 (5.50 mm)
Chunky, bulky	J/10 (6.00 mm)—K/10½ (7.00 mm)

■ Baby, Fingering, and Sock Weight: Used for lace work, light weight garments and other crochet projects. Most sock yarns are wool, reinforced with nylon to increase durability.

■ Sport Weight: Used for light-weight garments and heavier socks.

■ DK Weight: Contrary to popular belief, this commonly misunderstood yarn is not double stranded; rather, this yarn type actually falls in between sport and worsted weights. DK yarn is imported from Europe and is often worked using the same size hooks as those used for sport-weight yarn.

■ Worsted Weight: By far the most popular type of yarn. It is used to crochet everything from afghans to baby clothes, sweaters, hats, mittens, and even home decor items.

■ Chunky, Bulky: Much larger in diameter than other yarns. These yarns are mainly used for coats, jackets, rugs, and hats.

The weight of the yarn refers to the thickness to which the fiber is spun. In turn, the thickness of a yarn determines the gauge, or number of stitches and rows that can be worked per inch. Crocheting generally requires fewer stitches and rows per inch than does knitting—which consequently means you can produce the fabric faster. I've found that it takes approximately a third less time to crochet a sweater or afghan than it does to knit a similar project.

Yarn Categories

Yarns fall into two categories:

1. Craft Yarns
2. Fashion Yarns

Craft Yarns

Craft yarns are the yarns you find in craft and hobby stores. They are used for craft projects such as hats, bags, garments, afghans, and many other projects ranging from dolls and toys to home decor items as well. While you can find a few cotton yarns in these stores (mostly used for dishcloths), most craft yarns are made of synthetic (man-made) fibers.

Solutia, Inc. is the largest producer of acrylic fibers in the United States. Solutia's Acrilan fiber is often used for hand-knit and crocheted designs due to its softness and excellent colorfastness. The popular Bounce-Back fibers made by Solutia require no special care and provide unique benefits because they "bounce" back to their original shape when machine washed and dried. In fact, they must be machine dried to retain their original shape. Acrylic yarns expand considerably when wet and will maintain the exaggerated size if left to air dry. Man-made yarns tend to be durable and are often the choice of people who are allergic to wool or other natural fibers. Craft yarns are the least expensive yarns.

Fashion Yarns

Fashion yarns are often comprised of various fibers, but the highest fiber content is usually a natural fiber, such as wool, silk, alpaca, mohair, angora, cotton, linen, or cashmere. Some fashion yarns are blends of various synthetic and natural fibers. Many rayons, chenilles, and cotton blends are also considered fashion yarns.

> ▼▼▼▼▼▼▼▼▼▼▼▼▼▼▼▼▼▼▼▼▼▼▼▼
> ### Did you know???
> Eight strands of worsted-weight yarn equal a 2½-inch strip of fabric. Perfect for making a thick rug!
> ▲▲▲▲▲▲▲▲▲▲▲▲▲▲▲▲▲▲▲▲▲▲▲▲

Natural fibers tend to be softer and more durable than synthetic fibers; however, they are also more expensive and require more care. Fashion yarns are more expensive than craft yarns for a variety of reasons. Some of these higher-end yarns are imported from Europe. You find fashion yarns in yarn shops, catalogs, and on the Internet, but never in craft and hobby stores.

Fashion yarns come in a wide variety of textures and finishes: smooth, brushed, crinkled, looped, wrapped, bumpy, matte, shiny, slubbed, stringy, or hairy. Sometimes, different yarns are twisted together to form *designer* yarns, which are also called *novelty* yarns.

Fashion or Function?

When it comes to choosing yarns, both craft and fashion yarns have their pros and cons.

Many crocheters prefer to start off working with craft yarns, because they are less expensive, colorfast, easy to care for, and quite durable. For example, mothers tend to like to use craft yarns for children's garments, knowing their kids can play freely in them and they'll be able to toss grass-stained or muddied sweaters into the washer and dryer. On the other hand, craft yarns lack the rich feel and appearance of fashion yarns. Fashion yarns are more luxurious and drape better for garments.

Buying yarn is like buying anything else: You get what you pay for. Suppose you want to make an afghan, and your pattern calls for worsted-weight yarn. Before you actually buy all the yarn you need, first buy one skein of craft yarn and one skein of fashion yarn. Then work up a 4 × 4-inch swatch with each yarn and compare the two. The first thing you're likely to notice is that the fashion-yarn swatch looks and feels nicer than the craft-yarn swatch. You'll probably find that, depending on your tension and gauge, craft yarns are stiffer and less plush than the fashion yarns. The craft yarns are also easier to maintain and less expensive than their fashion counterparts.

Before you decide which kind of yarn to use for your project, take a good look at your swatch samples and ask yourself such questions as:

"Do I want the new afghan to feel soft?"
"Can I expect a lot of spills to happen?"
"How long do I expect to keep the same color scheme?"
"Is the yarn nice enough to use for a gift for someone I really care about?"

The answers to your questions and your swatch comparisons allow you to make an informed decision about which yarn best meets your needs.

Read the Label!

Crochet projects represent an investment of your time and money, so it pays to be an informed consumer. Always check all yarn labels for dye lot numbers. Although yarn is dyed in huge quantities and the same dyes are used for each dye bath, color shades can vary slightly from batch to batch, especially with natural fibers.

If possible, buy enough yarn of the same dye lot to complete your project. It's better to buy too much than too little. Most stores will accept full skeins of unused yarn that is returned within a reasonable amount of time, and will refund your money or allow you to exchange the unused yarn for other yarn. Make sure to ask about the store's return policy before you make your purchase and to keep your receipt.

What if you can't find enough skeins of the same dye lot for your project? Take two or more skeins, each from different dye lots, to the nearest window and examine them carefully in the natural light to assess how closely they match. Lighting in many stores distorts colors and can fool the eye. If you must buy from different dye lots, buy from no more than two. When working up your project, alternate skeins from each lot to make shade differences less noticeable.

Yarn labels also provide the recommended gauge and suggested sizes of hooks or needles to attain gauge. Please understand: These are recommendations only; they are not written in stone. When new yarns are introduced, they go immediately to designers, who work up swatches to determine the gauge each particular designer prefers. Give yourself permission to experiment with several different size hooks when working up a swatch to determine which gauge and hook produces fabric with the look and feel that most appeal to you.

Finally, check the label for care information. Most labels include written instructions or symbols indicating how to wash, dry, and block the yarn. Fashion-yarn labels typically feature symbols, which are straightforward and easy to understand.

Substituting Yarn

To avoid disappointment in the outcome and appearance of a crochet project, buy the recommended yarn as noted in your pattern. If your pattern calls for a pricey bouclé fashion yarn and you buy a flat, inexpensive yarn, the end result will not be the same.

Yarn-Care Symbols

⊔	Machine Wash	⊠	Do Not Wring (Dry Flat)
⊔	Hand Wash	🔲	Iron
○	Dry Clean	🔲	Iron Medium Heat
⊠	Do Not Bleach	🔲	Iron Low Heat
⊔	Delicate/Gentle Cycle	⊠	Do Not Iron

If you do decide to substitute yarns, select another yarn that is as close as possible to the recommended yarn in appearance, texture, weight, and feel. It's a good idea to buy one skein first and crochet a swatch to see how closely it matches the gauge and appearance of the recommended yarn. Using a shiny, flat rayon yarn for a pattern that calls for a fluffy mohair produces something entirely different from the original design. If the pattern calls for mohair yarn, your best bet is to choose a similar yarn, such as a brushed acrylic, to achieve the look you want.

What if your pattern calls for worsted-weight yarn, and all you have on hand is sport or DK weight? You'll find it extremely difficult to attain the required gauge if your pattern calls for worsted weight and you try to substitute a lighter weight of yarn. However, if you hold two strands of sport or DK weight together, you'll more easily obtain the correct gauge, because the two strands are equivalent to worsted weight. If you decide to *double-strand,* remember that you will need twice as much yardage.

Selecting the right type of yarn for a project can mean the difference between success and failure. Is your yarn choice suitable for the item and the intended use? For example, most wool yarns require hand washing, and they may irritate a baby's delicate skin. Is your yarn choice right for your climate? If you live in Canada or Alaska, you can wear a chunky wool sweater almost year around; however, if you live in Hawaii, you're unlikely to have many, if any, occasions to wear such a heavy garment.

Don't forget to also take the intended stitch pattern into consideration. Fancy and complicated stitches show best when worked with flat yarns of sport, DK, or worsted weight, or with flat threads. If you choose a textured yarn, such as mohair, bouclé, angora, or one with lots of slubs, a fancy stitch gets lost. When using textured yarns, it is better to stick to a plain stitch. Besides, experienced crocheters and designers know that you can create visual confusion when the yarn texture and the stitch pattern compete with one another.

Finally, when substituting yarn, make sure to match the yardage and not the weight of different yarns. For instance, wool

Converting Ounces to Grams

Use the formula: 100 grams = 3.5 ounces.

Yarn Conversion Chart

Ounces to Grams		Grams to Ounces	
1	28.4	25	$7/8$
2	56.7	40	$1 2/3$
3	85.0	50	$1 3/4$
4	113.4	100	$3 1/2$

yarn is much heavier than angora; thus, wool has less yardage per gram, or ounce, than angora.

What Makes a Good Yarn?

What makes a good yarn? That depends, to some extent, on whom you ask—and the answers are apt to be as varied as the yarns that are available. Ask another crocheter or any yarn shop owner, yarn rep, or yarn distributor, and you're likely to discover that each person offers a different opinion about which yarns are best and why.

The truth is, the "best" yarn is the yarn that suits a specific project—and your needs. A fine cotton thread is obviously a poor choice for crocheting an Aran sweater, but is suitable for a doily or a lace tablecloth. The best yarn is also determined by your own likes and dislikes. If you hate the feel of wearing acrylics, you'll probably prefer natural fibers for wearables. Most people agree that cashmere, a luxurious yarn, feels wonderful to both touch and wear. However, you might decide it is too expensive for your budget or that your lifestyle is too hectic to bother with yarns that require hand washing.

Many years ago I crocheted bikinis for my daughters. Those gaily colored little swimsuits were absolutely adorable—that is, until they hit the water, and then, they grew and grew! My poor little girls couldn't keep their swimsuits from falling off as they got in and out of the pool. I hadn't taken into consideration that acrylic yarn expands when wet—and so acrylic yarn is not suitable for swimming garments.

Be smarter than I was! Before buying yarn for a project, consider the following:

- Suitability
- Personal preference
- Expense

■ Care
■ Yarn characteristics

What to Expect When Working with Different Fibers

As previously mentioned, yarns and fibers vary in many ways. The information below describes specific characteristics of both natural and man-made fibers. Armed with this knowledge, as an informed consumer, you can make better buying decisions.

Natural Fibers

Natural fibers are made from plant or animal products.

Alpaca

The alpaca is a smaller relative of the llama, but its hair is more commercially desired and valuable than that of the llama. Very soft and light in weight, alpaca yarn doesn't felt (mat together) or pill easily. A versatile yarn, alpaca is absorbent, wrinkle-free, and a good insulator. It comes in 15 natural shades and also can be dyed. Alpaca yarns are expensive and can be hard to find.

Cashmere

This expensive and luxurious fiber comes from the undercoat of cashmere goats. It's expensive because each goat produces only a few ounces each year. Cashmere yarns are delicate and much more fragile than wool. Cashmere is often blended with other fibers to bolster its strength and durability. Highly prized, this ultra-soft yarn makes extraordinary garments and throws. Often a favorite of top fashion designers, cashmere enjoys recurring surges in popularity within both the garment and home-decorating industries.

Cotton

Cotton is a plant fiber that comes from the mature seeds of a cotton pod. Most cotton is white, but there are also green and brown varieties. Cotton is actually stronger than wool, and it feels and handles much differently than wool or acrylics. You'll discover this fiber has almost no give or elasticity. When working with cotton, you may find yourself struggling to maintain tension and gauge due to its lack of elasticity.

Cotton breathes and feels good to wear, making it suitable for year-round wear. A heavy fiber, its weight should be taken into account when choosing or creating a pattern. After completion, cotton garments tend to stretch somewhat in width, but not in length (up and down). Cotton, even mercerized cotton, also tends to shrink, so to avoid future heartaches, always work up at least a 4-inch-square swatch before starting a project. Then, wash and dry the swatch according to the label recommendations, measure it, and compare the washed swatch size to determine whether it has shrunk, and if so, by how much.

Linen

Linen comes from the flax plant family. Considered the oldest and strongest natural textile fiber known, linen use goes back in history an estimated five thousand years. While cotton yarns have a bit of elasticity, linen has none, although finished work may tend to pull down a bit. When measuring your work, measure your fabric suspended, rather than flat, to take into account linen's propensity to pull down. You can work ribbing with a strand of elastic thread combined with a strand of linen.

Like cotton, linen breathes well and is comfortable in both warm and cool weather, making it one of the most transitional and versatile fibers for garments. Linen is stronger than cotton and contains a subtle lustrous sheen that intensifies with age. Although woven linen garments tend to wrinkle, that is not the case with

Ribbing With Non-Elastic Yarns

Most experienced crocheters and knitters know it is all but impossible to create ribbing (pattern stitches often used at the bottom, top, and edges of a garment) with cotton or with linen, because of the lack of give in these fibers. However, if you carry a strand of elastic thread along with the strand of cotton or linen, you'll find it's a lifesaver when it comes to ribbing. This elastic thread comes in a wide variety of colors to match many different yarns. If you find it awkward to carry the two strands together, use this method for ribbing:

Work the ribbing as usual, then weave the elastic thread in and out of the ribbing for three or four rows on the wrong side of the fabric, and secure. Take care not to pull too tightly, or the elastic will break when you stretch the garment over your head or when someone tugs on your cardigan to get your attention.

linen yarn. Another positive attribute of linen is that it gets softer and more beautiful with age. Linen garments can be dry cleaned or hand washed. If you opt for hand washing rather than expensive dry cleaning, certain precautions should be taken. Use only a mild soap (never use harsh detergents) or a shampoo specifically made for sweaters and delicates. Before buying such a shampoo, check to see whether the label recommends the product for linen. Wash gently in tepid water, sloshing around the garment, without rubbing or pulling on it. Rinse gently, taking care to squeeze (not wring) out excess water. Rubbing, pulling, and squeezing can actually break linen fibers. Roll the garment in a succession of fluffy towels to absorb the excess moisture and lay flat to air dry.

Mohair

Mohair comes from angora goats. Most mohair is light and fluffy, but it tends to scratch and irritate when worn directly next to the skin. It's an excellent choice for outer garments, however, such as vests, cardigans, jackets, and coats due to its warmth and insulating qualities.

Mohair sheds dirt and doesn't felt easily. Despite its delicate appearance, mohair is very durable. It is usually roughed up to give it a fuzzy look and is often used for fluffy, lightweight garments such as sweaters, scarves, and stoles.

Because mohair is "hairy," it tangles easily and is difficult to rip back when you make a mistake. Although mohair is durable when finished, you must take care not to tug too hard on it when it becomes entangled while working with it, because mohair yarn breaks easily. Carefully plan your stitch patterns when using mohair. Large patterns, such as cables, work up nicely, but smaller and more delicate pattern stitches get lost in the hairiness.

I once crocheted a three-quarter length coat of luscious mauve mohair that I dearly loved. However, strange things began to happen to my beloved coat as I wore it. At first I thought it was my imagination: Every time I put on the coat, it seemed longer over the outfit I was wearing. I told myself my dress or skirt was shorter than the one I'd worn before. I soon realized it wasn't my imagination at all; my coat really had grown in length! By the time I was finally forced to quit wearing it, the coat was nearly 10 inches longer than the day I finished crocheting it—and ten inches on a less-than-five-foot frame makes a noticeable difference. So, remember to take the "growth" factor into consideration when making a garment of mohair. And remember that it stretches vertically, not horizontally.

Silk

Silk, as you probably know, comes from silkworms. The silkworm produces small amounts of this filament, with which it encases itself in the cocoon. After the silkworm abandons the cocoon following metamorphosis, manufacturers harvest the filament then unwind, wash, and spin the fibers into silk yarn, a time-consuming process.

Silk is one of the most beautiful and luxurious fibers in the world, and silk yarn is equally so. Because of the beauty and complex production process of silk, silk yarns also tend to be pricey.

On the positive side, you'll find silk yarns in a broad variety of textures and finishes, ranging from matte to shiny, with myriad variations in between.

A downside to silk is its lack of resiliency. Silk garments often stretch considerably. I once designed a gorgeous, long-sleeve Victorian sweater that landed on the cover of a national magazine. Only the editor, model, photographer, and I knew that the sleeves had "grown" several inches and had to be held in place with clothespins for the photo shoot.

When a pattern—or your own creativity—tells you to use silk yarn, use a silk blend. The other fibers help lessen silk's inclination to stretch. Elastic thread can be used to help stabilize ribbing worked in silk yarn. You also can place elastic thread strategically— such as running a couple of rows of it down the length of the sleeves, fronts, and back—to prevent a garment from growing too much.

Wool

Wool yarn comes from domesticated sheep. Beloved by fishermen for centuries, wool retains body warmth when wet and sheds water better than other yarns. It is also flame-retardant by nature. Wool yarn is probably the all-time favorite of most knitters and crocheters, for several reasons. Because of its natural elasticity, it is the most forgiving of all fibers. Wool is soft to work with and has a lovely "give" to it that is quite unlike any other fiber. Even when you work some stitches tighter or looser than other stitches, the wool conforms and creates a more even tension than do other fibers. If you find that your gauge is a bit off, you can block wool items to specific dimensions.

Flat wool yarns show off stitches in attractive ways. Wool yarns dye well and can be found in a variety of textures and a full spectrum of colors. Many of the wool yarns on the market today are "super-wash" wools, which means the yarn has been pretreated to remove excess lanolin, reduce shrinkage, and make it moth-resistant. Some of these super-wash yarns are hand or machine washable. Check the label for care instructions. Most wool garments return to their original shape when properly laundered. If washed in water that is too hot, wool felts or compacts dramatically.

Synthetic Fibers

Synthetic (man-made) fibers have different characteristics than do natural fibers. The yarns made from these fibers are less expensive and easier to care for, as well.

Acrylic

Acrylic yarns simply don't look, feel, or handle like wool. These synthetic yarns don't breathe, they are nonabsorbent, and they tend to pill. You know what that means: little fuzzy balls show up all over the place. Acrylic yarns do not have the elasticity of wool, but then, neither do some natural fibers. Acrylic yarns are the least expensive to buy. These yarns are probably the best bet for baby things and afghans, because you can throw them in the washer and dryer. Acrylic yarns are lightweight and don't wick away moisture, so they become less warm when wet.

Microfibers

Microfibers are made by means of new techniques that create extremely thin strands that stretch out many miles in length. These strands are then combined to create yarn that is extremely durable

The Burn Test

What if you come across some yarn at a yard sale or inherit a stash from a family member, and you have no idea which fibers make up the yarn's content? You can apply the burn test. The way the yarn reacts to fire will tell you something about its content. Different yarns react to a direct flame in varying and interesting ways.

EXERCISE EXTREME CAUTION WHEN APPLYING A BURN TEST. I recommend you use a lit candle and hold both the candle and the yarn over the kitchen sink for safety. Never, under any circumstances, allow a child to do a burn test!

Burn-Test Results

Cotton. Burns rapidly, emitting a yellow flame. Smells like paper. Continues to smolder with an afterglow. Leaves a brownish, feathery, ash-like residue.

Linen. Burns more slowly than cotton. Smells like rope. Also has an afterglow. Retains the shape of the swatch.

Rayon. Burns slowly. Smells like paper or rags. Leaves very little residue and a fluffy ash.

Silk. Burns slowly and usually self-extinguishes. Smells like burnt hair. Leaves a crushable black bead.

Synthetic Fibers. Most man-made fibers—including nylon, polyester, and acrylic—tend to melt and fuse. Nylon and polyester leave a hard gray or tan bead. Acrylic leaves a crisp, black mass.

Wool. Burns slowly and usually self-extinguishes. Smells like burnt hair. Leaves a small, brittle, black bead.

and a good insulator. Extremely soft and lightweight, microfiber yarns can be crocheted into garments that are comfortable to wear and easy to care for. They can usually be machine washed and dried. Be sure to check labels as some microfibers can be harmed by dry cleaning.

Nylon

Although you won't find many nylon yarns available, I've included it because it is so often combined with other fibers. Light in weight, nylon is strong and elastic, resists abrasion, and is easy to care for. Nylon doesn't stretch or shrink unless exposed to very high temperatures. When combined with wool, for example, it adds strength and elasticity.

Polyester

The most common type of synthetic fiber, polyester, like nylon, is used in combination with other fibers for strength. Polyester retains its shape and adds strength, durability, and resilience to other fibers. Polyester is easy to wash and comfortable to wear in moderate climates, although it tends not to breathe and can be uncomfortable to wear in hot weather.

Rayon

This fiber is produced from natural ingredients by artificial means. If that sounds like some kind of mumbo-jumbo to you, let me explain. Rayon is made with cellulose, a fiber that comes from wood pulp or cotton, which is then treated chemically until it can be drawn into filaments. These filaments are then plied, or twisted, into yarn. Although a rather weak fiber, rayon is absorbent and dries quickly. It is soft and comfortable and drapes well. Rayon is not prone to static or pilling. Dry cleaning is recommended, but if care is taken rayon can be hand washed and hung up or laid flat to dry.

Novelty Yarns

Some of the "novelty yarns" aren't truly yarns at all, but they can work well for crochet just the same.

Chenille

Chenille is cut from a specially woven fabric. Some chenille yarns shed from the cut edges. When used as a knit or crochet yarn, it also tends to twist, because it has no plies to oppose and stabilize it. When crocheting with chenille, it is difficult to maintain an even tension and gauge; in fact, chenille seems to have a mind of its own. For example, you may spend numerous hours trying to maintain an even gauge while working on an afghan, and when you put it down for the night your work looks great. But the next morning, you're likely to spot stitches that grew overnight into unsightly stitches that are much larger than the ones right next to them.

Eyelash or Fur

This novelty yarn is made from long filaments grouped together. The filaments stick out from the crocheted fabric and give the appearance of fur. Depending upon the length of the protruding filaments, some of these yarns can be very difficult to crochet with because you can't see the stitches to produce fabric of any length. However, they can be relatively easy to use for single-row edging.

Ribbon

It is what it's called: ribbon. A wide variety of ribbons can be found in yarn stores ranging from hand-dyed silks to metallics, cotton tape, tubular jersey, and the like. Wound on spools, novelty ribbons are used for edgings and other trims, as well as garments. You can also crochet thin ribbons found in the notions department of fabric stores, but they tend to twist badly. Ribbon has no elasticity, and fabric crocheted from it often looks irregular. Ribbon yarn is fine for edgings and trims, but you'll find it challenging to make a shell or sweater with it because of the twisting factor.

> **Handy Hint**
>
> When working with novelty yarns, use a small drop of Fray Check (available at fabric stores) at the beginning of the working yarn to eliminate fraying.

Other Material Choices

You can crochet with just about anything you can wrap around a hook. You might want to try some of the following: leather strips, twine, rope, string, cord, fabric strips, lacing, soft wire, or whatever strikes your fancy. If you can wrap it around a hook, you can try crocheting with it!

Other Helpful Tools for Crocheters

Although you could crochet with nothing more than a hook and some yarn, there are other useful tools that will help you successfully complete your crochet projects. You'll probably want to have most of these close at hand:

- Calculator
- Hook case
- Notebook
- Notepad
- Patterns
- Pins and pincushion
- Scissors
- Stitch checker
- Tape measure
- Tapestry or yarn needle

Calculator

A must-have that every crocheter needs to keep nearby. You'll use a calculator to quickly determine gauge, sizes, and lengths of crochet projects. When you must make changes in a garment, a calculator is a useful, time-saving tool.

Graph Paper

Essential to the design process for charting out schematics, sizing changes, stitches, and rows, as well as other design elements. Graph paper is also used to chart out color work and fancy stitch placement.

How Yarn Is Made

Let's start with the basics. Fiber is made up of strings and filaments that are processed into a strand long enough with which to work. Most yarn is plied material. A ply is a twisted strand of fiber. If the twist is firm, the yarn is fine. If the twist is too firm, the yarn kinks. If the twist is too loose, the yarn is soft, thick, and not as strong.

Interestingly enough, the number of plies in yarn has nothing to do with the yarn's thickness. Yarns made of four plies can end up being thinner than those made of only two plies. However, the number of plies does determine the strength and evenness of the yarn. Because yarn tends to twist as it's worked, it is usually plied (twisted) in the opposite direction of the individual strands to compensate for this natural tendency. Doing this helps to overcome slanting as the yarn is worked into fabric.

Many people erroneously think of worsted-weight yarn as sweater or afghan yarn. Worsted actually means a yarn whose fibers were combed prior to spinning. Yarns used to knit and crochet sweaters are known in Europe as double-knitting yarn.

Before natural fibers are spun into yarn, they are cleaned, untangled, brushed, smoothed (carded), and sometimes sorted by length. Then, bundles of these lengths are drawn into slivers. Slivers having a slight twist to them are said to be *roving*. Straight fibers are then separated from the roving and twisted into plies. The plies are then twisted together to produce different weights and types of yarns.

The length and quality of a fiber determines the texture, strength, luster, and feel of a yarn. Yarns made from longer fibers tend to pill less and also are smoother, stronger, more elastic, and lustrous. Blends are often not as strong as their 100% natural counterparts.

Hook Case

A hook case can be as simple as a plain zippered bag. It is used to store and keep crochet hooks together and easily accessible.

Notebook

Here's where you'll keep your crochet swatches, gauge information, as well as other helpful information such as tips, measurements of those for whom you crochet, and yarn preferences. Your notebook is the place to write down anything and everything pertaining to crochet that is important to you.

Notepad

Keep a notepad handy to list materials needed prior to shopping. I use notepads for simple, basic sketching, to make notes about a particular pattern, and for simple mathematical calculations.

Patterns

Patterns come in many different formats, sizes, and shapes. You'll find your stash of patterns growing incrementally along with your yarn cache. As your collection grows, it helps to organize your patterns in a way that is meaningful to you. I like to keep all the baby and toddler patterns together; likewise, I group patterns for children, women, and men. Maybe you'll want to keep all the afghan patterns in a group. Other groups might be hats, slippers, doilies and thread work, Irish crochet, purses, stoles, and pillows.

Pins and pincushion

Straight pins are used to pin crocheted pieces together during the finishing process. Pins that feature colored plastic heads are the most convenient choice as those without the heads sometimes imbed themselves in the stitches. With safety pins, it's best to use only the coiless ones for markers, because they won't catch or snag your work. Choose any shape or size of pincushion that you prefer for keeping straight, safety, and coiless pins together and close at hand.

Scissors

The size and shape of scissors you buy doesn't matter. But they do need to be sharp so yarns can be clipped cleanly. While any pair of scissors might do the job for you, you may want to check out the special scissors available for needlework. These include *snip* scissors that get under stitches, allowing you to snip without damaging fabric. Of course, the famous *stork* scissors continue to be a favorite among those who do all kinds of needlework. I feel more comfortable using small scissors instead of large, bulky ones; besides, small scissors fit nicely into my little supplies box. You're unlikely to ever lose your scissors again if you buy scissors on a chain or ribbon. If that doesn't work, you can even buy retractable scissors on a reel that you can pin to your garment.

Stitch Checker

Your stitch checker is needed to measure swatches and to determine gauge: the number of stitches and rows per inch. (See "Gauge" in chapter 4 for a complete discussion of the use of a stitch checker.)

Tape Measure

You'll need a tape measure to measure most crochet projects.

Tapestry or Yarn Needle

Tapestry or yarn needles are large needles with blunt tips. Always choose needles with blunt tips to avoid splitting yarn when joining crocheted pieces together. Unless instructions state otherwise, needles are always threaded with the same yarn used to make a crochet project.

Knowing about crochet hooks, about the various types and individual characteristics of yarn, and about the tools of the trade will help you to select the right materials for your projects. It also significantly increases your chances of a successful outcome.

Setting Up Your Personal Workspace

▼▼▼

ONE OF THE BEST THINGS about crochet is that—unlike sewing, quilting, woodworking, and cooking—you can do it just about anywhere. You don't need a studio or special room or to set aside a particular space for your work. Crocheting requires no special furniture; a comfortable chair is all you really need, and it can be any type of chair, in any location, that feels right to you. Still, there are some things you can do to get organized. After all, I can guarantee that your yarn stash will continually grow. You just need to figure out where to put all that glorious stuff.

I've lived in various homes in which I was able to devote an entire room to a studio/office and in other homes in which my "personal" space was more limited. Along the way, I've devised some methods for organizing my yarns, hooks, books, and other supplies that have worked for me and may work for you, too.

Like most designers/writers, I live with stacks of things—stacks of stitch dictionaries, stacks of magazines, and stacks of swatches—not to mention heaps of yarn. But those stacks get to me, because I'm a rather orderly person by nature, and I find chaos to be annoying. So, I try to minimize the number of stacks and the amount of time I live among them. When I'm swatching and sketching designs for publishers, for example, I need to keep a lot of items close at hand, but when I'm finished, everything goes back in place as quickly as possible.

Yarn Storage

When you first start crocheting, you'll probably just toss those bags of yarn in a closet and shut the door. But it won't take more than a few trips to the store before you'll discover your closets are bulging with bags and bags of yarn. Then before you know it, you won't be able to recall which yarn is in which bag, and you'll have to dig to find what you need or want.

Organizing Yarn

I like to organize yarns by type, brand, and color. Sound confusing? It's not. In fact, it makes for efficient organizing as well as for easy retrieval of whatever yarn you might need for a particular project.

Sorting by Type

Once you've completed a few crocheting projects, you'll realize that you prefer some types and brands of yarn over others. We all develop these preferences and soon find ourselves with a stockpile of several variations of these types and brands of yarn. It makes sense, then, to group yarns by brand and type. Then when you want to do a color project using these yarns or want to use up scrap yarns, they are all together.

For example, I keep all the baby yarns together in one section and all my worsteds in a separate section—the same goes for sport-weight yarns. I organize yarns the same way I do my closet. I like to keep the shirts and pants that go together next to each other, so I don't have to dig through the closet to put together an outfit. I also organize my closet by keeping sports outfits separate from business attire.

Sorting and storing by yarn type and brand also enables you to store the yarns you use most often in your most convenient storage areas. This is particularly advantageous when storage space is at a premium.

Sorting by Color

My youngest daughter, Dawn, laughs about how my sock drawer is arranged: all the socks are folded and placed in color families. I like to arrange my yarns, too, by color families within each yarn type, and place complementary color families together.

When it comes to sorting fashion yarns, I'm more interested in grouping the colors of the yarn than the types or weight of yarn because I must approach my designs differently. These differences are based on the needs and dictates of fashion yarn companies and needlework magazines. Sorting by color makes it quick and easy for me to find and select exactly the color I want for a particular project. Since I'm especially fond of making garments in monochromatics—colors of the same family—my sorting method lessens my color selection time. Designers tend to maintain larger caches of yarn than do those who crochet for a hobby. So, while this degree of organization works great for me, it might be unnecessary for you.

Storage Containers

Bookshelves can serve well as storage space for yarns and other crochet-related items. Another option is to buy plastic tubs, with or without covers, in which to store your crochet supplies.

I've found that plastic laundry baskets, which are lightweight and easy to lift, also work great to hold yarns. On the minus side, laundry baskets don't stack as neatly as covered tubs and bins. On the plus side, I like the laundry baskets because I can see which yarns and colors are in each basket without having to take off a lid and dig through a tub.

Hidden Storage Areas

Next to my desk and computer, I have set up a folding table measuring 4 feet long by 2 feet wide. My worktable is covered with a simple tablecloth that I made out of a raspberry and white pin-striped sheet, which has a gathered skirt that hangs to the floor. Hidden beneath the skirted tablecloth are boxes of crochet books, projects waiting to be shipped to publishers, yarns, and other crochet goodies.

In my living room, I have a three-legged table with a 30-inch diameter top. I've outfitted this table, too, with a long skirt and topper. Underneath this table, hidden from view by the skirt, I keep yarns, crochet hooks, and a little plastic box filled with various and often-needed items such as a calculator, an eraser, pens and pencils, a stitch checker, a pincushion, and scissors. If you peeked under that table, you'd also see stacks of crochet books hidden there.

Handy Hint

If yarn bobbins don't hold enough yarn, use a small plastic bag to hold each color.

You can sometimes effectively use baskets of yarn to complement your home décor, depending, of course, on your overall interior design. For example, if your family room is done in shades of bronze and green, a basket filled with yarn of various peach hues adds a visual complement to your color scheme. That basket of beautiful yarn also does something else: It adds a warm and inviting accessory to your home that reflects your personality and interests. It also is apt to serve as an icebreaker with guests, who are likely to ask about the yarn and how you use it.

That trunk at the foot of your bed is just begging to be filled with yarn. Why don't you put those extra blankets in the linen closet, where they belong, to make room in the trunk for your yarn stash? Do you have old collector-type suitcases stacked up in a bed-room? Or a collection of hat boxes or Shaker boxes? Fill up those empty spaces with yarn!

Got any extra room under your bed? Go to your favorite dis-count store and buy large plastic boxes with lids that are designed to hold gift wrap; these are deep enough to hold two layers of yarn skeins. You can use these same boxes to store extra yarn on a shelf in your coat closet, in the garage, in the basement, or on the top shelf in the guest room. Where there's a will, there's a space, and I know you'll find both!

Special Needs

Maybe you have special needs or just want some items that will make crocheting easier. If you have difficulty seeing your work, for exam-ple, you might want to acquire a number of products that are avail-able in needlework and craft catalogs as well as in some stores.

Magnifiers

Magnifiers help reduce eyestrain and come in a variety of styles. You can buy anything from adjustable, top-of-the-line floor lamp models to other, less expensive magnifiers. Some magnifiers fit around your head, freeing up your hands to crochet. Some have lights; others do not. Have you seen the Flip and Focus magnifier? It clips onto your eyeglasses and can be flipped up for normal vision or down for magnification. Other magnifiers hang around your neck and hover over your hands as you work.

Hand and Wrist Support

Do you suffer from carpal tunnel syndrome? Do your wrists get tired when you crochet for long periods of time? You might want to try elasticized mitts that slip over your wrists and hands, providing support while leaving your fingers free to work as usual. These fingerless gloves help to relieve the symptoms of repetitive motion stress on hands and wrists. The spandex fabric supports, massages, and increases circulation in the muscles, tendons, and ligaments.

Other Accessories

Have you ever heard of a yarn bra? Quite a handy little tool, the yarn bra is nothing more than a stretchy tube of mesh that slips over a skein of yarn. It is particularly helpful for controlling slippery yarns.

Here's another little something I'm sure you already have on hand: sandwich-, quart-, and gallon-size zip-sealing plastic bags. These are terrific to use when you take your crocheting with you. Put the yarn in the bag and when you're ready to begin crocheting, crack the seal just enough to allow you to pull the yarn through. This will keep your yarn clean and prevent it from rolling away as you work. Likewise, you can wash out a one-liter water or soda bottle, cut a slit from top to bottom, and insert a skein of yarn into the bottle. Then, you can draw out the yarn through the top opening.

Reading crochet instructions is easier if you use a stand to hold the pattern book. Some stands are magnetic and feature movable magnetic strips that can be moved from row to row, which enables you to keep track of your work. You can also buy line magnifiers that enlarge a single line, making it easier to read. Or, you might like a "line-minder" magnifier that features a red line that marks your place on graphs or directions while it also magnifies.

A gooseneck lamp can make it easier for you to see your crocheting, especially when you're working with dark-colored yarns.

Handy Hint

Make your own yarn bra with an old knee-high sock. Cut off the toe and place it around a skein of yarn.

Don't Just Wait—Crochet!

Taking your crocheting along with you can be a good thing—a very good thing, according to Arlene Ritzhaupt, owner of Ritzy Things Yarn Shop in Redmond, Washington.

"I always carry my crochet with me, so that I'm prepared and don't get upset if I need to wait," Arlene said. "Today was a good example. I checked in for a doctor's appointment and after 20 minutes of waiting was informed that an emergency had put the doctor behind schedule. I wasn't pleased knowing I'd have to wait longer, but I knew that the time I spent waiting wasn't going to be wasted. After all, I had a scarf to crochet."

Arlene grinned and continued, "I began to work, knowing that my crocheting was sure to be good for my blood pressure. Two other patients got up and left in such a huff, I thought they'd have heart attacks before reaching their cars. The bonus came when my work invited conversation from another crocheter and then a cross-stitcher joined our discussion."

Working with black yarn can be challenging even for those with the best eyesight.

Craft catalogs and stores sell various organizers, or caddies, that feature several compartments in which to store skeins of yarn. Most are designed with beveled edges and holes through which you can pull the yarn in use. They are especially handy for color work.

Similarly, plastic yarn bobbins are inexpensive and also convenient to use when doing small areas of color work.

You can buy or make any kind of yarn tote for your travel needs. I like the ones with lots of pockets for patterns, hooks, scissors, and other accessories. For working at home, you may find a knitting stand best suits your needs. Made of a wooden frame with fabric sides, knitting stands usually fold for easy carrying and storage. Most are large enough to contain all the skeins needed for a crochet project. There is also a pocketed holder that can be secured to your easy chair, keeping all those sundry crochet tools close at hand.

Now that we're organized, what are we waiting for? Let's start crocheting!

Creative How-To's

▼▼

IF YOU ALREADY KNOW how to crochet, you may choose to skip this chapter. However, if you learned how to crochet from someone other than an expert or a teacher certified by the Craft Yarn Council of America (CYCA), you may wish to review this chapter because of the professional techniques that are presented. You can read more about CYCA in the Resources chapter at the end of this book.

Before you start learning the basic crochet stitches, here are some tips to make your first endeavor easier.

Choosing Yarns and Hooks

Choose a flat-textured yarn in a light color for practice work and for your first project. I recommend that you choose either a worsted- or sport-weight yarn. Using a light-colored, flat-textured yarn makes it easier for you to see how stitches are formed. Dark and textured yarns tend to make stitches difficult to identify. The fiber content of your yarn is not nearly as important in the beginning as are the texture and color. It really doesn't matter whether you begin with an

49

inexpensive acrylic or whether you choose a wool, cotton, linen, or yarn blend.

Crochet consists of using a hook to pull loops from a continuous yarn or thread and working one stitch at a time with open spaces in between stitches. All crochet is based on a chain stitch foundation. Like learning anything new, it's all a bit confusing in the beginning. When using a flat-textured, light-colored yarn, you can see and understand more easily what you are doing as chains or stitches are formed.

The size of the hook is what determines the size of the stitches you crochet. First, try using a size H hook for worsted weight and a size G hook for sport weight. If you find that the fabric you crochet feels too stiff and rigid, try using a larger hook. If the fabric seems too loose and floppy, change to a smaller hook. All of the basic crochet-stitch swatches for this book were worked with worsted-weight yarn and a size H hook.

The Two Most Important Aspects of Crocheting

1. Understanding gauge
2. Learning to read instructions

Gauge

Your gauge is the number of *stitches* and *rows* you crochet per inch. Understanding the importance of gauge from the beginning will ensure that you make perfect-fitting garments all of the time, not just some of the time. Once you understand how critical gauge is, and how it affects the outcome of any crochet project, you'll never be afraid to crochet a garment.

Most crocheters learn the art of crochet from an accomplished family member or friend. Unfortunately, that someone often knows little, if anything, about the importance of gauge. And the importance of gauge cannot be stressed enough, it isn't just important—it's critical!

If you already know how to crochet, you have probably crocheted at least one garment in the past that didn't fit anything that remotely resembled a human body. Maybe the arms dangled nearly to the floor, or the neck was so tight you couldn't get it over your head. You can avoid such disasters when you understand the importance of gauge in relationship to the finished size of a garment. No one wants to invest time, money, and effort into a project that doesn't fit right.

Never begin a garment without taking the time to work a 4-inch-square swatch. You've probably heard it before, and it's true! Always make a swatch *at least* 4 inches square, and measure gauge accurately before crocheting any wearable design.

When making your model, continue to check the gauge periodically. You'll find, time and again, that your gauge has changed as you work. This typically happens because you tend to be more intensely focused when crocheting the swatch than when actually working on the crochet project; thus, that tension is reflected in a swatch that may be a bit tight. However, when you spend a half hour or so working on a project, you relax and so does your tension, resulting in a different gauge altogether. Generally, I work *at least three* swatches and then recheck my gauge every couple of inches to ensure that it is consistent.

When your measurements are off by even ¼ stitch, the end result can be disastrous. For example, let's say that you have determined your gauge to be 4 stitches per inch. To chart out the back of a sweater for a finished chest measurement of 40 inches, you divide 40 in half (by 2) to arrive at the required width of the back,

20 inches. To determine the number of stitches required for the back, you multiply the back width, 20 inches, by 4 (the number of stitches per inch and your determined gauge), for a total of 80 stitches. If your gauge is accurate, when the back is completed, it will measure *exactly* 20 inches in width. On the other hand, if your gauge is 4¼ stitches per inch instead, or off by just ¼ inch, the width of the back will be just under 19 inches wide. If your gauge is off by ½ stitch, or is actually 4½ stitches per inch, the finished back width will be a little less than 18 inches, which means your finished chest measurement will be 36 inches instead of 40! The same thing applies to measuring the number of rows per inch.

Handy Hint

If you tend to use the same brand and weight of yarn manufactured by a particular company, you can save crochet swatching time by creating a swatch notebook.

Measuring Properly

I recommend that you *not* use a ruler or tape measure to measure gauge. Instead, use a stitch checker, which you can find in most yarn and craft stores. Why? Because a stitch checker features a 2-inch open slot that *isolates* the stitches and rows (see figure 4.1). When using a ruler or tape measure, it is normal to begin to smooth out the swatch in an effort to get the stitch and the row count to match the gauge specified in a pattern. However, when you do so, you are manipulating the *true* gauge and are actually creating a *distorted* gauge instead, and the end result will be a garment that is based on that distorted gauge—it simply won't fit. Using a slotted stitch checker that you lay over your swatch isolates your stitches so you can see and count the true gauge.

To measure a swatch properly, lay it down on a flat surface and place the stitch checker on top of it. Count the number of stitches and rows within the slot. Identifying the individual stitches may be confusing at first. Look for the spaces between the stitches; if you can identify the spaces, you'll be able to see each stitch. Refer to the

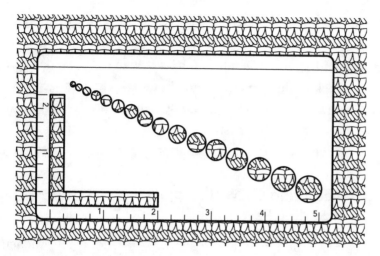

Figure 4.1. Stitch checker.

photographs in this chapter to see how each stitch should look. Count the number of stitches and rows within the 2-inch slots. (Measuring over only 1 inch will likely result in a misread gauge.) Then, using the ruler along the bottom edge of your stitch checker, measure and count stitches over 3 inches, and again over 4 inches to determine whether the number remains the same each time you measure. To get a true gauge, you must measure several times. If your swatch produces a gauge that is off by even ¼ stitch, it will alter the finished measurements.

Don't make the mistake of trying to adjust your tension to obtain a given gauge, because it is impossible to maintain an unnatural tension over any extended period of time. Within minutes, you'll relax and return to your natural tension without even realizing that you are doing so. Instead, take a few minutes to whip up a swatch to determine your true gauge to ensure perfect-fitting garments every time.

The type of yarn you use also affects the gauge. For example, if using wool, the most forgiving yarn of all, you can manipulate the swatch by blocking; however, it is a total waste of time and effort to block a swatch crocheted with acrylic yarn. Acrylic yarns have built-in "memory," which means that they are designed to return to the same size and shape of each stitch as it was crocheted. Trying to block a "memory" yarn to obtain the right gauge only temporarily manipulates the stitches. You are not getting a true gauge, because once you wash and dry a crocheted acrylic garment, it automatically returns to the true gauge.

Measuring Chevron, Ripple, or Scallop Pattern Repeats

It is much easier to learn how to accurately measure a complete pattern composed of several stitches, such as a chevron, ripple, or scallop, than it is to determine the number of single stitches and rows per inch. When measuring complete patterns, do not measure from the beginning to the end of each pattern; instead, make a swatch that has at least three repeats of the pattern and then measure from *the center of one pattern* to *the center of the second pattern* to get the true gauge. Do not smooth or manipulate your swatch in any way prior to measuring. Measure from the center of the first pattern to the center of the third pattern to determine whether your stitch and row counts were accurate the first time.

If you remember only one thing about crocheting, remember the importance of gauge!

Reading Crochet Instructions

If you are new to crocheting and have had the opportunity to look at crochet patterns and written instructions, you no doubt are wondering why crochet instructions are filled with abbreviations and terminology that seem to make no sense whatsoever. Although it may look like Greek to you, crochet abbreviations and certain terminology actually make it easier and faster to read—and follow—crochet instructions.

At first, you may need to refer to the abbreviation list (see sidebar below) to understand how to translate instructions, but reading instructions will soon become natural and easy for you.

I suggest that you make a copy of this abbreviation list and keep it handy while you are working on your first few projects so you can readily refer to it. Or, you can use the abbreviation page found in most crochet magazines.

Crochet instructions are always sequential—describing what to do, in what order, step by step and row by row. Don't try to read and understand an entire row at once; instead, read a *section* of instructions. Sections are divided by punctuation marks: a comma, a

Abbreviations

- Approx—Approximately
- Beg—Beginning
- CC—Contrasting color
- Ch(s)—Chain(s)
- Cl—Cluster
- Dc—Double crochet
- Dec—Decrease
- Ea—Each
- Gr—Group
- Hdc—Half double crochet

- Hk—Hook
- Inc—Increase
- Incl—Including
- Lp—Loop
- MC—Main color
- Oz—Ounces
- Pat—Pattern
- Rem—Remaining
- Rep—Repeat
- Rib—Ribbing

- Rnd—Round
- Sc—Single crochet
- Sk—Skip
- Sl st—Slip stitch
- Sp—Space
- St(s)—Stitch(es)
- Thru—Through
- Tog—Together
- Tr—Treble crochet
- YO—Yarn over

semicolon, a colon, parentheses, or brackets. Pause at each punctuation mark, and digest each section as you come to it, then work each step. Taking it one section at a time and following the instructions step by step allows you to grasp the instructions more readily. There is more about how to read, translate, and understand written instructions at the end of this chapter.

In the beginning, when you are first learning how to crochet, try to finish a row before laying your work down so you don't get confused about where you left off.

Let's Crochet!

Get your hook and yarn now and follow along.

Holding the Hook and Yarn

There are two main ways of holding a crochet hook: (1) like a pencil (see figure 4.2) and (2) like a knife (see figure 4.3). I prefer to hold a crochet hook like a pencil because I was taught that was the only proper way to hold it. I remember that the hook felt awkward and strange in my little girl hand, but my mother insisted I do it the "right" way—the only way, according to her.

Figure 4.2. Holding hook like a pencil.

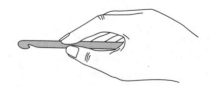

Figure 4.3. Holding hook like a knife.

When it comes to holding a hook, Arlene Ritzhaupt, who is a certified CYCA crochet instructor, says, "Listen to your hand." In other words, your hand will let you know which is the most comfortable position for you.

Lefties may wish to trace the figures here onto tracing paper and then turn the paper over to reverse all the examples.

As you work, hold the hook in your right hand and the yarn in your left hand to maintain a slight tension for an even gauge. If you are left-handed, hold the hook in your left hand and the yarn in your right.

Form a Slipknot

Leaving a 3- to 4-inch tail of yarn, form a slipknot by first forming a circle. Place the yarn that is coming from the ball (called the *working yarn*) under the circle (see step SK-1). Insert the hook under the bar just made (see step SK-2). Tighten the knot by gently pulling on both ends of the yarn, and slide the slipknot up to the hook (see step SK-3).

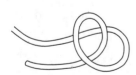

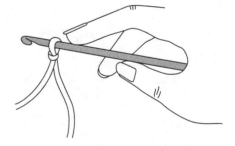

Step SK-1. Leaving a 3- to 4-inch tail of yarn, form a slipknot by first forming a circle. Place the yarn that is coming from the ball under the circle.

Step SK-2. Insert the hook under the bar just made.

Step SK-3. Tighten the knot by gently pulling on both ends of the yarn, and slide the slipknot up to the hook.

What To Do With Your Left Hand

Place the working yarn over the index finger of your left hand, holding it closely across the palm of your hand with the last two fingers. Hang onto the tail (next to the slipknot) with your left thumb and middle finger (see figure 4.4).

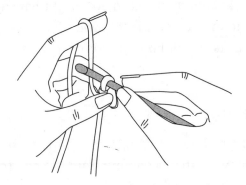

Figure 4.4. Holding the tail with left thumb and middle finger.

You may find it more comfortable to hold the yarn in a different way. The goal is to hold the yarn so that it can move freely and evenly through your fingers without becoming taut.

Yarn Over

Crochet stitches are worked on a length of stitches called a *chain*. Each chain stitch looks like a V as it is formed. A series of chains creates a foundation from which other stitches will be formed. The first chain begins with the slipknot, then the yarn is grabbed by the hook, forming a *yarn over* (YO). The yarn over is part of creating every crochet stitch. To yarn over, place the yarn *over* the top of the hook from the *back* to the *front* of the hook (see step CS-1). Grab the yarn with the hook and tilt the hook slightly toward you to pull the yarn into the hook's groove (see step CS-2).

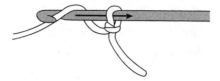

Step CS-1. To yarn over, place the yarn *over* the top of the hook from the *back* to the *front* of the hook.

Step CS-2. Grab the yarn with the hook and tilt the hook slightly toward you to pull the yarn into the hook's groove.

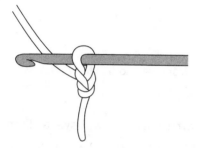

Step CS-3. Draw the yarn through the slipknot on the hook and onto the *working area,* to the right of the groove in the hook. You have made one chain and have one loop on the hook.

Step CS-4. Repeat this process until you are comfortable making chain stitches.

Chain Stitch

Draw the yarn through the slipknot on the hook and onto the *working area* to the right of the groove in the hook. You have made one chain and have one loop on the hook (see step CS-3).

Repeat this process until you are comfortable making chain stitches (see step CS-4).

The first line of crochet instructions generally instruct you to "chain loosely." This means that the loop on the hook should be loose enough for the hook to pass through easily. The loop formed should be close to the hook but not tight. Always bring the yarn over the hook from *back* to *front* as you form the foundation chain (see figure 4.5).

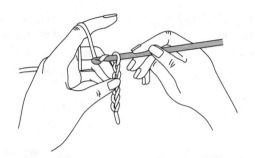

Figure 4.5. Yarn over hook from back to front.

At first, holding the hook and yarn may feel awkward. Don't worry—with a bit of practice, you'll soon feel more at ease. If the hook slips off your work, simply reinsert it through the last stitch without twisting the loop. As you form each loop, pull it onto the working area of the hook by pushing the hook forward to keep the loop loose. If the loops are not pulled onto the working area, they become too tight. If you find it difficult to make the loops loose enough, you may want to try using a hook one size larger for the chain only. As each chain is completed and moved onto the working area of the hook, the loops will be loose enough to work into later.

As you form more chains, continue to move your left hand slowly up the chain, about every four stitches, keeping it close to the hook to keep control of your tension.

When counting the number of chains formed, do *not* count the slipknot. Continue to practice the chain stitch, trying to keep your tension even and making stitches that are uniform in size. The loop that remains on the hook is not counted as a stitch. Once you have mastered the chain stitch, you are ready to progress to the single crochet stitch by working into the chain just formed.

Working into the Chain

Crochet stitches are *worked into* individual chains. Look closely at the chain you have just made. The front (right side of work) looks like a string of Vs. The back of the chain has a bump, called a *ridge,* behind each chain stitch.

There are two methods of working into the chain. The first method is the most common.

Method One

To work into the chain, insert your hook under both the top strand of a chain *and* into the back ridge of each chain (see figure 4.6).

Method Two

To create a smoother-looking edge, work into the back ridge of each chain (see figure 4.7).

Figure 4.6. Method One of working into the chain.

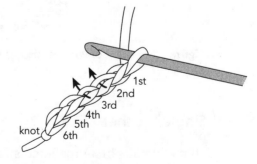

Figure 4.7. Method Two of working into the chain.

Basic Stitches

By now you are familiar with holding a crochet hook, forming yarn overs, and managing the yarn tension. Basic crochet stitches (and other stitches) are simply extensions of the techniques you have already mastered.

There are five basic crochet stitches: slip stitch (sl st), single crochet (sc), half double crochet (hdc), double crochet (dc), and treble crochet (tr). You use the same techniques to crochet these stitches as you do to make the chain stitch. Each individual stitch is made with one or more yarn overs and is completed by pulling the yarn through a loop or series of loops on the hook, according to instructions. The number of yarn overs determines the height of the stitch formed. The height of the stitch, in turn, determines the number of chains required to turn a row (see figure 4.8).

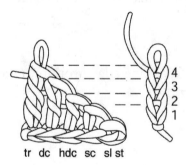

tr dc hdc sc sl st

Figure 4.8. Height of various stitches and the number of chains required to turn a row.

Single Crochet

To make your first crocheted swatch, chain 17 loosely.

Step One: Insert the hook into the 2nd chain from the hook (see step SC-1). The loop on your hook does *not* count as a chain.

Step Two: YO by wrapping the yarn around the hook and draw loop thru (see step SC-2).

Step Three: Draw the yarn thru the chain stitch. You now have two loops on the hook.

Step Four: Yarn over again (see step SC-3).

Step Five: Pull the yarn thru both loops on the hook (see step SC-4). You have just completed a single crochet (sc), and one loop remains on the hook. What if one of the stitches looks wrong? Simply remove the hook, and gently pull on the working end of the yarn, ripping back to the last stitch that was formed correctly. When you insert the hook back into the top loop of that stitch, be careful not to twist the chain.

To make the next single crochet (sc), insert hook into the next chain (see step SC-5), and repeat Steps Two through Five.

Continue in the same manner, making a single crochet (sc) into each chain, taking care not to twist the chain. At the end of the row, you have made 16 sc because the first stitch was made in the second chain from the hook. Remember that the loop on the hook is not counted. Each completed sc has two horizontal loops at the top of each stitch. These horizontal loops form Vs similar to a chain. You work through the top two loops of each stitch to form each stitch of the next row.

Step SC-1. Insert hook into 2nd chain from hook.

Step SC-2. Yarn over (YO) by wrapping the yarn around the hook and draw loop thru.

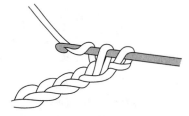

Step SC-3. Draw the yarn thru the chain stitch. You now have two loops on the hook. Yarn over again.

Step SC-4. Pull the yarn thru both loops on the hook. You have just completed a single crochet (sc), and one loop remains on the hook.

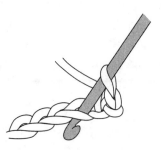

Step SC-5. To make the next single crochet (sc), insert hook into the next chain.

Swatching

Work each of the basic crochet stitches, using the number of beginning chains and stitches as written. When you are finished with each stitch, you will have a complete swatch to measure. Take out your crochet notebook and write down the following information:

- Type and brand of yarn used
- Size of crochet hook
- Gauge—number of stitches and rows per inch

To begin a new row (Row 2): Chain 1. This chain is used to maintain row height and is not counted as a stitch (see step SC-6).

Turn your work so the reverse side is facing you. Make the first sc into the last stitch of the last row by inserting hook under the top two loops of the stitch (see step SC-7). Always insert hook under the top two loops of any crochet stitch, unless otherwise specified.

Work 1 sc in each sc to end of row, making sure you work into the last sc of the row (see step SC-8). You should still have 16 sc.

Repeat Row 2, continuing to work in sc. Do not work into the turning chain as it doesn't count as a stitch in single crochet. Continue to work in sc until your swatch is as long as it is wide. Figure 4.9 shows a swatch worked in single crochet.

To end, cut yarn leaving a 3- to 5-inch tail. YO, pull tail thru remaining loop on hook, and pull tight. This secures the last stitch so the other stitches don't unravel. This technique is referred to as *finish off, fasten off,* or *end off* in written crochet instructions.

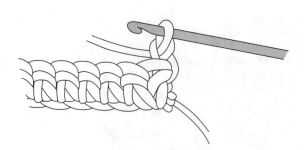

Step SC-6. Chain 1 to turn.

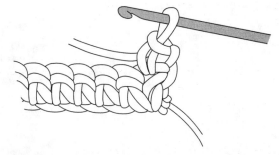

Step SC-7. Turn your work so the reverse side is facing you. Make the first sc into the last stitch of the last row by inserting hook under the top two loops of the stitch (first single crochet of second row made).

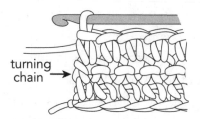

Step SC-8. Work 1 sc in each sc to end of row, making sure you work into the last sc of the row (end of 2nd row).

Check Your Gauge

Take out your stitch checker and measure your gauge as discussed earlier in this chapter. On the first page of your crochet notebook, write down your gauge—the number of stitches and rows per inch—and attach your swatch to the same page. I like to use glue sticks to attach the swatch, but it can be pinned to the page or stapled. Do not make the mistake of assuming that the gauge you obtained on this first swatch is your true gauge. You'll find that your tension and

Figure 4.9. Single crochet swatch.

▼▼

What to Do about Mistakes

Students often grow discouraged or distressed when they discover a mistake that requires them to rip back their work. But we're all human, and we all make mistakes. We make mistakes for lots of reasons: Maybe a step of the instructions was misunderstood. Sometimes a stitch is skipped. Perhaps two stitches were mistakenly worked into one stitch. You need to get into the habit of just ripping out imperfect work and redoing it. Ripping is part of crocheting, sewing, knitting, embroidery, or any other needle art. As you become more practiced and experienced, the need to rip back lessens, but it never goes away altogether.

I find myself ripping every day I crochet. Maybe I don't like the size of the stitches and think they would look better if they were worked on a smaller hook, so I rip. Perhaps I'm crocheting at night and not as alert as earlier in the day, and I may overlook a glaring mistake that is all too obvious in the morning. So, I rip back again. Why? Because I want my work to look handmade, but I don't want it to look "homemade" with obvious mistakes that lessen the quality of my work.

▲▲

gauge will change, sometimes dramatically, as you become more comfortable with crocheting.

Slip Stitch

The slip stitch (sl st) is the shortest of all crochet stitches and is rarely used on its own. This versatile stitch is used to join a chain into a ring, to join rounds of crochet, to reinforce edges, and for shaping without adding height. Whenever instructions say to "join," use a slip stitch.

   Step One: To make a slip stitch, insert hook into the top loops of first stitch of the next row (see step SS-1), YO and pull thru both loops on hook—1 slip stitch made (see step SS-2). Repeat this process according to instructions. Regardless of the stitch worked previously, slip stitches are always worked in the same way.

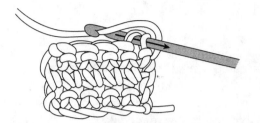

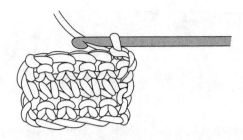

Step SS-1. To make a slip stitch, insert hook into the top loops of first stitch of the next row.

Step SS-2. YO and pull thru both loops on hook—1 slip stitch made.

Generally, you do not chain when completing a row and the next row begins with slip stitches. For example, if you are working the front for a sweater in double crochet (dc), instructions will tell you to begin shaping the armhole with a specified number of slip stitches. Do not chain when beginning a row with slip stitches, unless instructions tell you to do so.

Half Double Crochet

To Begin: Loosely chain 17.

Row 1—Step One: YO and insert hook into the 3rd loop from the hook. Both YO and one loop are now on hook (see step HDC-1).

Step Two: YO and pull a loop thru the chain only. You now have 3 loops on the hook (see step HDC-2).

Step Three: YO and pull yarn thru all 3 loops on hook at the same time (see step HDC-3). You have just made a half double crochet. Notice that the height of the half double crochet is slightly taller than a single crochet.

Continue to repeat Step Three, working one half double crochet (hdc) in each ch to end. You now have 15 hdc, plus 2 chains at the beginning of the row. These 2 beginning chains count as 1 hdc; therefore, you actually have a total of 16 hdc.

Row 2: Ch2 and turn the work so the backside of the first row is now facing. Note that the height of the ch2 equals that of 1 hdc

Step HDC-1. YO and insert hook into the 3rd loop from the hook.

Step HDC-2. YO and pull a loop thru the chain only.

Step HDC-3. YO and pull yarn thru all 3 loops on hook at the same time—1 hdc made.

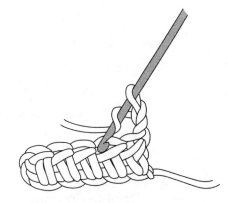

Step HDC-4. Skip the first stitch, YO, and insert hook under the top loops of the 2nd st.

and thus counts as the first hdc of the new row. (Single crochet is the only stitch in which you work into the first stitch of a row.) Skip the first stitch, YO, and insert hook under the top loops of the 2nd st (see step HDC-4), YO, and pull thru all 3 sts at once—half double crochet made. Work 1 hdc in each of the remaining hdc across the row to the beginning chain. Hdc into the top of the beginning chain. You now have completed 16 hdc on the second row, counting the beginning chain 2 as 1 hdc.

Continue to work in hdc until your swatch is as long as it is wide (see figure 4.10).

Figure 4.10. Half double crochet swatch.

Write down the number of hdc stitches and rows in your notebook. If you worked this hdc swatch with the same size hook as used for the single crochet swatch, your number of stitches per inch should be the same.

Double Crochet

The double crochet (dc) stitch is worked much like the hdc, only it requires one extra step. The double crochet is slightly taller than the hdc because of the extra step and is twice as tall as the single crochet.

To Begin: Loosely chain 18.

Row 1—Step One: YO and insert the hook into the 4th loop from the hook, keeping the YO on the hook (see step DC-1).

Step Two: YO and pull the yarn thru the chain. Do not pull thru the loops on the hook (see Step DC-2).

Step Three: YO and pull yarn thru the first two loops on the hook. You still have 2 loops remaining on the hook (see step DC-3).

Step Four: YO and pull the yarn thru the last 2 loops on the hook—one double crochet made (see step DC-4).

Step Five: YO and insert the hook into the next loop from the hook, keeping the YO on the hook (see step DC-5).

Repeat Steps Two through Five, working 1 dc in each ch across the chain. You should have 15 dc, plus 3 ch (counts as 1 dc) at the beginning of the row, for a total of 16 dc.

Step DC-1. YO and insert the hook into the 4th loop from the hook, keeping the YO on the hook.

Step DC-2. YO and pull the yarn thru the chain. Do not pull thru the loops on the hook.

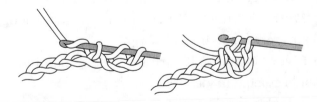

Step DC-3. YO and pull yarn thru the first two loops on the hook. You still have 2 loops remaining on the hook.

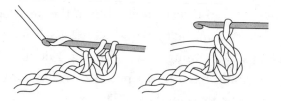

Step DC-4. YO and pull the yarn thru the last 2 loops on the hook—one double crochet made.

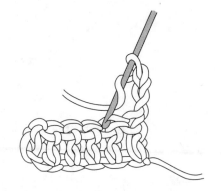

Step DC-5. YO and insert the hook into the next loop from the hook, keeping the YO on the hook.

Step DC-6. YO and skip first dc, insert hook under the top two loops of the 2nd dc.

Row 2—Step One: Ch3 and turn. At this point most written instructions will read as follows: Ch3 (counts as 1st dc now and throughout) because the height of the ch3 is equal to 1 dc. This means that you do *not* work into the 1st stitch of the row.

Step Two: YO and skip first dc, insert hook under the top two loops of the 2nd dc (see step DC-6).

Step Three: YO and pull yarn thru loop—3 loops on hook.

Step Four: YO and pull yarn thru the first 2 loops on the hook—2 loops remain on hook.

Step Five: YO and pull yarn thru the remaining 2 loops on hook—double crochet made.

Work 1 double crochet in each of the remaining dc across the row. Work the last dc in the top of the beginning chain.

Counting all of the stitches, including the beginning chain, you should now have 16 dc. Repeat Steps One through Five until your swatch is as long as it is wide (see figure 4.11). Write down the number of dc stitches and rows in your notebook. If you worked this dc swatch with the same size crochet hook as used for the single crochet and half double crochet swatches, your number of stitches per inch should be the same. But notice how the number of rows per inch lessens as you crochet taller stitches.

Figure 4.11. Double crochet swatch.

Treble Crochet

The treble crochet (tr) is taller than the double crochet because the treble requires one additional step to form each stitch.

To Begin: Chain 19 loosely.

Row 1—Step One: YO the hook twice, and insert the hook into the 5th chain from the hook (see step TC-1).

Step Two: YO and draw the yarn thru the chain. Do not pull the yarn thru the loops on the hook (see step TC-2).

Step Three: YO and pull the yarn thru the *first* 2 loops on the hook—3 loops remain on the hook (see step TC-3).

Step Four: YO and draw the yarn thru the *next* 2 loops on the hook. You still have 2 loops remaining on the hook (see step TC-4).

Step Five: YO and draw the yarn thru the remaining 2 loops on the hook. You have just made one treble crochet and have one loop remaining on the hook (see step TC-5).

Continue to work 1 treble crochet in each chain across. You now have 15 treble crochet, plus 4 chains at the beginning of the row that count as the first st, for a total of 16 tr.

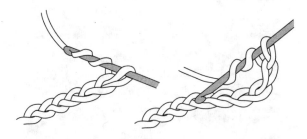

Step TC-1. YO the hook twice, and insert the hook into the 5th chain from the hook.

Step TC-2. YO and draw the yarn thru the chain. Do not pull the yarn thru the loops on the hook.

Step TC-3. YO and pull the yarn thru the *first* 2 loops on the hook—3 loops remain on the hook.

Step TC-4. YO and draw the yarn thru the *next* 2 loops on the hook. You still have 2 loops remaining on the hook.

Step TC-5. YO and draw the yarn thru the remaining 2 loops on the hook. You have just made one treble crochet and have one loop remaining on the hook.

Row 2—Step One: Ch4 (counts as first tr now and throughout); turn (see step TC-6).

Remember that when working *any stitch other than single crochet,* the beginning chain counts as the first stitch. Therefore, you always begin working the first treble crochet of Row 2 in the second stitch.

Step Two: YO twice, skip the first tr, and insert the hook *under* both of the top loops of the next tr (see step TC-7).

Step Three: YO and pull up a loop—four loops on hook.

Step Four: YO and pull yarn thru the first 2 loops on the hook—3 loops still on hook.

Step Five: YO and pull yarn thru the next 2 loops on the hook—2 loops remain on hook.

Step Six: YO and pull yarn thru the last 2 loops on hook—treble made.

Work 1 tr in each remaining tr across row, repeating Steps Two through Six, working last tr in the top of the turning ch.

Counting the beginning chain, you should have 16 tr. Continue to work in tr until your swatch is as long as it is wide. Again measure the swatch, and write down the gauge in your crochet notebook for future reference (see figure 4.12).

 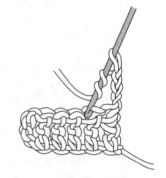

Step TC-6. Ch4 (counts as first tr now and throughout); turn.

Step TC-7. YO twice, skip the first tr, and insert the hook *under* both of the top loops of the next tr.

To Add or Join Yarn

Whenever possible, add new yarn at the *end* of a row. Crochet the last stitch until 2 loops remain on the hook. Cut yarn, leaving a

Figure 4.12. Treble crochet swatch.

6-inch tail. Complete the stitch by pulling the new yarn (leaving a 6-inch tail of the new yarn also) thru the last 2 loops.

Continue to crochet using the new yarn. Hold both tails on the wrong side of work, and continue to crochet using the new color and working over both strands of yarn until the tails are covered. If the stitches that you worked over the tails look too bulky or unsightly, pull the tails loose. After a piece is finished, thread the yarn tails into a tapestry needle and run the threaded needle through the tops of stitches to hide them; this technique is referred to as *weaving*. Weave yarn ends in *after* a piece is completed but *before* seaming.

Color Work

When doing color work, you use the same method as for adding or joining yarn. For example, if you are working in stripes, you change color during the last stitch. You work the last stitch until 2 loops remain on the hook, and then pull the new color thru the last 2 loops.

When following a chart or crocheting a multicolor pattern, colors must be changed *during* the row. If the *right* side of the work is facing, you work the last stitch of the old color until 2 loops remain on the hook and pull the new color through the last 2 loops. Do not cut colors that need to be rejoined and worked later. Each time you change color, make sure that all yarns not currently in use are placed behind your work on the wrong side. When colors are rejoined, a "float" thread appears on the wrong side as the yarn is carried across from one stitch to another. If more than 4 stitches are to be worked before rejoining the last color used, you can work *over* any yarns that must be carried along. The reason for working over the carried yarns is that it minimizes the length of floats, which can be easily caught and snagged.

When the *wrong* side of the work is facing and you are changing colors, be sure to keep floaters on this side of the work.

Handy Hint

When only small amounts of different-colored yarns are required for color work, rather than struggling to manage several different skeins of yarn at one time, you'll find it easier to wind small amounts of each color into a small ball or to use yarn bobbins.

Identifying the Right Side of Work

Sometimes the right side of the work depends on personal preference. Most pattern instructions specify which is the right side of work and tell you to mark the right side with a strand of yarn or a safety pin, making it easy to identify.

Look at both sides of the basic crochet stitch swatches you just completed. Notice that one side of the work is smoother in appearance, while the opposite side looks more bumpy and uneven. Generally, the smooth side is the "right" side of the work.

To Work in Rounds

Crochet work is either done in rows or rounds (rnds). When working in rows, you work back and forth as you did when making the swatches for the basic crochet stitches. To make circular, oval, or tubular pieces, you work in the round in a circular manner. When working rounds, you sometimes crochet without turning the piece.

Like crocheting in rows, when crocheting in the round, you must first make a foundation chain. There are two basic ways to work in the round. In the first method, you make a ring by joining a chain of a specified number and then work a designated number of stitches into the center of the ring. In the second method, you work the required number of stitches into the first chain.

> **Handy Hint**
>
> If the beginning tail of the chain is at the lower *left* of your work, you are working on a *right* side row.

Method One: Making a Ring

To make a foundation ring, make a chain of the specified number. For example, chain 4. To close the ring, slip stitch (sl st) into the beginning chain (see step MR-1).

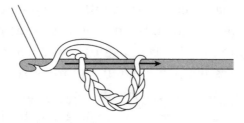

Step MR-1. To close the ring, slip stitch (sl st) into the beginning chain.

Beginning a Round

Your pattern instructions will tell you to chain a specified number. For example, chain 3 and work specified number of dc into ring (see step MR-2). The number of chains relates directly to the height of the stitch that is to be worked into the ring and usually counts as one stitch. You chain 1 to work in sc, 2 for hdc, 3 for dc, and 4 for tr.

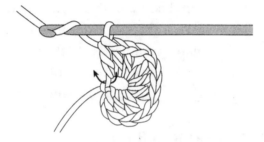

Step MR-2. Chain 3 and work the specified number of dc into the ring.

Rnd 1: Ch3 (counts as 1 dc); work 11 dc into ring. Because the ch3 counts as 1 dc, you now have 12 dc. When all the required number of stitches have been worked into the round, the first and last stitches are joined together. You do this by slip stitching into the top of the beginning chain. Do *not* turn your work when working in rounds unless instructions tell you to do so. When using this method of working rounds, *without turning* your work, you will notice that there is a definite visible joining line that is created where each round is joined. This line then begins to spiral to the left or right, depending on the type of stitches being worked. This line cannot be avoided (see figure 4.13).

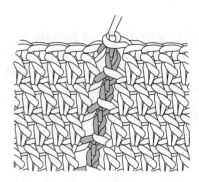

Figure 4.13. Joining line spiraling to the right.

Continuous Rounds Without Turning

When working continuous rounds, you do *not* join at the end of rows. To identify the ends of rounds, place a marker at the beginning of each new round. You can loop a different color length of yarn through your work for a marker, or simply attach a small safety pin as a marker. The marker is moved after each round is completed.

Continuous Rounds with Turning

When instructions specify that work is to be turned at the end of a round, the yarn is joined with a slip stitch, and then the work is turned at the beginning of the next round. When this method is used, the visible joining line remains straight (see figure 4.14).

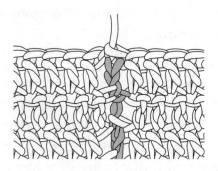

Figure 4.14. Joining line is straight.

Method Two of Beginning a Round

This method of working in rounds calls for all the stitches for the first round to be worked into the beginning chain. As the required number of stitches are worked, the stitches fill the first chain and form a circle.

More about Reading Instructions

Crochet instructions are written with punctuation marks. Pause after each punctuation mark and work as instructed; each step is separated by the punctuation marks.

Brackets and Parentheses

Brackets [ ] or parentheses ( ) indicate several things:

1. Sizing changes. Instructions are written for the smallest size, with other sizes following in brackets or parentheses in incremental sizes. Let's say you are reading instructions for the back of a pullover, and the instructions include four sizes—Petite, Small, Medium, and Large. If the instructions say to loosely chain 80 (84-88-92), you are to chain 80 for size Petite, 84 for size Small, 88 for size Medium, and 92 for size Large. You will find instructions easier to read and follow if you circle or highlight all the numbers pertaining to your size before beginning to crochet.

2. Repetition. A sequence for doing something is contained within the parentheses or brackets. For example, if you are reading instructions for making a Cluster, the instructions might read as follows: "Row 2: Ch3, turn; work Cluster in the next ch1 sp as follows: (YO, insert hook in ch1 sp and pull up a loop, YO and draw thru 2 loops on hook) 3 times, YO and pull thru all 4 loops on hook—Cluster made." This means

that you do everything within the parentheses 3 times to make a Cluster.

3. Specifications. If the Right Side row is not the smooth side of work, as is usual, it will be noted on the first right side row as follows: "Row 2 (Right Side)."

4. Explanations. When working fancy crochet stitches, you sometimes work several stitches into one stitch to create a fancy pattern stitch. For example, make a shell as follows: skip 2 dc, work (2 dc, ch1, 2 dc) in next dc. The sequence of stitches within the parentheses are all to be worked into the same stitch to make a shell.

Asterisks

Asterisks (*) are used to shorten instructions. Work all instructions following an asterisk as many *more* times as instructed. For example, instructions might read: *2 dc, ch1, skip 1; rep from * 3 more times.

Why Crochet Instructions Are Written the Way They Are

Crochet instructions are written with abbreviations to make reading easier and quicker. At first, you may need to refer to the abbreviation list to understand how to translate instructions, but it will soon become easier for you. As you will see in the following examples, certain basic steps are assumed in written instructions.

Instructions: Loosely chain 16.

Translation: Make a slipknot. Then make 16 chains that are loose enough for the hook to pass through easily. Written instructions assume that you know that *all* crochet begins with a slipknot. When the instructions say to chain "loosely," it is assumed that you know that each chain must be loose enough for the hook to pass through easily on the next row.

Instructions: Row 1: Ch3 (counts as first dc now and throughout), turn. *skip next 2 chs, 5 dc in next ch, skip next 2 chs, dc in next ch; rep from * across.

Translation: When instructions say "Ch3 (counts as first dc now and throughout)," you must remember this first ch3 counts as 1 dc as noted in the parentheses. The instructions to count the ch3 as 1 dc are only given one time. "Skip next 2 chs" is self-explanatory—you simply do as it is written: you skip two chains and do not work into them. "5 dc in next ch" also means what it says and assumes that you know how to do the double crochet stitch—you work 5 double crochet into the same chain stitch. "Skip next 2 chs" is again self-explanatory. "dc in next ch" means that you work 1 dc in the next chain. "Rep from * across" means that you do everything in sequence beginning with the asterisk and then continue to repeat those same sequences as many times as neccessary until the row is finished.

Basic crochet stitches can be combined in hundreds of ways to create different pattern stitches. When written instructions require you to crochet anything other than the basic stitches, the instructions are sometimes presented in a separate section prior to the beginning of a crochet project. Other times, instructions for pattern stitches are included as you read along. For example, if you are following a pattern that has a popcorn pattern stitch, instructions might be written as follows: "5 dc in next sc, drop loop from hook, insert hook (from front to back) thru the top loops of the 1st and 5th dc, YO and pull tog, ch1 to close—Popcorn (PC) made." From this point forward, every time you need to make another popcorn, the instructions will be written as PC and will not describe the process again.

Edging in Single Crochet

Single crochet is the most common edging. When instructions tell you to single crochet *evenly* across or around a piece, you need to take care to space your stitches so as to keep the piece flat. If you find that the edge is flaring out, you need to rip back and space your stitches farther apart. If you find that the edge is puckering or pulling together, you need to rip back and place your stitches closer together. Your goal is to keep the edging as smooth, even, and flat as possible.

Blocking

Blocking smoothes and "sets" a crocheted item, giving your work a professional-looking finish. Before blocking, check the yarn label for special instructions. Some acrylics and other artificial blends can be damaged by blocking.

There are three ways to begin the blocking process:

1. If the item is hand washable, launder and rinse it without wringing or twisting. Then roll the item in two or three towels (in succession) to remove excess moisture.

2. Spray the item with a spray bottle, taking care to only dampen the piece. Don't get it sopping wet.

3. Steam the item.

For the first two methods, lay out several large, fluffy towels, and then place the pieces to be blocked on top. With the *right* side up, gently pat and smooth the piece to the desired shape and measurements. Pin into place and allow to air-dry. When dry, the blocking is completed.

Steaming is a good, and much quicker, method of blocking. Turn the item *wrong* side up and pin it to the correct size on an ironing board or table covered with several thicknesses of towels. Hold a steam iron or steamer over the piece, and steam it thoroughly, *never* actually touching the iron to the fabric. Touching the fabric will flatten stitches, and holding the iron on the fabric can

Handy Hint

Always use rustproof pins when blocking!

"kill" the yarn, meaning that the heat destroys the yarn's natural resiliency forever. After steaming the piece, allow the garment to cool and dry completely before removing the pins.

When blocking acrylic yarns, you can steam lightly, but never touch the iron to the fabric because it is the most likely yarn of all to be killed by heat. It can literally melt the stitches together. The easiest and safest way to block an acrylic item is to place it in a dryer with a damp towel and allow to tumble for 5 to 10 minutes. When you remove the item from the dryer, lay it out on a flat surface, and then smooth and pat it into the desired shape.

Creating Your Crochet Projects

▼▼▼▼▼▼▼▼▼▼▼▼▼▼▼▼▼▼▼▼▼▼▼▼▼▼▼▼▼▼▼▼▼▼▼▼▼▼

NOW THAT YOU'VE LEARNED the fundamentals of crochet—stitches, techniques, how to read instructions, and how to determine gauge—it's time for you to make a few useful crocheted items. You may want to start with some simple projects you can make without a pattern or written instructions.

Squares

If you made the swatches of the basic crochet stitches in chapter 4, you already know how to crochet a square. You can make many different items out of squares. Look over the ideas here. Many different wearables and home decorating items can be made by crocheting one square or by joining several squares together.

No-Pattern Hat

This is one of my all-time favorite projects for beginners. Kids love it, too, whether they make the hat for themselves or receive it as a gift (see figure 5.1). You don't even need to count the number of chains or stitches to start crocheting this hat. It's that simple!

Figure 5.1. No-pattern hat.

For this project, you make two identical squares. I recommend that you use worsted-weight yarn and an H hook. You have already learned how to crochet several basic crochet stitches, and while you can use any of them to make this hat, I recommend that you use double crochet. Double crochet works up much faster than single crochet or half double crochet. Treble crochet is really too loose for a hat.

Begin by making a chain that fits comfortably around the head. Fold in half and mark the center with a small safety pin. Pull back the chain to the safety pin. Remove the safety pin, and make 2 more chains. Work in double crochet, just like you worked your swatch, until the length of the square is the same as the width. Half your hat is already made. Now that you're gaining confidence in your crochet work, a second square can probably be worked up more quickly than the first.

To make sure that both squares are exactly the same, count the number of double crochet stitches on any given row of your first square and write down the number of stitches, then add 2 to that number to determine the required number of chains for the second square.

Now crochet the second square, and sew both squares together with the right sides facing. Work one round of sc around the lower edge. Make or buy two tassels and attach them to the upper corners. The weight of the tassels causes the corners to droop slightly in a most whimsical and charming way. To get a different look, you can work the squares in a solid color or stripes of equal or varying widths.

Pillows

You can make a pillow by crocheting and then sewing two squares together. Either fiberfill or a premade foam pillow form can be inserted.

Let's say you are going to make a pillow that is 14 inches square. How do you figure out how to crochet a square that size? It's easy. Just choose one of the basic crochet stitches and look up your gauge: the number of stitches and rows per inch. If your gauge is 3.5 stitches per inch, then multiply 14 inches $\times$ 3.5 = 49 stitches. You need to make a chain of 49, then add 1 more chain if you are going to work in single crochet, add 2 chains for half double crochet, add 3 chains for double crochet, and add 4 chains for treble crochet. Just crochet until your fabric is as long as it is wide.

> ### Handy Hint
>
> When working with dark-colored yarn, lay a white pillowcase on your lap so stitches show up more clearly.

If you use a premade pillow form, do not go by the measurements given on the package. Take the time to measure the form to get accurate measurements. Do not be concerned about the depth of your pillow. Crochet fabric is stretchy by nature, so your squares will plump up nicely when stuffed or filled.

After making two squares, sew them together with the right sides facing, leaving an opening wide enough to insert either the pillow form or fiberfill. Using a tapestry needle and matching yarn, close the opening by sewing it together.

You can use one square to make a triangle-shaped pillow. Fold the square diagonally to create a triangle. Sew the edges together, leaving an opening to insert fiberfill, and stitch closed after stuffing.

You can adorn even the simplest of pillows with such embellishments as ready-made cording and tassels to create classy home accessories that have a custom look.

Purses

You can create purses by simply crocheting two squares and sewing them together, using whatever color, weight of yarn, or stitch that suits your fancy. Sew on rayon cording for a shoulder strap, or add a length of beads or metal chain for a different look. If you prefer a handheld bag, make a chain, loop in half, and sew the ends together in one corner of the bag.

Baby Blocks

Stuffed crocheted blocks make wonderful soft toys for babies, and this is a great way to use leftover yarn. Just crochet six small squares, sew them together, and stuff them with fiberfill. Make the squares all one color, or use several colors. Embroider a letter of the alphabet on each square. If you like, spell out a new baby's name or initials in cross-stitch. Make a set for a unique gift, or make two tiny baby blocks to embellish the top of a wrapped gift.

Coasters

You can easily whip up a set of coasters, each made from a single crocheted square. Mix and match colors as you like. Try edging the squares in a different yarn or a complementary color.

Rectangles

Using the same techniques as for a square, continue to add rows until you reach the desired length for your project.

Scarves

Begin by making a chain the width of your choice, and work in one of the basic crochet stitches until the scarf measures the desired length. Add tassels or fringe to the ends, if you like.

Table Runners

Using the same principle as for a scarf, make a chain of the desired width, and continue to crochet until you reach the desired length. Add rayon cording to the edges, tassels to the corners, or fringe on the ends.

Placemats

Here is a good project to tackle if you want to practice changing colors. Try crocheting place mats with stripes or checks.

Other Ideas for Crocheted Squares and Rectangles

- **Earwarmers.** Crochet a 3- to 4-inch wide strip until it's long enough to fit around the head. Sew ends together. Embellish with tassels, flowers, ribbons, bows, charms, or other decorative embellishments. Crocheted earwarmers work up quickly and take only a small amount of yarn. This little project is another good way to use leftover yarn. Especially quick to crochet, earwarmers make good last-minute stocking stuffers for Christmas.

- **Rugs.** Hold several strands of worsted weight yarn together, and use a large hook to make square or rectangular rugs for the kitchen, entryway, bedroom, or bathroom. Rugs can also be crocheted using strips of fabric and are usually crocheted using large hooks such as sizes P or N.

- **Dishcloths.** Dishcloths are another good way to use leftover yarn, but it's best to crochet them with cotton yarn for frequent laundering. Make them any size that suits you.

- **Mantel Scarves.** Especially popular for the holidays, mantel scarves can be worked in sparkly or metallic yarns for a festive look.

- **Bibs.** Using soft, washable, and colorful leftover yarn, you can crochet bibs in a snap. Just add ties to a square.

The Granny Square

One of the most familiar and versatile crochet squares is the all-American granny square. Easy to make, multiple squares can be joined together to make an almost endless array of projects. I think you'll find the granny square interesting and fun to crochet.

You can use any color or kind of yarn or thread to crochet a granny square. Typically, each round of a different granny square is worked in a different color; however, colors can be combined in hundreds of different ways. You can let your imagination take over when working granny squares.

Granny squares were invented by American pioneer women to simulate the look of a quilt while using up scraps of leftover yarn. As these women traveled westward, new yarn was too expensive to buy, so they often ripped out old sweaters and reused the yarn.

Granny squares begin with a chain that is joined to form a circle and then quickly becomes a square. When working a granny square, you do *not* turn work unless instructed to do so.

How to Make a Basic Granny Square

Loosely chain 4 and join into a ring.

Rnd 1: Ch3 (counts as 1 dc), work 2 dc into ring, ch2, (3 dc into ring, ch2) 3 times, join to top of ch3. Cut yarn. Do not turn. (See figure 5.2.)

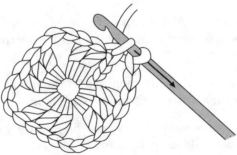

Figure 5.2. Granny square round 1.

Reusing Old Yarn

You begin by using the infamous Frog Stitch—rip it, rip it, rip it! When you unravel yarn, you'll notice that it is full of kinks. To remove the kinks, wrap the yarn around a large plastic container, such as a bowl, taking care not to wrap too tightly. Or you can wrap the yarn around a plastic cutting board, spreading out the yarn as much as possible. Place the wrapped yarn in the bathroom as near to the shower or tub as possible. Run hot water until the room fills with steam. Close the door and let the steam go to work—it magically straightens out the kinks. When the yarn is completely dry, wrap it into balls, taking care not to wind too tightly. If you wind too tightly, the yarn stretches and loses its natural resiliency.

Rnd 2: Join new color into any ch2 space (see figures 5.3 and 5.4), ch3, work (2 dc, ch2, 3 dc) into same ch2 sp, ch1, (3 dc, ch2, 3 dc) into next ch2 sp 3 times, ch1, join to top of ch3. Cut yarn.

Figure 5.3. Tying in new color.

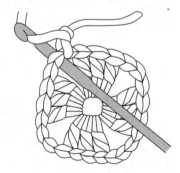

Figure 5.4. Pulling yarn through to begin a chain.

Tie new color into ch2 sp, leaving a 3-inch tail. Insert hook into ch2 sp and pull thru a loop.

Rnd 3: Join in a third color in the same manner as before. Ch3 (2 dc, ch2, 3 dc) into first ch2 sp, *ch1, 3 dc into next ch1 sp, ch1

(3 dc, ch2, 3 dc into next ch2 sp); rep from * 3 times, ch1, 3 dc into next ch1 sp, ch1, join to top of ch3. Cut yarn.

Rnd 4: Join new color in any ch2 sp. Ch3 (2 dc, ch2, 3 dc) into same ch2 sp, *ch1 (3 dc into next ch1 sp) twice, ch1 (3 dc, ch2, 3 dc) into next ch2 sp; rep from * 3 more times (ch1, 3 dc into next ch1 sp) twice, ch1, join to top of ch3. Cut yarn.

Rnd 5: Join new color in any ch2 sp. Ch3 (2 dc, ch2, 3 dc) into same ch2 sp, *(ch1, 3 dc into next ch1 sp) 3 times, ch1 (3 dc, ch2, 3 dc) into next ch2 sp; rep from * 3 more times (ch1, 3 dc into next ch1 sp) 3 times, ch1, join to top of ch3. Cut yarn.

Granny Square Projects

The fascinating thing about granny squares is that you can continue to work rounds, making any size you like. By joining granny squares in clever ways, you can use them to create boxes, clothing, Christmas stockings, tote bags, and a myriad of other things. You can create crocheted items of just about any size with granny squares. Listed here are just a few of the wide range of things you can create with granny squares.

One Granny

Single granny squares make great coasters and dishcloths. Or you can make one large granny square for a baby blanket or an even bigger granny for an adult-sized afghan. Make a granny square to use as a table topper.

Two Grannies

Add ribbon ties to the sides and shoulders of two granny squares and voilà—you've created a vest for a favorite doll! Make two larger matching granny squares to make a vest for the doll's mommy.

Crochet and sew two tiny granny squares together to make a doll hat. Add tassels at the corners.

Three Grannies

Make three granny squares, using fine thread, and sew them to-gether to make bookmarks for the family bookworms. Crochet three grannies; join them, and you have a rug.

Four Grannies

Make and join four granny squares for the front of a pillow, photo album, or book cover. Four joined grannies might end up as a pet blanket, car throw, tablecloth, or welcome mat.

More Grannies

Make nine granny squares to create a doll blanket. Multiple grannies can be joined to create vests, sweaters, hats, purses, stoles, scarves, and other items. Try making new chair pad covers; while you're at it, why not crochet a matching table runner? I'm sure you'll think of many other ways to combine grannies.

Fancy-Thread Grannies

Solid-colored pillow shams become a thing of beauty when grannies are added over them, letting the color show through.

Make grannies of white thread for window curtains. Sew white or ecru thread grannies together to make a window valance. Add small thread grannies, all in a row, to edge the bottom of a dust ruf-fle for a room done in a Victorian or Americana style. Thread grannies can be joined into table toppers, mantel covers, table-cloths, and so on.

Ways to Sew Seams and Join Grannies

There are a variety of ways to join crocheted pieces together. The method you choose depends on how you want the finished product to look.

Whip Stitch

Whip stitching can be done from either the right or wrong side. Most pattern instructions will state the preferred method. To whip stitch, sew through both pieces at the same time (see figure 5.5).

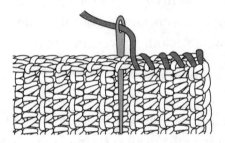

Figure 5.5. Whip stitch seam.

Using a threaded yarn or tapestry needle, insert the needle from the *back* to the *front* bringing the needle and yarn up, over, and around the upper edge, leaving a 3-inch tail to weave in later. Make 2 stitches (one on top of the other) at the beginning to secure yarn. Continue along the edge, being careful to match stitches.

Backstitch

Backstitching makes a firm and secure seam. It's the method I always use when joining garment pieces (see figures 5.6 and 5.7). Place right sides together, pinning pieces into place at one inch intervals, taking care to match stitches. Secure yarn by stitching over the first stitch a second time, leaving a 3-inch tail to weave in later. Insert the needle from *front* to *back*, working through the top two loops of each stitch. Be patient and let the needle find its way into the stitches; don't force the needle through or you're apt to split the yarn. Bring the needle one crochet stitch forward, and push the needle through to the *front* of work. Insert the needle back into the stitch where the first stitch forward began, and bring forward one crochet stitch on the back. Push needle through to the front of work. Continue in this manner across both pieces, securing yarn at the end of seam with another double stitch.

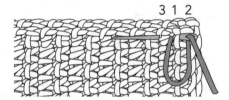

Figure 5.6. First stitch of back stitch seam.

Figure 5.7. Back stitch seam in progress.

Weaving

Begin with *right* sides facing you. Line up the edges evenly. Sew through both pieces twice in the same place to secure yarn before beginning the seam, leaving at least a 3-inch tail to weave in later. Insert the needle from *right* to *left,* going through only one loop/strand on each piece (see figure 5.8). Bring the yarn over, and continue to insert in the same manner, drawing the seam together about every 2 inches as you work. This method is often used to join pieces that are worked with intricate stitches because the right side is always facing you, making it easier to see that stitch patterns match perfectly.

Weaving is sometimes called "whip stitching" when instructions refer to joining grannies. When assembling squares, you begin with *wrong* sides together and the *right* sides facing out. Whip stitch the squares together going through the outside, *back* loops only. Take care not to draw stitches together too tightly. The desired result is two squares that lie flat yet are butted together neatly.

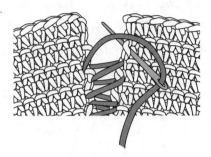

Figure 5.8. Weaving a seam.

Crochet with Slip Stitch or Single Crochet

You can join motifs or garment pieces together by crocheting the seam. Crocheting the seam forms a ridge. Most often the ridge, like any other seam, ends up on the inside (wrong side) of a garment; however, it is sometimes worked as a decorative feature so the ridge shows on the right side of the work. This "seam side out" look is often used for shoulder and side seams and sometimes around sleeves as well.

To crochet seams together, you can work the seam with slip stitches to lessen the ridge or work in single crochet to emphasize the ridge. Place *right* sides together, with pieces lined up evenly (see figure 5.9). Working through the top loops of each stitch, insert hook through both pieces, and work either a slip stitch or single crochet into each stitch to the end of the seam.

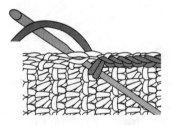

Figure 5.9. Slip stitch seam.

Crochet with Slip Stitch and Chains

This method of joining is most often used for motifs and grannies; however, it can also be used as a novel seam finish for clothing. Place *right* sides together, and line up pieces evenly. Attach yarn with a slip stitch in an end stitch or corner of a motif and chain 2, slip stitch into corresponding stitch of the other piece, ch2, skip 2 stitches on the first motif and work 1 sl st, ch2, skip 2 stitches on the second motif and slip stitch into the corresponding stitch of the second piece (see figure 5.10). You can vary this method by changing the number of chains in between slip stitches and you can slip stitch at desired intervals.

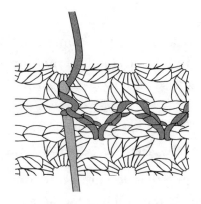

Figure 5.10. Using slip stitch and chains to join.

Size, Fit, and Adjusting Patterns

Before you determine which pattern size is right for you, let me give you a few hints about sizing. Most of us think of ourselves as being a certain size. Maybe you consider your size to be Medium. What is a size Medium? Maybe you assume that there are standards when it comes to sizing—that's one of those things that is kinda/sorta true. No doubt you've noticed that sizing varies from brand to brand when you purchase ready-made clothes. The same applies

Think Creatively

Before you start one of the projects in this book, remember that you can use any color of yarn you like. Now, that may seem like a perfectly silly thing for me to say, but research shows that 90% of crocheters make a pattern in exactly the same color as the original. A reader once wrote to an editor friend of mine, "I just love the sweater design in your latest issue, but pink isn't my color. Could you design the sweater in blue?" I want you to start thinking creatively from the get-go.

Each of my designs includes tips about how you can change or vary the design to create a different look. Most written patterns don't include "Designer Tips"; I'm including them to help you see the creative possibilities in any basic pattern.

to crochet garments and patterns. Sometimes garments vary according to a company's basic standard measurements; sometimes the sizing differs because of the way the garment is meant to fit the body.

Measure, Measure, and Measure Again

Since we are assuming that you are a size Medium, take a look at the sizing for Project 1, the Pullover Sweater. The instructions state that the finished bust measurement for a size Medium is 44 inches. Instead of making the mistake of thinking that sounds about right, take out a favorite pullover sweater, T-shirt, or sweatshirt and your tape measure. Lay the garment down flat on a table, and smooth it down, making sure it has no wrinkles. Measure across the chest, from armhole to armhole. Double that measurement to get the finished bust measurement. Compare the finished bust measurement of your favorite garment with the finished bust measurement of the pattern. Is the measurement 44 inches? Or is it larger or smaller? If you want to duplicate the fit of your favorite garment, choose the pattern size that is nearest to that measurement. Prior to starting any garment, follow the same procedure.

Remember, the garment you measure should be similar to the pattern of your choice. Let's say you are going to crochet a blazer. Compare the pattern to a similar blazer from your wardrobe. Measure the chest, underarm length, armhole depth, sleeve length, and back neck of the jacket from your wardrobe and compare the measurements to the crochet pattern, noting differences between features such as lapel width, style of pockets, and cuffs.

Based on your comparisons, determine whether you need to adjust sizing or make other changes to your crochet pattern. Obviously, you can easily change the total length (back neck to hem) by adding or omitting rows, but what about the sleeves? If the pattern features sleeves with ribbing and the jacket from your closet does not have ribbing, then you must consider how ribbing affects the length of a sleeve. Ribbed sleeves are longer in length than straight sleeves and have more ease. Straight sleeves fall to the wrist without any ease.

The time taken to check details such as ease, features, and measurements before you start to crochet any new garment helps ensure that your finished product will look and fit right. When you

Ease

The next time you go to the yarn shop, take a good look at the sizing for various patterns. Notice that some patterns include *actual* bust measurements as well as *finished* measurements. "Ease" is the difference between actual and finished measurements. You may be surprised to see that some patterns only allow 2 inches of ease. A garment with only 2 inches of ease fits close to the body and restricts body movements. Preferences for ease are highly personal, so you may need to adapt your crochet pattern to ensure the fit is right for you.

take the time to plan ahead, you can enjoy crocheting a garment more, assured that you'll be satisfied with the end result.

Reading Schematics and Adjusting Patterns

Crochet patterns in books and magazines often include *schematics*—outline drawings of each garment's pieces. Schematics also include measurements, the number of starting stitches, and other information. See figure 5.11 for a typical schematic for a drop sleeve.

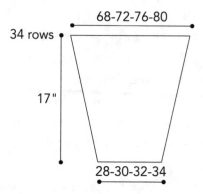

Figure 5.11. Example of a drop sleeve schematic.

As with written instructions, the numbers shown on a schematic cite the first size first, with the other sizes following and separated by hyphens or brackets. The schematic shown is a typical example of a sweater pattern featuring four sizes: Small, Medium, Large, and Extra Large. The numbers over the horizontal line at the bottom of the sleeve indicate how many stitches are required to begin the sleeve (this number for crocheted garments is *not* the same number required for the beginning chain). The vertical line going from the bottom of the sleeve to the top indicates the total length of the sleeve (17 inches in this example). The horizontal line across the top of the sleeve indicates the total number of stitches required to achieve the required width of the sleeve and should be twice as wide as the armhole depth. Each sleeve will be folded in half, with the center matching the shoulder seam when the sweater pieces are sewn together.

When crocheting a drop sleeve, most instructions tell you to work to a specified length; sometimes they say, "or to desired length." If you want the sleeves to fit properly, work to the length that is right for you. To determine the sleeve length that is the most comfortable for you, measure the sleeves of a similar garment that fits you well.

A designer must follow some kind of sizing standards when creating a design, but let's face it—there is no such thing as a typical body shape! Maybe you have a wide waist, big hips, short arms, or narrow shoulders. None of us has a perfect body. Many people need to make adjustments to patterns to achieve a good fit. Luckily, that is much easier to do with a crocheted sweater schematic than it is with a sewing pattern.

Let's continue with the assumption that you are a size Medium. The second number (30) shown at the bottom of the drop sleeve schematic is the number of stitches you need to begin the sleeve. After all the increases have been made, you will have a total of 72 stitches (second number at top of sleeve). But when you compare the measurement of the upper arm of a sweater that fits comfortably to the pattern, you realize if you follow the instructions and make the sleeve according to the pattern, it's going to be uncomfortably tight. Write down the measurement that is comfortable for you next to the sleeve schematic.

Subtract the difference between your desired measurement and the pattern measurement to determine how many inches need to be added. Let's say the difference is 2 inches and your gauge is 4 stitches per inch. Multiply the gauge (4) by the number of inches that need to be increased (2). You need to add 8 stitches to the total number of stitches (72) given on the schematic. For the sleeve to fit properly, you need a total of 80 stitches.

Each sleeve has two sides, so next you need to determine how many increases need to be made on *each* side of the sleeve to achieve the total number (80) stitches. In this case, you need to increase 4 stitches (half the number of stitches added) on each side of the sleeve. Determine how many rows need to be worked to attain the desired sleeve length. For example, if you want to crochet a sleeve length of 17 inches and your gauge is 2 rows per inch, you need to work 34 rows to reach 17 inches. Look at the drop sleeve schematic to determine the specified number of beginning stitches for your nearest true size, Medium. According to the schematic, you begin with 30 stitches at the wrist and increase until you have a total of 80 (your adjusted total number of stitches).

Subtract the beginning number of wrist stitches, 30 from 80, to determine how many stitches must be increased in all—50 stitches. To determine how and when to work the increases, divide 50 by 2 (the number of sides). You need to work 25 increase rows. Increases are worked on *each* side of the sleeve. You have 34 rows in which to make those increases. Divide the total number of rows (34) by the number of increases, 25, to get the answer: 1.36. To simplify the increases, you increase 1 stitch, *each* edge (in both the first and last stitch), *every* row 25 times to achieve a total of 80 stitches, then work 9 rows even.

Now that the sleeve length is settled and you've written down your changes on the schematic, you're almost ready to start crochet-

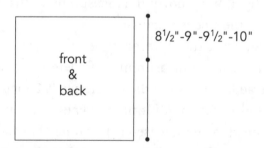

Figure 5.12. Example of a sweater schematic (front and back).

ing your sweater—but not quite yet. Don't forget that the width of a drop sleeve must match the armhole depth exactly!

According to the schematic (see figure 5.12), the armhole depth for a Medium is 9 inches. The armhole depth is exactly half the measurement of the total sleeve width: 9 inches × 2 inches = 18 inches upper sleeve width. But you need 2 inches added to provide the required upper sleeve width. Your adjusted upper sleeve measures 20 inches. When you divide 20 inches (the adjusted sleeve width) by 2 (half the sleeve width), your adjusted armhole depth is 10 inches. If you were to leave the armhole depth at 9 inches, your upper sleeve would be 2 inches larger than the armhole opening and thus would not fit properly. Therefore, you must add 1 inch to the armhole depth for both the front and back pieces to coincide with the adjustment made to the upper sleeve width. Adding 1 inch means that you need to work 2 additional rows on the front and back since your gauge is 2 rows per inch. Write down these changes on your schematic. If you need to make any other adjustments to crochet patterns, just follow the principles given here. When adjusting one piece of a garment, make sure you make adjustments to the other pieces accordingly so that pieces fit together properly in the construction process.

Prior to beginning Project 1, my Pullover Sweater, take time to review the finished measurements and the schematic to determine whether you need to make any adjustments. If any adjustments are necessary, follow the method described above.

Pullover Sweater

The yarn used for the Pullover Sweater, Samoa, is a sport-weight cotton with a lovely sheen, imported from Italy by the Skacel Collection, Inc. I chose cotton for all the reasons discussed earlier in the book about this natural, feel-good fiber. If you wish to use a substitute yarn, please refer to "About Yarns" in chapter 2.

The length of time it takes you to make this T-shaped sweater depends on your skill level and experience with crochet. Most crocheters can complete this sweater in 8 to 12 hours. Notice that I've included a broad range of sizes so you can make the sweater for just about any body size or shape.

As I've mentioned before, I always have beginning students make a short-sleeve pullover for their first project. Making each piece—back, front, and sleeves—involves nothing more complicated than making basic rectangles (see figures 5.13 and 5.14). Once you have crocheted a few inches of the back, I'm sure you'll agree that this project is simple and fun to make.

Instructions are provided for 8 sizes; measurements under each size are *finished* bust measurements.

XPetite	Petite	Small	Medium	Large	XLarge	XXLarge	XXXLarge
32″	36″	40″	44″	48″	52″	56″	62″

Instructions are written for size Xpetite, with sizes Petite, Small, Medium, Large, XLarge, XXLarge, and XXXLarge following in brackets. Instructions will be easier to read if you circle or highlight all numbers pertaining to your size.

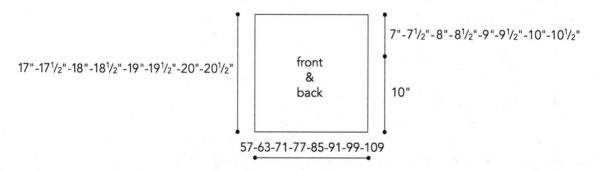

Figure 5.13. Pullover Sweater front and back.

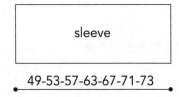

Figure 5.14. Pullover Sweater sleeve.

Materials

6 (7 - 8 - 9 - 10 - 11 - 12 - 13) Skeins Samoa, Color 88 Medium
  Green, 50 grams, 105 meters (115 yards), sport-weight
  cotton yarn*
Tapestry needle
Crochet hooks sizes E & H or sizes required to obtain gauge
*As shown in color insert.
Note: Other sport-weight yarns can be substituted. When making
substitutions, be sure to check labels for both weight and yardage to
ensure you buy the right amount of yarn.

Instructions

Gauge using larger hook: 7 sts & 4 pattern rows = 2 inches

Back

Using larger hook, loosely chain 59 (65 - 73 - 79 - 87 - 93 - 101 - 111).

   Row 1: Dc in 4th loop from hook and in each ch to end, 57 dc
(63 - 71 - 77 - 85 - 91 - 99 - 109).

   Row 2: Ch3, turn; (counts as first dc now and throughout), dc
in 2nd dc and in each dc to end.

   Row 3: Ch1, turn; 1 sl st in first, *1 tr, 1 sl st; rep from * to end.

   Row 4: Ch3, turn; dc in 2nd dc and in each st to end.

   Rep Rows 2 - 4 until 17 (17½" - 18" - 18½" - 19" - 19½" - 20" -
20½") or desired length. Cut yarn and end off.

Designer Tips

- Omit the sleeves for a vest.

- Work in stripes, alternating colors every two rows.

- Work in three colors, working 1 row of each color.

- Add knitted ribbing to the bottom for a European designer look.

- Work each piece in a different primary color.

- Work to a longer length for a long pullover or tunic.

Front

Work the same as back.

Sleeves

Using larger hook, loosely chain 51 (55 - 59 - 65 - 69 - 73 - 75 - 79).

Repeat Rows 1 - 4 as for back, then rep Row 4 two more times. Cut yarn and end off. Make two.

Finishing

Sew front and back together, with RS (right sides) facing, leaving center 7½″ - 8″ open for neck.For sleeve placement, place markers 7″ (7½″- 8″ - 8½″ - 9″ - 9½″ - 10″ - 10½″) on either side of shoulder seam. Fold sleeve in half and pin center to shoulder seam with RS facing, and match sleeve edges to markers. Sew in sleeve. Sew sleeve and side in one continuous seam.

Edging

Using smaller hook, with RS facing, attach yarn with sl st to side seam, ch1, sc in same st as joining, *ch15, sc in next st at bottom of sweater; rep from * around sweater, join with sl st to beg sc. Cut yarn and end off.

Sleeve Edging

Rnd 1: Using smaller hook, with RS facing, join yarn with sl st to seam, ch1, sc in same st as joining, *1 sc in each of next 3 sts around lower sleeve, 2 sc tog; rep from * around. (You may not be able to work complete repeats for all sizes. If you end up with a few odd number of sts, work them in sc.) Join with sl st to first st.

    Rnd 2: Ch1, sc in first st, 1 sc in each sc around, join. Cut yarn and end off.

2 Baby Afghan

Worked in a bulky-weight yarn with a fairly large hook, size J, you'll find that the pattern stitch is easy to memorize and the blanket works up quite quickly. How long it will take to make the blanket will vary from person to person, but you should be able to complete this project in 10 to 12 hours.

    Finished Measurements: 31″ × 42″

Materials

4 Skeins Mondial Junior, 06 Lt. Aqua, 50 grams, 60 meters (66 yards), 60% new wool, 40% acrylic, bulky weight*

4 Skeins Mondial Junior, 01 White, 50 grams, 60 meters (66 yards), 60% new wool, 40% acrylic, bulky weight*

5 Skeins Mondial Junior, 10 Purple, 50 grams, 60 meters (66 yards), 60% new wool, 40% acrylic, bulky weight,* Main Color (MC)

Crochet Hooks sizes I and J or size required to obtain gauge

*As shown in color insert.

Designer Tips

■ Make and edge with the same color.

■ Make afghan in one color and edge with a complementary color.

■ Add tassels to corners.

■ Fringe all around instead of working edging.

■ Alternate two colors, working 2 rows in each color.

■ Try using the new Baby Bright colors.

■ Alternate solid-color stripes with complementary variegated stripes.

Note: Other bulky-weight yarns can be substituted. When making substitutions, be sure to check labels for both weight and yardage to ensure you buy the right amount of yarn.

Instructions

Gauge using larger hook: 1 pattern repeat = 3 inches

Afghan

Note: To make long dc (ld), YO, insert hook as instructed, YO, pull loop thru and lift up even with last st worked (YO and pull thru 2 loops) twice.

Using larger hook and MC, loosely ch 75.

Row 1: Dc in 4th loop from hook and in each next 2 ch, *ch3, skip 3 ch, 1 dc in each of next 5 ch; rep from * to within last 6 chs ending ch3, skip 3 ch, 1 dc in each of last 3 ch, 73 dc. Change to Aqua.

Row 2: Ch3, turn (counts as first dc now and throughout) 2 dc, * To make shell, work 3 dc in 2nd skipped ch, 5 dc; rep from *, ending shell, 3 dc.

Row 3: Ch3, turn. 6 dc, * ch3, skip 3 dc, 5 dc; rep from *, ending 7 dc. Change to White.

Row 4: Ch3, turn. 6 dc, *shell in corresponding dc 2 rows below, 5 dc; rep from *, ending 7 dc.

Row 5: Ch3, turn. 2 dc, *ch3, skip 3 dc, 5 dc; rep from *, ending ch2, skip 3 dc, 3 dc.

Continue to repeat Rows 2 - 5, after working 2 rows with each color.

Work even in established pattern until afghan measures 39 inches in length, ending by working the last row in MC.

Edging

Using smaller hook and MC, attach yarn to any corner st. Ch7, dc into 4th ch from hook, dc in same st as joining, *skip 3 sts, 1 dc in next st, ch4, dc into 4th loop from hook, dc into same st; rep from * around. Join to 3rd ch of beg chain. Cut yarn and end off.

Floppy Brimmed Hat

The Floppy Brimmed Hat is also worked in an imported Italian yarn, imported by the Skacel Collection, Inc. I chose this yarn because it has a crisp, crimped finish similar to the look of crepe fabric. I held two strands together to create a worsted weight while working throughout with a smaller-than-usual hook size to obtain the firmness and stability needed for a hat. If this is your first circular crochet project, I think you'll enjoy trying out this new technique.

The Floppy Brimmed Hat has openwork stitches, called *meshes*. You can clearly see these open spaces if you turn to the color insert in this book. In this pattern, meshes are formed by skipping one stitch and working one chain over the space skipped. This is the simplest way to make lacy crochet. You can make various pattern stitches by altering the combinations and numbers of stitches and spaces.

One size fits most.

Materials

4 Skeins Dakar, 474 Navy, 50 grams, 120 meters (131 yards),
    90% cotton, 10% polyamide, sport weight*
1 Skein Filati Baerta Gue Zip, 100 White, 50 grams, 90 meters
    (98 yards), worsted weight*
Crochet hook size F or size required to obtain gauge
3 Silk flowers (optional)
*As shown in color insert.
Note: One strand of worsted-weight yarn, or two strands (held together) of DK or sport-weight yarn can be substutited. When making substitutions, be sure to check labels for both weight and yardage to ensure you buy the right amount of yarn.

Instructions

Gauge: 11 dc & 5 rows = 3 inches

Crown

Hold two strands together throughout. When working in rounds, do not turn at the end of rounds.

Loosely chain 4 and join into ring.

Rnd 1: Ch3, 2 dc into ring, *ch2, 3 dc into ring; rep from * 3 more times, ch2, join to top of ch3. Do not turn.

Rnd 2: Ch3, 1 dc in first dc, 1 dc (in next dc), 2 dc in next dc, *ch2, 2 dc in next dc, 1 dc, 2 dc in next dc; rep from * 3 more times, ch2, join to top of ch3.

Rnd 3: Ch3, 1 dc in first dc, 3 dc, 2 dc in next dc, *ch2, 2 dc in next dc, 3 dc, 2 dc in next dc; rep from * 3 more times, ch2, join to top of ch3.

Rnd 4: Ch3, 1 dc in first dc, 5 dc, 2 dc in next dc, *ch2, 2 dc in next dc, 5 dc, 2 dc in next dc; rep from * 3 more times, ch2, join to top of ch3.

Rnd 5: Ch3, 1 dc in first dc, 7 dc, 2 dc in next dc, *ch2, 2 dc in next dc, 7 dc, 2 dc in next dc; rep from * 3 more times, ch2, join to top of ch3.

Rnd 6: Ch3, 1 dc in first dc, 9 dc, 2 dc in next dc, *ch2, 2 dc in next dc, 9 dc, 2 dc in next dc; rep from * 3 more times, ch2, join to top of ch3.

Rnds 7–9: Ch3, 1 dc in each of next 12 dc, *ch2, 12 dc; rep from * 3 more times, ch2, join to top of ch3.

Rnd 10 (Mesh Row): Ch4, skip 1 dc, *1 dc, ch1, skip 1 dc; rep from * around, ending ch1, join to top of ch3—38 meshes.

Designer Tips

- Use grosgrain ribbon instead of the crocheted cording to weave in and out of mesh stitches.
- Use satin or rayon cording instead of crocheted cording.
- Make a tailored bow instead of tying cording into a floppy bow.
- Hold one strand of very light-weight metallic yarn or thread with one strand yarn.
- Use multicolored yarn.
- Use novelty yarns: chenille, slubbed, or other texture.

Rnd 11: Ch3, 1 dc in each dc and ch1 sp around—75 dc.

Rnd 12: Ch3, 2 dc, *2 dc in next dc, dc in the next 3 dc; rep from * around, 95 dc, join to 3rd ch of ch3.

Rnds 13–15: Ch3, 1 dc in each dc around. Join to top of ch3.

Rnd 16: Ch1, 1 sc in same st as joining, *skip 2 dc, 5 dc in next dc—shell made, skip 2 dc, sc in next dc; rep from * around, join and cut yarn.

Cording

Using a single strand of Zip, make a chain long enough to fit around Mesh Row and to tie into a double bow. Cut yarn. Weave cording in and out of mesh and tie double bow. Pin or sew flowers just above bow. Brim can be manipulated to turn up or down to suit you.

4 Matching Hat and Bag

I used the same yarn for the Matching Hat and Bag as I used for the Floppy Brimmed Hat because it worked so well the first time. Again, you'll need to carry two strands of yarn together throughout for both the hat and bag.

Materials

6 Skeins Dakar 186 Tan 60 grams, 120 meters (131 yards), 90% cotton, 10% polyamide, sport weight* (6 Skeins are required to make both hat and bag)

Crochet hooks sizes E & F or size required to obtain gauge

Tapestry needle

Two ½" diameter wooden beads

One large snap

⅓ yard fabric for lining (optional)

*As shown in color insert.

Note: One strand worsted-weight yarn, or two strands (held together) of DK or sports-weight yarn can be substituted. When making substitutions, be sure to check labels for both weight and yardage to ensure you buy the right amount of yarn.

Instructions

Gauge holding 2 strands tog throughout: 3 Cl & 4 rows = 2 inches

Bag

Finished measurements: 8¾" × 7"

Using larger hook, loosely chain 32.

Row 1: Sc in 2nd loop from hook, *ch1, skip 1 ch, 1 sc in next ch; rep from * to end—15 ch1 sps.

Row 2: Ch3, turn. (YO, insert hook in ch1 sp and pull up a loop, YO and draw thru 2 loops on hook) 3 times, YO and pull thru all 4 loops, Cluster (CL) made, *ch1, work Cl in next ch1 sp; rep from * across, dc in last sc: 15 CL. Mark as RS row.

Row 3: Ch1, turn. 1 sc in first dc, *ch1, 1 sc in ch1 sp (between Clusters); rep from across, sc in top of beg ch.

Repeat Rows 2 - 3 five more times. Repeat Row 2 once more. Make two.

Finishing

With WS (wrong sides) facing, using smaller hook sc around sides and bottom of bag, working 3 sc in each lower corner, join. Cut yarn and end off.

Shoulder Strap

Attach yarn to side seam of bag, work a chain to desired length, sl st to seam on opposite of bag, sl st into st next to first sl st, ch1, turn.

Sl st into 2nd ch from hook and each ch to end, sl st into st next to st where yarn was attached. Cut yarn and end off.

Optional Lining

Cut out a 15″ × 18½″ rectangle from fabric. Fold in half and sew ½″ side seams. Insert lining into bag, fold upper edge down ½″ and pin to upper edges of bag. Slip stitch into place using sewing needle and matching thread.

Motif

Chain 6 and join into ring.

Rnd 1: Ch2 (YO, insert hook into ring, pull yarn thru, YO and pull thru 2 loops) twice, YO and pull thru all 4 loops on hook, ch5, *(YO, insert hook into ring, pull yarn thru, YO and pull thru 2 loops) three times, YO and pull thru all 3 loops on hook—Cluster made (Cl), ch5; rep from * six more times, join to top of ch2.

Row 1: Ch3, work 2 dc into ch5 sp (1 dc in top of Cl, 3 dc into ch5 sp) twice.

Row 2: Ch3, turn; work in dc across. Cut yarn and end off.

Designer Tips

- For a spring look, pin small, matching silk flowers to center of hat and motif on bag.
- Work Cluster Pattern Stitch, alternating two colors for a striped effect.
- Omit the shoulder strap.
- Sew a large brass ring to one corner for a handle.
- Work up several sets to match outfits, jackets, or coats.
- Instead of wooden beads, try fancy buttons for a glamorous look.

Sew bead in center of motif. Sew or crochet motif to center back of bag. Sew snap to lower motif and front of bag.

Hat

One size fits most.

Crown Motif

Chain 6 and join into ring.

Rnd 1: Ch2, (YO, insert hook into ring, pull yarn thru, YO and pull thru 2 loops) twice, YO and pull thru all 3 loops on hook, ch5, *(YO, insert hook into ring, pull yarn thru, YO and pull thru 2 loops) three times, YO and pull thru all 4 loops—Cluster made (Cl), ch5; rep from * six more times, join to top of ch2—8 Cl.

Rnd 2: Ch1, work *1 sc in first ch5 sp, ch6; rep from * 7 more times, sl st into first sc.

Rnd 3: Sl st into first ch6 sp, ch3 (counts as 1 dc), work 5 dc into same ch6 sp, *ch3, work 6 dc into next ch6 sp; rep from * 6 more times, join to beg of rnd.

Rnd 4: Ch3, 1 dc in each of next 5 dc, *3 dc in ch3 sp, 6 dc; rep from * 6 more times, join to top of beg ch.

Sides

Rnd 1: Ch1, 1 sc in same st as joining, *ch1, skip 1 dc, sc in next dc; rep from * around, ending ch1, join to beg of rnd.

Rnd 2: Ch2,(YO and insert hook into first ch1 sp, and draw loop thru, YO and draw thru 2 loops) twice, YO and pull thru all 3 loops on hook, *ch1, skip 1 sc, (YO and insert hook into first ch1 sp, and draw loop thru, YO and draw thru 2 loops) three times, YO and pull thru all 4 loops on hook—Soft Cluster made (Cl); rep from * around, ending ch1, join to top of first cl.

Rnd 3: Sl st into top of ch2 at beg of previous rnd, *1 sc in ch1 sp, ch1; rep from * around, join to beg of rnd.

Rep Rnds 2 & 3 of Soft Cluster Stitch 3 more times, join.

Brim

Rnd 1: Ch1, working 1 sc in each Cl and in each ch1 sp, join to beg ch1, 85 sc.

Rnds 2 & 3: Ch3, dc around, join.

Rnds 4 & 5: Change to smaller hook and work Rnds 1 and 2 of Cluster Stitch. Join and cut yarn.

Sew bead to center of motif. Turn up brim as desired.

Advanced Techniques

The following techniques are apt to be encountered in written instructions for a wide variety of crochet projects.

Back or Front Loop Only

Sometimes written instructions tell you to work into either the back or front loops only. Depending on how stitches are worked, interesting effects are created. See figure 5.15 to see the different ways to insert the hook. When working into the *front loops only*, the unused loops create a horizontal ridge. If you are later instructed to work into the *free loops*, these unused loops are the free loops. When you work into the *back loops only*, a woven effect is produced.

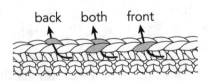

Figure 5.15. How to identify loops.

Increasing

Increasing the number of stitches in a given row is a method used to shape a garment to fit the contours of a body. For example, sleeves are often increased (widened) from the wrist to the underarm. Increases are created when two or more stitches are worked into the same stitch to widen the fabric being crocheted. Increases are used to enlarge a piece in other ways, such as when working in the round, to make the circle larger with each round. Increases are often worked into corners when a garment is being edged to create a sharp or rounded corner.

Increases are shown in double crochet in figures 5.16 and 5.17, but instructions will tell you which stitch to use when increases are called for in a pattern.

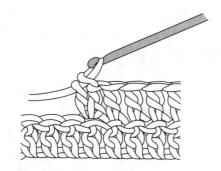

Figure 5.16. Increase within a row or round.

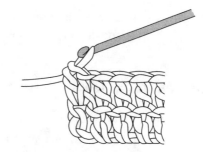

Figure 5.17. Increase at the beginning or the end of a row.

Sometimes increases are made by making additional chains at the end of a row. When you are instructed to add on stitches at the end of a row, the instructions will tell you how many chains to make.

Decreasing

Decreasing is a method used to reduce the number of stitches in a row or round to shape the piece being worked. As you recall, crochet stitches vary in height based on the number of steps that are required to form stitches. Therefore, decreasing the number of stitches is also based on the number of steps required to form a stitch.

Decreasing in Single Crochet

To decrease in sc, insert hook into next st, YO and draw a loop thru. Yarn over and draw thru all 3 loops on hook—1 dec made (see step DES-1).

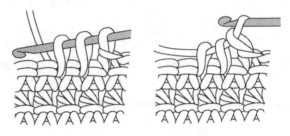

Step DES-1. To decrease in sc, insert hook into next st, YO and draw a loop thru. Yarn over and draw thru all 3 loops on hook—1 dec made.

Decreasing in Double Crochet

To decrease in double crochet, YO, insert hook into next st, YO and draw a loop thru—3 loops on hook. YO and draw thru 2 loops on hook—2 loops on hook (see step DED-1).

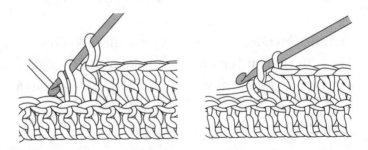

Step DED-1. To decrease in double crochet, YO, insert hook into next st, YO and draw a loop thru—3 loops on hook. YO and draw thru 2 loops on hook— 2 loops on hook.

To continue to decrease in double crochet, repeat step DED-1 into the next stitch—3 loops on hook (see step DED-2).

YO and draw thru all 3 loops on hook—one decrease made (see step DED-3).

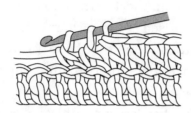

Step DED-2. To continue to decrease in double crochet, repeat step DED-1 into the next stitch—3 loops on hook.

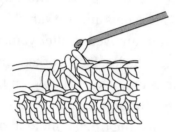

Step DED-3. YO and draw thru all 3 loops on hook—one decrease made.

Decreasing in Other Stitches

To decrease in other stitches (hdc, tr, etc.), work each stitch up to the last step above and then YO and draw thru all loops on hook.

Counting Rows and Stitches

There are various methods of keeping track of the number of rows worked. You'll find it easiest to track rows if you make your markings immediately *after* each row is completed. To protect your pattern, slip it into a plastic sleeve and make your markings on the outside plastic. If you use a washable marker, you can simply wash the markings off the plastic sleeve when you are finished and reuse the plastic sleeve for another pattern.

Other ways to keep your place and avoid writing on patterns include marking rows with Post-It notes or by sticking a large pin with a colored head into a page to mark the row or sequence of stitches being worked.

Better yet, go to your local yarn shop and ask about counting devices. You'll be surprised at the vast array from which to choose. There are hand-held counters that keep a running count as you click at the end of each row. Other counters slip onto knitting needles or crochet hooks.

Be sure to ask about coiless pins—they are worth their weight in gold when it comes to marking rows or stitches in the needlework. Because they are coiless, they prevent yarn from tangling or getting caught in a stitch. Coiless pins are also valuable when it comes to preventing your work from unraveling after you lay it down. Simply slip the coiless pin through the last loop worked and gently tighten it.

Split plastic rings are also available and can be placed on the fabric to mark the beginning of shaping, color placement, or stitch sequences.If you are having trouble memorizing a pattern stitch sequence, write out the sequence of stitches on a little tag with a string and attach it to the right side of the fabric.

Stitches should be recounted every time instructions mention the number of stitches that should be in a row. For optimum results, it's a good idea to recount your stitches every few rows to make sure you haven't lost any stitches and to avoid having to use that nasty Frog Stitch: Rip it! Rip it! Rip it!

Multiples

Fancy stitches—those other than simple, basic single crochet, half double crochet, double crochet, and treble crochet—are created by a series or sequence of stitches that creates one repeat of a pattern stitch, such as a shell stitch. The number of stitches required to make one shell is called a *multiple*.

Stitch Dictionaries

If you're interested in using your love of crocheting to earn money, stitch dictionaries are a necessary part of your crochet library. When choosing crochet stitch dictionaries, be sure to look for those that include clear illustrations and instructions for making unusual stitches and stitches that are new to you. Leaf through the pages, closely noting the quality and clarity of the stitches before making your selection.

For example, the instructions to make a simple shell might read as follows: "Dc in 4th ch from hook and in next 3 chs, *skip next 2 chs, (2 dc, ch2, 2 dc) in next ch—Shell made, skip next 2 chs, dc in next 5 chs; rep from * across."

Multiples often have a few extra stitches that form a partial pattern at each edge so that when pieces are sewn together, the pattern is intact. Therefore, instructions then state that the pattern stitch is a multiple of 10 + 7, for example.

Unfortunately, different publications state the stitch count for multiples in different ways, which can make it confusing for even the most experienced crocheter. Let's say you have a terrific stitch dictionary that is filled with hundreds of crochet stitches, and you find the perfect multiple to make a simple afghan. It's easy enough to figure out how to attain a certain width—you work a swatch and figure out the gauge for each pattern repeat and multiply your given gauge by the desired width of your afghan. However, one publication may say "multiple of 6 + 2," meaning that each repeat contains 6 stitches and 2 extra stitches are required for the edges. Other publications may say "multiple of 6 + 2 sts," but they mean that you need to chain 6, plus 2 for the beginning chain. How do you know what to do?

If a symbol chart is provided, you can count out the stitches to determine the correct number of chains to make. But if there is no such chart, this is the method I use: I make several extra chains more than the number stated. I know that I should work at least 3 pattern repeats to get a true gauge. If the multiple is 6 + 2, then I must multiply 3 × 6, or 18 stitches. Because I'm not sure whether the +2 means actual stitches or the number of chains required, I make 5 or 6 extra chains.

After the first row is completed, according to written instructions, I may have a few chains left over. That's easy enough to take care of. I simply undo the beginning slip knot and slowly, carefully pull out the extra chains and resecure the chain in the right place, and then I just continue to work in the pattern as instructed.

Your Crafts Vision

▼▼

BY NOW YOU'VE LEARNED how to crochet and, I'm willing to bet, have joined the legions of us who are hooked on crochet!

Crochet offers many positive things. It relieves tension: The cares of the day just seem to pass away as the yarn, or thread, moves through your fingers. It provides a challenging and enjoyable creative outlet. If you're like me, as you look at the glorious colors and textures of the yarns you are working with, your imagination begins to take over, and you are soon thinking of other ways to crochet something new. That's how you get hooked—you can't help but look forward to the next new, exciting, and creative project.

Some of you may never want to do more than crochet strictly for the fun of it. Crocheting garments, afghans, and other items for family, friends, and yourself may satisfy you for now and possibly forever. But I'm certain some of you are already thinking of ways you might turn your love of crochet into a way to help others or to make money.

Crocheting for Charity

Maybe you aren't even thinking about making money for yourself, but are instead thinking of a way you can contribute to your club, church, or other organization with your crochet talents. Many charities are looking for volunteers, such as Warm Up America, Caps For Kids, and the Linus programs.

Maybe you'd like to participate in the Children In Common (CIC) project. This organization exists to supply children in eastern European orphanages with warm clothing. The greatest needs are for knit or crochet hats, mittens, scarves, socks, and sweaters for newborns to children 16 years of age. CIC is a support organization started in 1992 for parents who are adopting children from eastern Europe: Russia, Lithuania, and provinces that used to be part of the U.S.S.R., such as Siberia and Georgia. It operates under the guidance of Adoptions Together, Inc., based in Maryland, which places hundreds of these institutionalized children in loving homes. One of the group's main functions is to raise funds to help support the orphanages where the children spend their first months or years.

Knit and crochet items and other supplies are also taken to Europe either by parents who are traveling to complete an adoption or by the bi-annual Mrs. Santa Goodwill tour in late December. Yarn, needles, hooks, instructions in Russian, and other materials are sent to the children to teach them the skills of knitting, crocheting, sewing, tailoring, and woodworking, so they can support themselves when they are required to leave the orphanages at age 16.

Jeannie Dykstra, owner of Elegant Stitches yarn shop in Miami, Florida, supports Children In Common by soliciting donations of yarn from distributors as well as crocheted items, knitted items, and quilts from individuals. She also holds an annual holiday boutique, both in her shop and on her Internet site, where handmade items are offered for sale, with a portion of the money received being donated to the fund. If you'd like to participate in this program, see the Resource chapter at the back of this book.

Jeannie Dykstra has a special interest in CIC, because her sister, Janice Pearse, is the one who started the program after experiencing a difficult adoption herself. Janice went on to start the international adoption program at Adoptions Together, Inc., and she has placed more than 600 children in loving homes in America. The fact that Janice was instrumental in opening up adoptions in Lithuania is of special interest to these sisters, whose grandparents are Lithuanian.

> ### Did you know???
> The average crocheter makes 18.7 projects per year.

For some crocheters, the profit that comes from crochet is simply and solely the satisfaction that comes from extending a helping hand to others less fortunate. Delphia Dennis of Bellevue, Washington, spent a full year in Nome, Alaska, as a volunteer missionary working at a Christian radio station. One night a week she went to a shelter for abused women that served not only Nome, but also 40 villages throughout western Alaska.

Delphia recalled, "We sat around the dining table and did wonderful handwork. We crocheted, knitted, or worked with beads and shared experiences. In the beginning the women were reticent, waiting to see how I reacted to what they had to say or to their customs and traditions. I found that it took time to build friendships and trust."

Delphia continued with a thoughtful tone, "Most of the women's work was done in the traditional patterns that had been handed down by mothers and grandmothers. I felt that the most helpful thing I had to offer them was to teach them how to read patterns. They, in turn, taught me how to do beadwork, using two needles and thread. It became what I call 'an exchange of ideas.' Sometimes the exchanges included much more than fiber arts, and, after all, I enjoy learning as much as I do teaching. I found that when abused women work with fibers and share ideas, it's a healing experience."

At the fiber arts sessions, donated yarn is passed around, and most of the yarn is sent to villages to be used in Suicide Prevention Programs in which older women teach younger women and girls the skills of various needle arts. Yarns are donated by other churches and by those who hear of this program by word of mouth and are given out according to need. Sometimes the hats, scarves, mittens, and other handmade items made from the donated yarns are sold to buy heating fuel for the church or for other community projects.

Delphia has also done volunteer teaching at a day shelter for homeless women in Seattle, which also receives donated yarn. Although some of the women struggled to learn how to make a basic chain—and some did nothing more than make a chain, rip it out, and make it over repeatedly—they felt a sense of accomplishment. Some go on to crochet items—from afghans to house slippers and hats—that they sell on the street or through local consignment shops to earn money to feed their children. There are those who make small items for themselves or for gifts. Once a week they come back to pick out new yarns and, perhaps more important, to talk about what they want to make.

Delphia discovered that learning how to crochet made a similar difference to both groups of women. "I could sense an intangible feeling of success as the women learned something new, challenging, and useful at a time when they were perhaps at the lowest levels of self-esteem," she said. "The joy that comes from sharing knowledge and seeing others' satisfaction does a lot for me, too. It generates true enjoyment, benefit, and synergistic power when women meet to work and share together. Best of all, as they focus on learning to crochet, the women tend to put aside their suspicion and hostility."

Earning Cash with Crochet

Perhaps you'd like to make some extra money. Or maybe you want to launch a new part-time or even full-time career following your crochet passion. The reasons for wanting to earn income from crochet are as varied as all of us crocheters and the conditions of our lives. Maybe you'd just like to have more spending money, pay for ballet lessons for your little girl, or buy that band uniform for your high school son. You might want to put aside money for a few luxuries you can't afford right now, like a dream cruise or a trip to Europe. Perhaps you want to make your own money to invest or just to sock away in a savings account. Maybe you dream of using your crochet to become more financially stable or even to become financially self-sufficient.

The reasons don't matter. What does matter is that wherever need or desire exists, so too can be found the foundations on which dreams are built. My own career started with a dream and a list of things I love to do. Crochet won, hands down!

About the same time my girls grew weary of all those crocheted sweaters, my independent spirit was yearning for freedom. I knew I wanted a business of my own. Unsure of what that might be, I drew up a list of my skills, talents, and abilities. When finished, I looked at the list and asked myself a final question: What was the one thing on the list that I'd most likely feel passionately about the rest of my life? That's when I knew a life of crocheting was for me, and I've never regretted that decision.

For Noreen Havens of Edmonds, Washington, her job at the Boeing Company led her into the "crochet business" in a way that satisfied her passion for crochet and her desire to share her craft with others. Noreen explained, "It's amazing what you can get done during your breaks and lunchtime, even before and after work. At first, I crocheted for my own pleasure, but as others saw what I was doing, they wanted to know more. I had an audience! From there, the business of crochet began for me. I sold many of the items that I crocheted, such as garments and afghans, but the highest demand was for my lace work."

In the early seventies, Noreen designed and crocheted a dress for one of her daughters, but after it was finished her daughter decided she really didn't care for it. Noreen took the dress to work and sold it to a coworker.

"It fit her to a tee, and she looked like a million dollars in it," Noreen recalled. That led to requests for her to make twelve more dresses that were similar to the first one. The first dress took Noreen two weeks to make; she finished the last one of the series in eight hours flat.

"I remember crocheting that last dress on a snowy day in February as I sat in front of the fireplace, when I couldn't get out of my house to go to work," Noreen said.

More rewarding to Noreen than making money with her crochet, however, were the requests for her to teach others how to crochet. The satisfaction of sharing with others was all that mattered to her; she never gave a thought to charging her coworkers for her classes.

The "business of crochet" often begins, like it did for Noreen, in the workplace. However, for Jenny King of Queensland, Australia, business began during her college days more than 20 years ago. Today, Jenny is the best-known crocheter and crochet-book publisher in Australia. It all began when she designed and crocheted bikinis to earn spending money while she was in college. Those itsy-bitsy bikinis took only four hours to make and sold for a tidy profit. In fact, that young college girl had a sharp pencil—she sold those bikinis for five times more than the French cotton thread cost her!

Business sometimes comes about in strange ways that change lives forever. Kathie Power Johnson, a prominent knit and crochet designer, taught herself to crochet while in college. Years later, she found herself needing a break from a demanding scientific research job and fell into teaching crochet as a result of getting acquainted with yarn shop owners in the Sarasota, Florida, area.

"I discovered that teaching knitting and crocheting came naturally to me," states Kathie. "I found it so rewarding that I never returned to my other career."

What about your dreams? Do they include crocheting? Crocheters sometimes start out by dreaming of making a little money on the side just so they can buy more yarn. We've all heard the adage that when you do the thing you most love, the money follows. That is often true when it comes to the love of crochet. One thing seems to naturally lead to another, whether it's a crocheted dress that you sell to a coworker or a set of Christmas tree ornaments you

Crochet Dream-Maker Questionnaire

If you're dreaming about ways to profit from your love of crochet, maybe it's time for you to start making your wish list. Begin by asking yourself some questions.

- How much time do I want to devote to crocheting?

- What kinds of crocheted items do I enjoy making the most?

- What do I do best: design, teach, write instructions, or create items?

- Who is likely to buy my crocheted items?

- What are my financial, personal, and career goals?

donate to your church bazaar. The word spreads quickly if you have something to offer that others desire.

Take some time to analyze your goals. Are they realistic? What do you need to do to achieve them? Writing down goals is easy to do, but achieving goals means taking a series of steps to get from here to there. The clearer you are about the necessary steps, the sooner you are likely to achieve your goals.

Obviously, your goals—and your crocheting—are important to you. Otherwise, you wouldn't be considering moving into or increasing your stakes in the moneymaking realm of crochet. It's important, then, to take the time to fine-tune your goals and to investigate the opportunities and the challenges. Throughout Part II of this book, you'll discover how others profit from crochet as well as valuable guidelines on the business aspects of the needlework industry. I think you'll be surprised at some of the ingenious ways others profit from crochet while having fun at the same time.

Part Two

For Profit

Profiting from Your Creations

▼▼▼

AS YOU LEARNED IN CHAPTER 6, there are dozens of ways to earn money with your craft, either through your crochet expertise or your crocheted items. This chapter focuses on the crocheted items you make. However, the issues and principles discussed here apply to all the ways in which a crocheter might make money with crochet.

One of the most important, and sometimes perplexing, aspects of selling is knowing how to price and how much to charge for your finished pieces. Most consumers know how much they are willing to pay for any given item before they check the price tag, and the consumers of crocheted items are no exception. You need to have that same information—to know what your potential customers are willing to pay for your crocheted products—before you can determine your prices.

However, pricing for *profit* involves more than choosing a price that will light up your customers' eyes and open their wallets. It requires knowing the "five Cs" of effective crafts pricing and marketing:

Your Customers. The consumers most likely to value and buy
 your crocheted items. The items and features customers

want. The price range they are willing and able to pay for items similar to those you want to sell.

Your Competition. The volume, nature, quality, characteristics, availability, and going prices of crocheted items on the market. The most successful crochet entrepreneurs and the "secrets" to their successes.

Your Costs. The actual cost to market, produce, and sell your crocheted items, plus the "overhead" costs of doing business: the combined costs of production (your labor), materials, equipment, workspace, marketing, taxes, and miscellaneous business expenses.

Your Capabilities. The nature, quality, and volume of what you can produce, based on your talent, knowledge, productivity (how fast *can* you crochet?), resources, available time, and goals.

Your Creativity. The "value-added" creativity you bring to your crocheting projects.

Though this approach to earning money with crochet may seem like a five-eyed monster, it is really just taking a close, commonsense look at basic information. Chances are, if you've already been immersed in crochet for a while, you probably already know much of this information or can readily access it. Now, you just need to do a little research, pull together all the information, think it through—perhaps even write it out on paper—and come up with a pricing formula that appeals both to your customers and to you.

Many crafters seeking to turn a hobby into a moneymaking venture start by—and sometimes stop with—focusing on customer needs. The most successful arts and crafts entrepreneurs launch and build their businesses on a different foundation: *What do I want?* That means looking first at your capabilities. Otherwise, how can you effectively target your customer base, accurately estimate your costs, put the right value on your creativity, or profitably price your products?

Define Your Capabilities

The first step is to establish your goals. For example, do you want to create a for-profit business or simply "pay the way" of your hobby? Once you define *what* to do, you can set forth manageable steps (including pricing) that delineate *how* to achieve your goals.

Only you can determine your personal goals and what you can do to reach them, but completing the following exercises should help point you in the right direction.

How Much Income Do I Want to Earn?

I'd like to earn enough money from crocheting to:

- ☐ Cover my craft expenses
- ☐ Set aside a slush fund for "extras" and special occasions
- ☐ Supplement my household income
- ☐ Provide a full income

How Much Time Can I Invest?

I am willing and able to devote the following time to making and marketing my crocheted items:

- ☐ Up to 10 hours a week
- ☐ Up to 20 hours a week
- ☐ Up to 40 hours a week
- ☐ More than 40 hours a week
- ☐ Weekdays
- ☐ Evenings

☐ Weekends

☐ Other _____

You might also want to draw up a projected schedule or mark off a calendar, showing which days and times you intend to spend on your crochet "business."

What Will I Crochet for Sale?

Check all that apply and jot down any other items you are interested in making and selling. You might also want to keep an idea notebook that you can add to as concepts for new things to crochet come to you.

Garments & Accessories

☐ Bags/Purses

☐ Coats/Jackets

☐ Dresses/Skirts

☐ Hats

☐ Mittens/Gloves

☐ Ponchos/Vests

☐ Shawls/Scarves

☐ Socks

☐ Sweaters

☐ Other _____

Home Decor

☐ Afghans/Blankets

☐ Curtains

☐ Doilies

☐ Pillows

☐ Table Runners/Placemats

☐ Tablecloths

☐ Other _____

Novelties

☐ Doll Clothing and Accessories

☐ Dolls

☐ Stuffed Animals

☐ Other _____

Items For

☐ Infants and Toddlers

☐ Children

☐ Teenagers

☐ Women

☐ Men

☐ Other _____

Which Freelance Strategy Will I Use?

☐ Speculative (make it, then sell it)

☐ Order (market/take orders for specific items)

☐ Custom (design/make to order)

☐ Original (create from your own designs)

Other Issues to Consider

■ Do I have the resources necessary to cover initial material and supply costs?

■ Can I work well with customers?

■ Are my tools and workspace conducive to creating crocheted items for sale?

- Do I have sufficient experience and skill to meet my moneymaking goals?

- Do I enjoy making things for others?

- Do I have the flexibility and creativity to adapt my crochet work to the style and color preferences of others?

- What are my crocheting strengths and weaknesses?

- What are my marketing strengths and weaknesses?

- What, if any, limitations do I foresee in terms of what I am willing and able to crochet for sale?

After going through these exercises, you should have a pretty good handle on the crocheted items you are willing and able to create for sale. The next step is to find customers who align with your goals and capabilities.

Identify Your Customer Base

Part of your market research consists of identifying those people who are most likely to buy what you have to offer. Many beginners mistakenly think that "everyone" will want to buy their crocheted items, which is never true of any product. If you specialize in lace table runners, for example, you can't realistically expect these items to appeal to consumers who prefer, say, an art deco or African motif. On the other hand, people who lean toward country or Victorian decor are probably prime potential customers for you, because lace table runners are likely to fit in nicely with their decorating style.

To ensure the success of your crochet business, you'll need to define your customer base by identifying potential buyers and gathering specific information about their likes, dislikes, and purchasing habits. You can go about this in one of two ways: identify the market for the things you like to crochet or identify what you could crochet for a specific market. Some enterprising crocheters use both strategies in their market research. For example, you might research the types of crocheted items that would sell well in consignment shops in your immediate geographic area, while at the same time researching the potential venues for your 1970s "retro" apparel or collector dolls.

To pull together enough information to identify a target customer base, you will probably need to turn over and examine several market-research stones.

Who Are My Potential Buyers?

With some amateur snoop work—such as talking with fellow crocheters, visiting consignment shops, skimming magazines, and surfing the Internet—you should be able to put together a profile of the type of buyer who is just waiting to pay you the asking price for the privilege of taking home one of your crocheted creations. Here are a few clues to uncover in your customer investigation:

- Who might buy the things I crochet? Consumers? Retailers? Pattern publishers? What types of individuals within each category are most likely to buy what I crochet?

- What are the demographics of my potential customers: age, gender, geographic area, income level, profession, personal interests?

- How do potential buyers typically purchase crocheted and other craft items?

- In what ways do the styles of potential buyers resemble and differ from that of my creations?

- What items do potential buyers need and want that I could provide?

- What price range are potential buyers willing and able to pay for items similar to what I crochet?

Where Will I Market My Products?

☐ Art galleries

☐ Arts and crafts co-ops

☐ Bazaars/flea markets

☐ Classified ads

☐ Consignment shops

☐ Craft malls

☐ Craft shows

☐ Community bulletins/directories

☐ Gift shops

☐ Holiday/seasonal boutiques

☐ Home shows

☐ Internet directories

☐ Kiosks (malls, outdoor markets, shopping centers)

☐ Mail order

☐ Novelty/specialty shops

☐ Referrals/word of mouth

☐ Special order

☐ Telephone directory

☐ Tourist attractions/shops

☐ Web site

☐ Yard/garage sales

Doing your customer homework can prevent you from wasting time and effort creating items for which there is little or no market available and marketing your perfectly wonderful and ultimately saleable crocheted items to people who simply don't want them. Your market research is just as certain to uncover prospective buyers, creative opportunities, and ripe market niches you might never have imagined otherwise.

Sometimes serendipity happens—and a money-making crocheting opportunity just falls into your lap when you least expect it and may not even be looking for it. (Remember Noreen Havens from chapter 6, who ended up crocheting 12 dresses for her coworkers at Boeing?) That's why it pays to wear and display your projects and to give crocheted gifts whenever possible. You never know who might "discover" your work and where it might lead.

Check Out Your Competition

Crocheters tend to regard fellow crocheters, even those we've never met, as kindred spirits. We universally applaud, support, and share with one another. So, the term *crocheting competitors* may seem like a contradiction. Certainly, "competition" among crocheters is different than it is among other arts and industries. But it does exist, and it is a good thing. Why? Because we can all learn from the hits and misses of those who've "been there and done that." When you're looking for an example of what to do and not to do, who better to learn (and borrow) from than those who've achieved a measure of success.

What Do I Need to Know About and From Competitors?

Are you ready to check out the competition? Look through magazines, newsletters, and Web sites; talk to your friends and associates in crochet classes, online chat groups, and yarn stores; cull whatever resources are available to you to find out as much as you can about how other crocheters earn money with their crocheted items. Your investigation should include the following:

- Who are the most successful crocheters in your community? In the category (or categories) of crocheted items you intend to sell?

- What do these top performers crochet and sell?

- How do they create the products they sell?

- How do they sell their crocheted products?

- Where do they sell their work?

- What types of advertising and promotion do they use?

- How do they price their products?

- What are the price ranges of their crocheted items?

- How do they purchase their supplies?

- Which design, production, pricing, and marketing techniques have worked best for them—and why?

- Which techniques haven't worked out—and why?

- How long did it take to reach their goals? To make a profit?

Research your "competitors" as thoroughly as you would your prospective buyers. Then, follow those examples that make sense to you; adapt other approaches to suit your needs and sensibilities; and innovate when a new or better way reveals itself to you.

Determine Your Costs

When you start to earn money from your crocheting, you need to estimate and track your expenses both to establish your prices and to help you determine what items and sales venues are, and are not, profitable. (You also need this information for tax purposes; see the sidebar on record keeping.) If you intend to sell your work only as a sideline, with minimal expenses and income, you can base your pricing and marketing formulas primarily on your *direct costs.* But if your intent is to create and operate a craft "business" that either supplements or provides a living income, you'll also need to factor in your *indirect costs,* especially when it comes to tax time and to evaluating the profitability of your venture.

Direct costs include all of the labor, materials, supplies, patterns, tools, and consignment fees incurred exclusively for a specific item you create for sale. It is up to you to put a dollar value on your time (labor), but most crocheters base this figure on their individual experience and expertise as well as on the creativity and difficulty of the particular piece. Make sure to include in your labor costs any time spent designing or on design alterations. Direct costs might also include a portion of the cost of any purchased item or service that is used for two or more of your crocheted items—for example, hooks and advertising.

Indirect costs are all those "overhead" expenses that you incur during the course of setting up and running your money-making crochet venture. This includes office supplies, design supplies, craft supplies (pins, markers, etc.), crochet tools, special equipment (magnifiers, lamps, wrist supports), mileage, postage, long-distance phone calls, catalogs, pattern books, subscriptions, class fees, membership dues, price tags, garment labels, Web site, advertising, and furnishings for your workspace. If you have a workspace or studio that you use primarily for crocheting, whether within or separate from your home, you might also want to factor in the lease/mortgage and utility costs for that space.

Some crafters record these figures in spiral notebooks or columned "accounting" sheets. Others use computer software, such as Quicken. Others use index cards stored in a recipe box. Use whatever expense recording method that suits you, but do pay attention

Record Keeping

If you thought the crochet business was exempt from bookkeeping and filing, think again. Just like any other "businessperson," once you start to charge for your crocheted items (or services), you'll need to keep your records in order.

Tax Records. Regardless of whether crochet brings you a little or a lot of money or whether an annual profit or loss, you must keep written records of both your expenditures and income for tax purposes. Keep your expense receipts, sales receipts, check stubs, and copies of your invoices. Keep a log of your auto mileage. It can be easy to overlook and exclude small expenditures, such as a new crochet hook, a special set of buttons, or a crochet magazine, but they add up at the end of the year!

Always check with your accountant or tax official about tax-deductible items!

Tax-deductible items include:

- Tools: crochet hooks, needles, pins, bobbins, calculators, software, scissors, magnifiers

- Materials: yarns, buttons, trims, beads, purse handles, sewing thread, snaps, and other notions

- Resources: patterns, instructions, catalogs, magazines, how-to books

- Subscriptions and Memberships: magazines, newsletters, organizations

to the costs associated with making each item as well as your overall expenditures.

Maximize Your Creative Edge

All other things being equal, the creative aspect of your crochet work not only gives you a marketing edge—meaning it makes it easier to sell—but it also helps to garner a higher price for your products. The creativity quotient (for lack of a better word) depends on

- Education: courses and classes directly related to furthering your craft or business skills

- Overhead: long-distance phone, postage, shipping, workspace, faxes, Internet, utilities (%)

- Marketing: price tags, garment/textile labels, consignment fees

- Office supplies: paper, pens, staples, invoices, blank sales receipts, envelopes, computer disks

- Travel: auto mileage, airfare, hotels, meals, taxi fare, tolls

Customer Records. If you do custom or special order work, you'll probably want to keep track of each customer's purchases, yarn preferences, and body measurements. If you sell your work through several consignment shops, gift stores, and other retailers, you'll need to keep track of which items you've consigned or sold to each shop, any ordering or merchandising information specific to each shop, and how well items sold at each shop.

Project Records. For each new item you create, whether on a custom or general-use basis, keep track of your materials costs, the time required to design and/or make the item, and the number of the item sold. Make sure to retain a clean copy of the written instructions for each of your original designs and for each customized (modified) pattern.

how the market perceives the originality of your design, or of your individual interpretation of a pattern. Unique and compelling use of color, style, patterns, and texture is especially critical to an item's perceived creativity value. Devotees of crochet might also consider the technical complexity of the work and/or its unusual application (that is, using crochet to create something not typically done in crochet) in valuing an item's creativity.

Because this value-added component to pricing and market positioning is subjective, it can be somewhat tricky to determine. The key determinants are: Does the design "work" on all levels (form and function)? Does it distinguish your work from that of the "crochet crowd" in a complimentary way? Does it increase the demand and value/price of your crocheted item?

You have nothing to lose and much to gain by following your muse and flexing your creative muscle. Go ahead—experiment widely with color! Try different fibers! Create new stitch combinations! Modify contours! Mix styles! Add trim and accessories! Start your own trends! Most important, enjoy yourself—never losing sight of your customers, your capabilities, your competition, and your costs.

Handy Hint

You can use patterns to get creative ideas as well as to keep up with current trends, yarns, and styles. However, never copy or use commercial patterns to create commercial products, because doing so could constitute copyright infringement.

Pricing Your Creations

The approaches used to price crocheted items are as widely varied as the people who crochet them. For example, a senior crocheter who crochets for hire mainly to earn extra spending money might base her fees on the number of skeins used for a particular product. On the other end of the spectrum, a crocheter who's trying to earn a living selling her craft might use a complex formula that factors in materials costs, time and effort, market demand, percentage of overhead, and the amount of customization required.

The most common pricing methods used in crochet include:

- **Per skein of yarn used.**
- **Percentage over cost.** Usually four to five times your cost per skein.
- **Hourly.** Based on your personal needs, going rates for your area, or what the market will bear.
- **Minimum per item, plus incidental expenses.**
- **Cost of materials, plus per-yard charge.**
- **Per item, based on what the market will bear.**

Pullover Sweater

Baby Afghan

Jeanne: Nonscientific Approach to Pricing

"My son, the MBA, says I'd be better off selling half as many items at twice the price, but that's easier said than done," says Jeanne Leech of Bellevue, Washington. "I base my prices on what I'd be willing to pay. I also figure in my costs for craft fair table rentals, insurance, materials, and other expenses. It's not a very scientific method."

Most of Jeanne's work is lace thread crochet. She digs around at flea markets for old crochet books, from which she reproduces old-fashioned lace potholders, lace collars, yokes, and other novelty items. Her lovely lace angels sell so well year round, she can't keep up with incoming orders.

Jeanne currently sells only at craft fairs, while she and her husband, both retired, travel all summer in their motor home. Traveling has afforded many selling opportunities in RV parks around the country. Though Jeanne has had great success selling her work at a rented space in a craft mall, she found it too difficult to maintain while traveling. Prior to retiring, both she and her husband sold items to coworkers and received special orders. Having discovered that her work sold well in an office setting, Jeanne and another friend, who still works, make items together, which Jeanne's friend continues to sell to coworkers. Do you remember the Sunbonnet Sue patterns from years ago? Jeanne makes a crocheted refrigerator magnet version that she can't finish fast enough to meet demand.

Another of Jeanne's friends is a talented ceramist who makes egg-shaped heads with marvelous faces. Jeanne buys the heads, and then she designs and makes varied hats for these delightful creatures. The hats range from a big sun bonnet to a football helmet. A choir member once bought one with a big Easter bonnet and an open mouth as if it were singing. Children are naturally drawn to the characters, and a child psychologist bought several to use in therapy sessions as examples of various emotions. These intriguing heads draw customers to Jeanne's table at craft fairs. Customers tend to spend a great deal of time playing with them and trying different hats on the eggheads. As they linger, they usually notice the other items Jeanne has to offer. As a result, she makes more sales.

Jeanne crochets three to four hours a day, mostly for fun, and makes no effort to earn a living from crochet.

"It's very satisfying when people love and buy the things I make. And I love making them," she says. "Much of the money I earn with crochet is spent buying yarn and fabric for my charity work."

Joy: Original Pricing

Joy Bauer, of Cissna Park, Illinois, creates lovely doilies and custom filet-crochet pictures which she inserts into frames. Each picture features unique decorative touches, the family's name worked into the filet crochet, and a caption of the customer's choosing. For example, one picture containing a picture of a house says, "Bauer home, est. 1957" and features a delicate lacy edging.

Joy uses only her own designs and customizes the wording to her customer's specifications. She generally charges approximately four times the dollar amount she has invested in making the item.

Joy has previously placed her crochet work in craft booths, but they did not sell well in that venue. Living in a small town, she is able to successfully sell strictly by word of mouth. Her only marketing tool at present is a color flyer showing her designs, which she slips into each filled order. However, she is considering the Internet as a way to reach a broader market in the future.

At one time, Joy and her mother owned a yarn shop in Cissna, a rural community where they sold yarn and craft kits.

"It was great fun. I really enjoyed seeing all the things other people did," Joy says. "But we closed the shop because we were spending too many hours for the amount of money we were earning."

Noreen: Time + Costs + Value = Price

According to Noreen Havens, who freelances as a pattern editor for many top designers and has done a considerable amount of custom crocheting, "Some beginners who are trying to establish themselves end up doing the work for pennies an hour, whereas well-known "artists" can command equitable, sometimes even lucrative, prices for their work.

"I feel it is in the best interests of aspiring artists and their fellow artisans not to work for 'nothing,' because it sets a precedent that hurts not only themselves but also others in the business."

When Noreen owned a yarn shop and sold her crochet work twenty years ago, her pricing formula was three times the cost of the material.

"That formula is no longer workable," she claims. "Today, the cost of material is usually incidental to the value of the item and to the cost of hours to produce the item. It now seems more appropriate to base the price on the cost of material *plus* the time and effort required to create an item, rather than only on the cost of materials."

The for-hire crocheter must know how long it takes to crochet an item before attempting to set a price. Labor costs, then, set the base prices for basic items, with the costs of custom designing (if necessary), materials, and unusual problems or stumbling blocks expected to arise during execution added to that base.

Nancy: Time and a Half

Nancy Nehring, of California's Silicon Valley, is a highly regarded crochet expert well-known for her crochet designs, articles, lectures, and books. Her collection of old crochet hooks and their fascinating histories make an intriguing slide presentation. Nancy's real love is writing, and her first book, *50 Heirloom Buttons to Make* (Taunton Press, 1996), contains an entire chapter on crocheted buttons.

Equally fascinating is Nancy's approach to pricing, for she times and writes out instructions for everything she crochets. She begins by crocheting a swatch and noting the time it took to do. She uses the time sample to calculate how long a project will take. Then, she divides that figure in half and adds that to the estimated time to give herself ample time to finish the project by the deadline. She quotes customers a flat per-piece price that is based on an hourly rate. If she finds that her asking price was too low, she absorbs the loss. If her price was too high for the amount of time it actually took to crochet an item, she sometimes lowers the price.

Nancy is adept at finding ways to diversify and multiply her crochet income. When doing custom crochet design work for which the buyer doesn't require exclusive rights, Nancy often makes a duplicate and sells the design to a magazine.

Vicky: Yarn x Three

Vicky Turek, a custom crocheter who lives in Highland Village, Texas, takes a different approach to pricing based on the type and amount of yarn she uses. She charges three times the cost of the estimated amount of yarn needed to complete the custom crochet work. Although Vicky knows approximately how much time is required for a particular project, she doesn't keep track of her hours.

Because she uses only her own unique designs, never the patterns of others, Vicky first asks potential customers several questions to determine what they want. She shows them pictures of her previous work, computer sketches of designs, and colors of yarn. For first-time customers, she requires a 25% deposit, even though she has never had a customer refuse to buy one of her finished designs.

All of Vicky's custom crochet work is generated by word of mouth and brings her between fifteen to twenty hours of work per week.

Tarie: Show, Tell, and Price Well

Due to unfortunate life circumstances during the 1970s, at the tender age of 14, Tarie Dillard-Williams became an emancipated teen living independently in California, working two jobs, and putting herself through school. Tarie had learned crochet basics as a young girl from her grandmother, and she turned to crochet during her mid-teens when she didn't fit in with her peers or adults and spent considerable time alone.

"That's when I started crocheting blankets for friends and people who were kind to me," Tarie recalls. "Everyone seemed to love the things I crocheted and I started getting orders. At first, my blankets were simple ripple-stitch afghans, then I started designing afghans with people's names on them. At that point, I didn't even know how to read a pattern."

Everywhere Tarie went, her crocheting went with her. When, during her senior year of high school, she was required to crochet an afghan for her home economics class, Tarie received an "A" for her afghan and never had to attend home ec again!

Tarie grew bored with blankets and began to branch out. She experimented with crochet thread vests and was soon designing, crocheting, and selling them for $50 to $75 each—realizing a profit of $35 to $60 per vest! Of course, during that time, she still used dime-store yarns, because she didn't know of any other kind. Tarie continued to try to find ways to make a living doing what she loved most—crocheting! She knew she couldn't support herself by crocheting and selling only vests and blankets.

"It took too long to finish projects," Tarie explains. "To this day, I feel crocheters do not receive adequate compensation for the time and talent they invest."

During a sad time later in her adult life, Tarie visited a friend in Montana to regroup from her personal crisis and to figure out which direction to take with her life next. At the time, she worked in a corporate atmosphere, still bringing along her crocheting everywhere she went: business meetings, lunches, company events. While taking a drive in the country while visiting Montana, Tarie and her friend came across a billboard advertising a yarn shop.

"Bless my friend. She took me right to that yarn store," Tarie recalls. "I felt reborn! All of a sudden, I knew my purpose, and the rest is history."

Returning to Texas three months later, Tarie opened a "yarn store," so-called because she didn't yet know how to knit. The community's curious came calling , and when they saw Tarie's crochet work on display, customers started placing special orders. Some of her best customers were men buying handmade treasures for their wives or mothers. A local policeman paid $300 to have her make a vest for his sister and then came back to order two custom afghans at $600 each! Customers have also ordered her christening sets, sweaters for children and adults, and other items.

Tarie's pricing formula is quite unique: She charges the retail amount of the yarn, plus 15 to 25 cents per yard, depending upon the project and level of difficulty.

After three years of educating her customers on different yarns and crochet, Tarie has customers who are willing to pay $720 just for the yarn to make a sweater or $800 for the materials for a jacket.

"It helps if shop owners promote the more expensive yarns," Tarie says. "I show people the less expensive yarns and then the expensive yarns, and I always have samples made up in the better yarns. The yarns sell themselves because customers can see that the nicer the yarn, the nicer the end product."

Tarie is determined to have one of the largest yarn stores in the United States. Dedicated to passing along the skills of knitting and crocheting, she sponsors "Craft Camp for Kids" once a year in her shop. For five days, Monday through Friday, children come from ten in the morning until four in the afternoon. The classes are filled to overflowing every year.

"Two nine-year-old girls I taught to crochet are now making their own sweaters and vests. They even made baby hats for our local community hospital," Tarie says proudly. "And I have two nine-year-old boys in the camp that could put women my age to shame when it comes to how well they crochet. My camp kids keep coming back, year after year."

Despite her success and experience, Tarie, like many others, has found that pricing is a tricky business and that her standard pricing strategies don't always work. For example, she recently restored a 95-year-old afghan made of stiff cotton thread. Though she stuck to her quoted fee of $150, she realized after completing all the time-consuming, tedious work that she should have charged twice that amount.

Susan: What the Market Will Bear

Susan Allen of Virginia Beach, Virginia, makes and sells crocheted Christmas ornaments year round. It began 26 years ago when Susan wanted to make something different for Christmas and found an old leaflet with instructions for four ornament covers to fit over Christmas balls. For years she experimented with different threads and colors until finally, while living in England for three years, she discovered the Twilley's Goldfingering thread that she uses and sells today.

By 1997, Susan had developed nine designs of her own and had made hundreds of ornaments. One day her husband looked at her and at all her ever-multiplying Christmas ornaments and said, "Honey, I don't think we know this many people."

Susan took photographs of nine of her designs, wrote instructions, and put everything into a book that she started publishing on her computer at home. She began selling her finished ornaments and the Twilley's Goldfingering thread at local craft fairs during the months of October through December. But when she tried to sell them to a local Christmas shop, the buyer flatly refused as soon as she mentioned the word "crochet." Though taken aback at the response, she decided it was the buyer's loss and meant more profit for her.

"At my first craft fair, my table was in a great spot," Susan recalls. "I sat and crocheted and waited for my first sale. Everyone was telling everyone else about my ornaments. Customers kept walking up to my table and saying, 'Oh, you're the lady with the balls everyone is talking about.' I was a little embarrassed at first to be called the 'lady with balls.' But from that day on, I acquired a new title that continues to follow me to every craft fair since. I'm known as the 'lady with balls,' Christmas balls, that is."

Susan stressed that if you decide you want to crochet items for profit, you should do a lot of research before investing your time and money. She says that knowing your target market is critical. Take the time to visit your local craft fairs to see what is selling and what is not selling.

"Remember that your taste may not be everyone's taste," Susan emphasizes. "When I first started selling finished ornaments at craft fairs, I kept with the traditional colors of red, green, and blue trimmed in either gold or silver thread. People asked me for every color imaginable, including black ornaments with gold. Now, I'm in touch with an ornament maker who keeps me up to date with the current colors, and I sell them all—even black."

When it comes to pricing, Susan bases her prices on what the market will bear, after much research. She finds that if she bases her pricing on an hourly wage plus materials, the ornaments are too expensive to sell.

"I'm a firm believer that if you price affordably, customers will buy," she says. "Customers do not care how many hours it took for you to make your product, and they don't realize your time is as valuable as their time. Standard formulas do not work for me."

"I often overhear women at the fairs say that they watched their grandmothers or mothers crochet, but they don't have the time. I can't imagine not having time to crochet," says Susan. "I feel that crochet is becoming a lost art."

Profiting from Your Expertise

▼▼▼

MANY CROCHETERS ENJOY EARNING MONEY by selling their crochet expertise in addition to, or instead of, selling their crochet creations. Profiting from your expertise simply means providing a crochet-related service for a fee. How can you profit from your crochet expertise? Let me count the ways: teaching, designing, pattern testing and editing, stitch testing, and writing—to name just the most common freelance jobs for crocheters.

Those of us who profit from our crochet talents usually discover we can make more money per hour doing this type of for-hire work than we can selling crocheted items. Another thing that this group has discovered, as you'll see when you hear from the crocheters in this chapter, is that profiting from your crochet expertise requires the ability to diversify. If you want to "make it" as a crochet expert and make money at it, you'll probably need to market more than one talent.

Many of the marketing principles discussed in chapter 7—understanding your customers, capabilities, competition, costs, and creativity—apply to parlaying your crochet expertise into money-making services. There are, of course, some differences, most of

159

which will become apparent when you read about crochet service opportunities in this chapter.

One of the main differences between selling crocheted items versus crochet expertise is that you generally have less control over the amount of money you receive for your services than over the fees you charge for products. Whereas you determine the price to charge for each item you make and market—albeit, based on some factors that you can't completely control, such as market demand and materials costs—you seldom have the luxury of setting prices for your crochet expertise. The fees paid for crochet expertise, for a design or a magazine article, are almost always dictated by the client. Let's say, for example, that you are one of several instructors chosen to teach crocheting classes at a large national trade show. You will receive the same amount per hour, or per day, as all the other teachers participating in the show. You either accept the rate of pay offered, or you don't. There is no room for fee negotiations. The good news is you're likely to get up to $50 per hour or $500 per day.

In some cases, you'll be asked to quote your fee for a certain "freelance" service. If you expect to get the work, your fees must be competitive with other crochet experts providing these services. If you charge too much, clients will likely choose another expert who charges less; if you charge too little, your client may undervalue your work or question your expertise.

In the beginning, you'll have to solicit most of your work from publishers, yarn companies, and other potential "clients." Once you've established yourself as an expert provider of a certain service, these clients might come to you—or will at least be more receptive to your proposals.

When contacting a prospective client, it is important to type your letter on letterhead, because editors tend to dismiss queries that are handwritten, which take longer to read and say "unprofessional." You definitely want your first impression to appear professional. No one ever gets to make a *second* first impression! If you have access to a computer, you can use it to create your own personalized letterhead and then just print it out. You can also buy a few sheets of nice paper from an office supply or copy service store (most sell designer stationery in several businesslike styles) and then personalize it with your name, address, and phone number.

There are many ways to profit from your crochet talents. Read on to learn about how you might parlay your crochet expertise into enjoyable money-making opportunities.

Designing

If you frequently come up with original ideas and make up your own distinctive designs, design work might appeal to you, as it did to me. The start-up costs are minimal. You need nothing more than a stamp, a sheet of letterhead, and your design talent to get the process rolling.

Pattern-book publishers are a prime market for freelance designs. Design work is highly competitive. Only experts need apply, but that doesn't mean you can't learn how to become an expert, too.

In the beginning, you'll probably do design work on a part-time basis simply due to the logistics involved. It takes time to establish a relationship with editors and to gain a reputation for your work. It also takes a while to gain the experience necessary to determine how many hours to allot to various design duties.

As a freelance designer, you will routinely perform the following activities:

- Swatching and sketching
- Writing query letters
- Market research

- Charting
- Mathematical calculations
- Instruction writing
- Sizing
- Instruction editing

How to Write Instructions

Crochet instructions are written in a technical language, unlike how-to instructions for other crafts or hobbies. The only way to learn this unique language and its strict rules is to read and re-read crochet instructions as they appear in magazines, books, and other published patterns. However, you'll find there are minor differences in phraseology when you compare the patterns of one publisher to another. You may also spot differences in the rules for ending or beginning a row, but the rules about abbreviations, when to capitalize or not capitalize words, and the order in which instructions are written are standard.

While I've taught classes on how to write crochet instructions for the Crochet Guild of America (CGOA) to other professionals, I do not know of other resources available for learning this technical language. It's something that is usually self-taught, in spite of the complexities.

Sizing Standards and Measurements

While there are a few publishers who have strict sizing standards and measurements for each size, most do not. Comparing sizing changes and the measurements of one publisher to another is helpful, but you'll find differences, sometimes vast differences in the measurements when it comes to armhole depth or the back neck to hem length of garments. Some of these differences are based on how the garment is intended to fit the body. For example, most outer garments such as cardigans and jackets allow more ease than

What a Designer Needs to Know

- How to write instructions
- Sizing standards and measurements
- The importance of gauge
- How to calculate multiple stitch patterns
- What other designers are doing
- Crochet design trends
- Color theory
- Fiber characteristics

do pullovers. Other differences in measurements can be directly attributed to a garment's style or shape.

The Importance of Gauge

One of the most important components of good design work is the ability to determine true gauge. Accurate gauge is critical to a designer in determining sizing differences when charting out a crochet design. Each size and each measurement, as shown on a schematic, must be exact. Suppose you crochet and submit a model (to be photographed), in a size Petite, along with written instructions to a publisher. When your model is received, someone in the design department is likely to measure the shoulder width, armhole depth, wrists, total length, etc. and compare those measurements to your schematic to ensure that they match exactly. Your gauge will also be double-checked.

How To Calculate Multiple Stitch Patterns

Knowing how to calculate multiple stitch patterns is more complicated than is gauge when it comes to adhering to sizing changes. In determing where and when to start shaping for an underarm or neckline, advance planning and calculations are required to maintain a multiple stitch pattern. You need to plan out the sizing changes, at the same time maintaining a multiple stitch pattern, so each finished garment has integrity. For example, if your multiple stitch pattern takes ten rows and four inches to complete, that is a real challenge when it comes to shaping armholes, because armhole depths are most often increased by only one half inch for each larger size.

Adjustments must often be made to finished chest measurements, as well as other measurements, to ensure that multiples remain intact. These adjustments are difficult to determine and often come down to a judgment call on the part of the designer. If multiple pattern stitches do not match at the underarms or shoulder seams, the finished garment will not look professional. Making such adjustments requires that each stitch and row be charted for each size prior to beginning your crochet project.

Because of the complexities of designing crocheted garments, many designers stick to afghans, baby blankets, and other items that do not require sophisticated shaping and strategic mathematical calculations.

What Other Designers Are Doing

Savvy designers know they need to be aware of what kinds of designs other designers are marketing. In addition, if you design garments, you need to keep in touch with fashion trends in general, not simply crochet trends. Designs are most often created and accepted a year prior to publication; if you submit a crochet design based on a current fad, that fad is likely to have passed over the following year.

Color Theory

Not everyone does crochet color work. If doing so appeals to you and you've not been trained in color theory, you can buy color wheels from most yarn shops. These handy tools make it easy to determine perfect color combinations at the spin of the wheel.

Fiber Characteristics

Publishers expect designers to not only know about various yarn and fiber characteristics, they expect us to make appropriate choices. The yarns chosen need to be suitable for both the style and purpose of a design.

Getting Started

First, you'll need to identify potential buyers of your freelance designs. The fastest and easiest way to do this is to leaf through crochet, knitting, and craft magazines. Look for magazines that feature crocheted items, and ads that feature U.S. yarn manufacturers (foreign countries do not hire designers from abroad), and that feature crochet patterns, clubs, and books. You're not ready to query editors about design possibilities until you research the crochet marketplace. Familiarize yourself with your favorite crochet magazines by reviewing several issues, preferably for a full year. Then compare one publication to another, noting the differences in editorial content, advertising, and projects. Take the time to thoroughly read written instructions for featured crochet projects to get a feel for each publication's style, format, and wording.

To get a feel for the editorial focus and crochet designs of each magazine, gather the following information for each:

■ How often is the magazine published?

■ Are the projects easy and quick, suitable for beginners, or are the projects for advanced crocheters?

■ Are the yarns used generic or low-end, or are they fashion yarns?

- Which types of yarns are advertised: low-end, mid-priced, and/or high-end?

- Which kinds of crocheted items are featured in the magazine's designs and articles: home decor, garments, gifts? Are they for men, women, children, infants/toddlers?

- Are the projects and techniques conventional, innovative, or niche? Are they varied or focused on specific style(s)?

- Are the projects theme-based?

- Is the magazine published by an organization? (If so, you may need to be a member to submit designs.)

- What market demographics (age group, income level, geographic region, educational level, etc.) does the content seem to target?

Analyzing and understanding as much as possible about a magazine not only provides you with valuable market research, it also increases your chance of acceptance! Now, take those magazines that, based on your analysis, would be a good fit for your designs. Make a list of the editorial addresses (not the subscription addresses) and the names of the editors. Make a second list of yarn companies that advertise in the same magazines, again writing down addresses also. You'll also notice that publishers of crochet patterns and books also advertise in magazines, and you can find their mailing addresses.

Write a *query letter* to each editor or yarn company on your list. Don't forget to use your "professional" letterhead. When querying magazines, insert the name of the appropriate editor in the salutation. When writing to publishers and yarn companies, it is perfectly acceptable to address your query, "To Whom It May Concern". Ask whether they are interested in considering or reviewing designs from freelancers and, if so, to send you their *writer/designer guide-*

▼▼

Freelance Designer Must Haves!

Writer/Designer Guidelines. Specific information about how articles or designs are to be submitted to a publication.

Editorial Calendars. Schedule of editorial themes and description of needs, usually for a full year.

▲▲

lines and *editorial calendar*. You don't need to ask yarn companies for writer's guidelines or editorial calendars, because they seldom have them. Some pattern publishers have guidelines and others do not. Always ask for the guidelines and if a company doesn't provide them for designers, they are likely to send you a letter or give you a phone call to explain their design needs.

Always enclose a business-sized self-addressed, stamped envelope (SASE) with every query letter!

Writer/Designer Guidelines

When the writer/designer guidelines and editorial calendars you requested arrive (in your SASE), review the guidelines first. These guidelines tell you exactly how to submit designs to a particular magazine.

For example, the guidelines might state the following design submission requirements:

- Type and double-space all patterns.

- Sketches must be dark enough to copy.

- A swatch must accompany each design.

- Enclose a SASE with sufficient postage to ensure the return of your submissions.

- Specify skill level required to produce the item.

- Send a photo of the item or items.

Guidelines vary a great deal from one magazine to another. Some editors require that you include return postage when submitting a design package to help defray their immense shipping costs. You may be surprised to learn that a return rate of 75% is common, with only about 25% of submissions actually being published.

Now, listen very carefully! Many crocheters assume that most designs are rejected because they're not good enough, clever enough, or professional enough. While that is sometimes the case, the *number one* reason for rejection is the design failed to meet editorial needs. It's simple: if you don't give editors what they need and want, they aren't going to buy your design!

Editorial Calendars

Like writer/designer guidelines, editorial calendars also vary considerably—in fact, even more so than guidelines. Most calendars list issues chronologically, and cite the theme of and list of items needed for each issue.

Editorial calendars also provide a *submission date* for each issue. That doesn't mean you have to, or should, wait until the specified date to submit a design; it means the editor must receive your submission on or before, and absolutely *no later than,* the given date.

You'll see another set of dates on the editorial calendar: the dates when the finished models and instructions for each issue must be in the editor's office.

You may at first be surprised to discover how far ahead magazines plan their content. Many publications schedule by issue themes and major topics a year or more in advance. Beginning designers sometimes find it difficult to get used to thinking about holiday designs on a hot summer day 18 months in advance. It takes mental discipline to put yourself in a creative mood based on an editor's needs rather than on what is happening around you or on what you "feel" like creating.

Let's say it's late summer, and a publication is seeking a dressy openwork shawl design for its May issue, some eight months away. The submission date for swatches and sketches is October 10. Once the submissions are received—by October 10—an editorial staff panel reviews all of the submissions and picks out their favorites based on the magazine's design criteria. The editors then send letters out to those designers whose designs are being considered for the May issue, requesting completed models and written instructions submitted by a specified deadline. Generally the designer will be given a couple of weeks to comply. How can you increase your chances of your design being chosen over the other submissions? By doing market research, of course! The more familiar you are with a magazine's needs, the more likely you'll give them a design that meets, or exceeds, their expectations. If you submit a great pattern for a warm, close-textured shawl in a heavy tweed yarn in response to the magazine's call for a dressy, open-work shawl—you're just wasting your time and the editor's time. Although your warm, heavy shawl might be just the ticket for an issue focused on designs suitable for cool autumn days and activities, it clearly doesn't fit the bill for a light, elegant shawl for a spring concert.

If you give editors what they want, they will come back for more!

Terms and Conditions

When a magazine (or other buyer) accepts one of your designs, the editor (or other official) sends you a contract spelling out the terms and conditions of the offer to acquire certain rights to your design. Read the contract carefully and address any questions or concerns you might have before you sign and return the contract. If you don't understand the wording or take issue with any of the terms, consult with an attorney for clarification or advice. Once you sign and return a contract, you have agreed to all the terms as stated. Sometimes contract terms can be negotiated. For example, most contracts state that the model itself becomes the property of the publisher. Some companies will return models, if requested to do so, but this must be added in writing to the contract. Any fee negotiations take place before a contract is sent out and usually are discussed over the phone well before a contract is mailed to you. Typical contract terms include:

- Description of design
- Verification of design originality
- Design fee offered
- Rights being purchased
- Terms and conditions of sale (including payment method)
- Specifications for delivery of finished design

Design Originality

The contract will include a statement that the designer (you) guarantees that the design is completely original and has not been published elsewhere.

Design Fees

Editors will sometimes tell you upfront how much they are willing to pay for a design, but usually they'll ask you to quote them an asking price. If you're a beginner, how do you know how much to ask for? Although it may appear you have now entered into a negotiation process with the editor, that isn't exactly the case. Most editors maintain a standard price list of designs for all basic crocheted items—sweaters, hats, afghans, doll clothing—which specifies the fee ranges to be paid for each category. Interested buyers are likely to ask you to quote a price in the hopes you'll request less than the higher end fees and thus will save the editor money. If your asking price is too high, the editor is likely to either decline to pay that amount or suggest a lower price. There are no tried and true formulas when it comes to the going rates for design fees. Design fees are always controlled by the client and are typically based on a combination of factors: intricacy of execution (skill level), estimated time to make, sizing changes that require extra time to calculate and write instructions for, and so on. However, some publications pay a flat fee for specific items—for example, an afghan—regardless of the quality, complexity, or creativity of the design or stitch pattern. Flat fees can vary greatly, but a moderate fee for an afghan would be $300 with some publishers offering much less and others offering more. Design fees are usually closely guarded secrets between buyers and designers and among designers themselves. However, becoming a member of an association, such as CGOA (Crochet Guild of America), enables you to begin networking with other designers who may be willing to share their design fee secrets once you've established a level of trust with them.

Initially, it is best to settle for less than to ask for too much. Why? Because the sooner and the more often your designs are published, the more leverage you have in selling your designs and increasing your fees for them. The first goal, then, is to get your designs in print. Whenever one of your designs is published, you will receive at least one free contributor copy of the issue (or other publication) in which your design appears.

If you have written for other magazines, you'll be surprised to learn that there are differences when writing for needle art magazines. For example, when writing for other kinds of publications, the magazine page(s) where your work appears are referred to as "clips." Writers often cut out and photocopy clips as evidence that they have been published. However, crochet projects are shown in color and generally do not photocopy well. Therefore, designers often purchases extra copies of the issues that feature their designs, and tear out those pages. Designers refer to these torn out pages as "tear sheets" and use them as verification that they have been published and are professionals. They also insert tear sheets into their portfolios.

Believe me, those tear sheets are invaluable. When you query another editor, you'll want to include a tear sheet as evidence that you have been published and to provide examples of your personal style.

Once you get an idea of the range of design fees, you can determine how many designs you need to produce monthly to meet your financial needs and to establish a regular cash flow. To make a living at design work, it is often necessary to devote a substantial amount of time to making design submissions.

Rights

Your contract states which rights the magazine or yarn company is offering to buy: for example, first rights, all rights, exclusive first North American rights, nonexclusive, or all ownership rights. A contract that seeks first rights only allows you to publish your patterns again in books, videos, Web sites, or other non-serial publishing opportunities. Writers often prefer to sell only first rights or nonexclusive rights, because it enables them to sell their articles to other publications either after the article is originally published (first rights) or anytime, anywhere (nonexclusive). However, that doesn't seem to apply to crochet designs. I know of no publications that reprint crochet patterns. While other kinds of magazines sometimes pay more for all or exclusive rights than for nonexclusive or limited rights, that is not the practice with crochet patterns.

Once you sign a contract, the rights to your pattern (written instructions) as specified on the contract belong to the magazine. If you granted anything other than first rights or nonexclusive rights, you cannot publish the instructions elsewhere for monetary gain. You can reprint the instructions only if you give them away and then you must include information about where and when the pattern was originally published.

Copyright law is a complicated aspect of publishing, with rights being defined by innumerable exclusions and conditions, making it subject to misunderstanding. When in doubt, consult a copyright attorney.

Payment

One of the most important things specified in a contract is the payment terms. In publishing, there are three basic terms of payment:

1. **Upon execution of contract**
2. **Upon receipt of finished article/design**
3. **Upon publication**

Upon execution of contract means you'll get paid after any contract negotiations are finalized, you sign and return the contract, and the publishing official(s) sign the contract. That, however, doesn't mean the magazine (or yarn company) immediately writes you a check the day they receive your signed contract. It usually takes 30 days, sometimes longer, for your payment to go through the accounting process.

Upon receipt actually means after receipt, review, and acceptance of the finished article/design—a process that can take a few days, several weeks, or more. Once the acceptance process is complete, you can expect to wait another 30 days or so for the payment to make its way through the accounting system. Some accounting cycles are shorter, but don't count on it.

Other magazines pay upon publication, meaning you don't get paid until your design is actually published. In that case, you

When Mistakes Happen

Have you noticed the "corrections" columns in most needlework magazines? We're all human; sometimes the designer makes a mistake, sometimes the publisher. Regardless of who slips up, it is the designer's reputation that is most affected when readers find flaws in patterns.

Once mistakes are published, it can be difficult to undo the damage, as I found out when the instructions for one of my afghan designs appeared in a popular magazine with a problem—that became a big problem!

The pattern stitch featured in this particular afghan was a six-row repeat, with the first row being a foundation row. The instructions I'd submitted read "Repeat Rows 2–7." Somehow, during the magazine's editing process, the instructions for working Row 7 mysteriously disappeared. When readers got to "Repeat Rows 2–7," they were unable to do so, because there were no instructions for working Row 7.

The e-mails and letters poured into the editor's office, and she contacted me. Within minutes, I emailed her a copy of my original instructions, exactly as submitted—with Row 7 intact. The editor called back to confirm the magazine's mistake. Assuming

---

are likely to receive your contributor copies two to three weeks before you receive payment. When contracting for payment upon publication, you need to realize that it may take a full year for your design to be published and for you to receive payment. You should also be aware that, despite all that advance scheduling, editorial calendars do occasionally change unexpectedly, which could result in your design being published earlier, but it is as likely to be delayed.

Testing and Editing Your Patterns

All written crochet instructions should be carefully read, worked, and edited, as needed, to ensure that every stitch and step is clear and accurate. Most novice designers try to test and edit their own instructions, because when your cash flow is still tight (or nonexistent), it is difficult to justify the expense of paying someone else to

the magazine would include the correction in a future corrections column, I put the matter out of my mind.

You can imagine my surprise when a week later I received an envelope stuffed with e-mails and letters from readers. Enclosed was a note from the editor, thanking me in advance for contacting everyone who had written to explain the problem. I was not pleased with the dilemma this presented.

On one hand, I wasn't eager to remedy the magazine's mistake. On the other hand, refusing to do it would probably mean the editor would never accept any of my designs again. I also knew that editors exchange information with one another, and I didn't want to get a reputation for being difficult to work with.

In the end, I wrote a form letter apologizing to readers and explaining that Row 7 had inadvertently been omitted from my original design when it was published in the magazine. Of course, I provided the missing Row 7. All the while, I grumbled about the time, effort, and stamps the episode had cost me.

I take comfort in knowing that I'd submitted clean instructions, because I'd had them tested and edited. When the magazine made the mistake, I did what I could to rectify the problem with readers and to protect my career.

check your work. But when you check and double-check your own work, it is all too easy to overlook errors, omissions, and sizing mistakes. For your own protection, I strongly recommend that you bite the added-cost bullet and hire a pattern tester or editor. Just think of it as a necessary expense of being in the design business. Your reputation is at stake, and you don't want to get a bad reputation for writing instructions loaded with mistakes.

Considering that a full year may pass before you see your design in print, during which you created many other designs, you are likely to have forgotten the details of the design. If you get a phone call after a year's time inquiring about whether a specific phrase in your instructions is written correctly, it will be a challenge and will take time to review the instructions and seek out possible errors. Hiring a pattern tester or editor can save you many hours of frustration.

SHARON'S STORY

Sharon Blosch of Dublin, California, is a pattern tester/stitcher for Crochet Trends & Traditions, a partnership formed by Brenda Stratton and Carol Alexander. She has been crocheting for 40 years, having as a young girl been taught by her Canadian grandmother how to improve her tension. Sharon became acquainted with Brenda Stratton through the Crochet List and Crochet Partners Web site, which posted a "help wanted" ad for stitchers. "Brenda asked me to provide samples of my work, so I made three different dishcloths, figuring she'd have something to use even if she didn't like my work," Sharon said. Though some time passed before Sharon received her first assignment, as soon as she began, she immediately found she liked the work.

"I enjoy editing the pattern even more than doing the stitching," Sharon said. "It's a thrill to see something straight from the designer's mind and to be part of the process of getting a design published."

Along with the written instructions and yarn, Sharon also receives the materials list, gauge, instructions for specialty stitches, and a sample swatch. "The swatch is a godsend, because I can refer to it for gauge and for clarification of instructions," Sharon said.

Pattern Testing/Stitching

Due to rising business costs, fewer publishing houses hire pattern testers today than in the past. However, freelance opportunities for pattern testers/stitchers still exist.

These days, a growing number of designers are self-publishing their patterns in an effort to increase their shares of the profits. These small publishers sometimes hire pattern testers who do dou-

During her many years of crocheting, Sharon has often felt the frustration of encountering poorly written or edited crochet patterns, and feels she has always been a proofreader at heart.

Now, when she finds spelling and "typo" mistakes in the patterns she's testing, she makes notations directly on the instructions. When she finds construction errors, she contacts the designer to determine whether she has misunderstood something or whether the instructions contain errors or omissions.

The most difficult part of the job, according to Sharon, is having not only to switch hook sizes, but sometimes she must manipulate her stitches to match the gauge of the designer.

"It takes some effort to develop consistency, and I tend to be a perfectionist when it comes to working on designs," she said. "This is really work!"

Sharon finds freelancing as a pattern tester to be the perfect venue for her talents, even though she doesn't earn enough to support a family.

"It provides travel money so I can attend CGOA conventions," she said, "but I mostly do it for fun."

ble duty—crocheting and proofreading. Designers also occasionally hire stitchers to do nothing more than produce models of their patterns. I prefer to use local stitchers, but many designers hire stitchers from around the country.

So, what exactly is a pattern tester/stitcher? Ask different folks, and you're likely to get different answers. Some publishing houses employ pattern testers to do the obvious—check patterns for accuracy. These pattern testers rarely work an entire crochet project, but instead carefully read, or *proof*, the instructions. When errors, omissions, or mistakes are spotted in the written instructions, the pattern tester corrects the instructions accordingly. Sometimes, the pattern tester actually works a few rows of the crochet pattern to make certain she understands the designer's intentions. The pattern tester/stitcher is given written instructions and a sufficient amount of yarn to work a crochet project, whether it's an afghan, sweater, stole, or whatever.

Getting Started

Some national organizations and guilds, such as the Crochet Guild of America (CGOA), maintain a list of crocheters who are interested in freelancing as stitchers and pattern testers (as well as editors, custom designers, etc.). People get on the list based on information they provide when filling out their CGOA volunteer sheet (if they fill one out).

Designers, publishers, and any others who are interested in hiring contract crocheters often contact CGOA. CGOA then puts out the word to as many of the crocheters as it can reach, passing along the call for contractors with contact information for the person seeking help. Any of these freelancers who are interested in the job then contact the person seeking a tester directly. If you think you might enjoy doing this kind of work, you also might want to send out query letters to designers or yarn companies. You'll also find lots of ads in the back of needlework magazines.

Payment Terms and Conditions

When you work as a freelance pattern tester for a small pattern publishing company, the business practices tend to be rather informal. Though some companies, such as Crochet Trends & Traditions, provide written contracts when hiring pattern testers, others do not.

What Pattern Testers/Stitchers Need to Know

- How to read and comprehend written instructions

- How to spot and correct mistakes in instructions

- Proper terminology when rewriting instructions

- How to produce perfect crochet work

- How to accurately check gauge

- How to double-check mathematical calculations

- How to meet deadlines

Generally the person who is doing the hiring sets a deadline for when the completed project must be in her hand. At the same time, she offers a flat rate to the pattern tester. The pattern tester then decides whether to accept or reject the offer. Rates for this type of work are rarely negotiable. The rates for pattern testers/stitchers are lower than are design fees, for obvious reasons. The designer comes up with the original design, does all the charting and mathematical calculations, and writes the instructions.

The payment terms are usually *upon project completion* and the on-time receipt of the corrected instructions and, if applicable, the finished model. If your test/stitch project arrives after the agreed-upon deadline and prevents the designer from meeting her deadline with the publisher, the designer doesn't get paid—and you shouldn't expect payment either. Also don't expect payment for work that doesn't pass the quality muster.

When the tester/stitcher fails to meet a deadline or his or her workmanship is not up to par, some publishers and/or designers allow her to keep the model in lieu of payment. However, many designers work with yarn companies in developing knit and crochet patterns for publication in national magazines. In many of these cases, the yarn company provides the yarn and agrees to pay half of the design fee in exchange for having their yarn mentioned. This is especially true of yarn companies who do not have big advertising budgets; providing yarn in exchange for an endorsement is much less expensive than buying advertising space.

Yarn companies are not in the business of giving away free yarn and do so only with the expectation that their yarn will be mentioned. If your missed deadline causes a designer to lose an opportunity to publish her design, the yarn company will be unhappy with the designer and might never work with her again. If your tardiness affects a designer's income, the designer, in turn, is unlikely to want to work with you again.

Teaching

Now and then, yarn companies sponsor well-known designers to travel around the country putting on trunk shows and teaching workshops. Some companies also hire established designers to appear on national television craft shows.

Most teaching and workshop opportunities are found locally, primarily through needlecraft organizations and shops in your geographic area. Crochet courses are sometimes offered at community colleges and high schools, which are non-credited and continuing education classes for the community at large. However, you may discover, as I did, that the amount of time required to fill out all the paperwork, make models, create handouts, and drive to and from the class greatly reduces the small hourly fees paid for these community-sponsored classes. After my first quarter of teaching,

Teaching Opportunities

- Clubs and organizations
- Continuing education programs (high schools/community colleges)
- Craft guilds
- Craft stores
- Local yarn shops
- Regional or national needlework conferences
- Trade shows

when I tallied up my time and costs, I was actually only making $2.17 per hour!

Getting Started

Increasingly, yarn shops are hiring only those instructors who are certified by the Craft Yarn Council of America (CYCA) to teach crochet and knitting. Why? Because these programs turn out well-trained instructors who are especially adept at teaching others. The CYCA's Certified Instructor Program (CIP), which has been in existence since 1984, teaches crocheters and knitters how to teach others. Their new CIP program focuses on providing graduates with the tools to teach professionally in stores and other venues. If you love to crochet and have advanced beginner skills and enjoy teaching, this program may be for you. CIP courses are offered at both CGOA and The Knitting Guild of America (TKGA) conferences and conventions, which are held at various locations around the country throughout the year. The cost for the 17-hour program is reasonable—only $35. This rigorous and intense course is taught over several days. Graduates of CIP courses are then asked to volunteer 15

What a Teacher Needs to Know

- Crochet techniques, terms, materials, tools, range of items that can be created with crochet
- How to determine the skill level required for specific projects
- How to teach effectively
- The varied ways in which different people learn new skills
- How to encourage and inspire students

You'll also need to have patience and genuinely enjoy working with people to succeed as a crochet instructor.

hours of teaching before being awarded certification. The council feels this is an important way to strengthen teaching skills and to give back to one's community.

Terms and Conditions

The rate of pay for teaching is generally determined by where you teach. For example, if you teach on a local level, then the rate of pay tends to be less than if you teach on a regional or national level.

Local Teaching

Do you remember Lester Vaughn from chapter 1? At nearly 80 years of age, she is CYCA-certified, and her teaching schedule is always full. However, Lester teaches at local yarn shops, craft stores, and schools, which are more apt to pay by the hour or by a flat fee for the class taught. Some of her teaching engagements are strictly volunteer. For example, it is illegal to charge a fee when teaching in public schools. Sometimes the parents contribute a few dollars for gas for her car, but she receives no teaching fees whatsoever. It's the love of her craft and of teaching crochet to children that rewards Lester.

Most yarn shops, craft stores, community colleges, and other schools collect the class or workshop fees from students and then pay the instructor on an hourly or per-class rate. Once in a while, you'll be contracted to teach by a generous sponsor, like I was when I taught classes for several years for a yarn shop owner in eastern Washington. Regardless of the number of students, she gave me all the class fees, because she knew the classes kept her customers interested and coming back for more. Besides, she assured me that the amount of money they spent on yarn for each class was more than the cost of the classes. Of course, I also created original designs for each class that I taught in her shop, which she then used as store displays to encourage class sign-ups for each new class. These displays also helped promote her yarns.

Instructors often receive side benefits too, such as discounts on their yarn and other purchases, which most stores offer to their teachers.

Karen Klemp, a retired Foreign Service officer who lives in Arlington, Virginia, has always crocheted everywhere, in the car, on planes, in front of the television, and on her lunch hour at work.

"When we lived in Germany, I started to make a wonderful afghan from a romantic pattern with a pineapple border. I began with the border, rolling it up as I worked," Karen recalled. "Then we moved to Croatia, where we were in the midst of a war and I was the U.S. government's refugee coordinator to the former Yugoslavia. I took numerous trips where flak vest and helmet were required garb and traveled in armored vehicles and helicopters trying to dodge enemy radar. It was during those trips that I made the center of the afghan.

"When I unrolled my work and took a really good look at it, the edging I had worked earlier was nearly six times larger than the middle, and the middle section was crocheted so tightly, it felt like cardboard. I had to rip out the whole thing, and then I made a different afghan altogether. That one turned out perfect, and I gave it as a wedding gift to a Serbian woman from Vukovar, who married one of the American Foreign Service officers at the Embassy." For years, Karen dreamed of making crochet her primary occupation.

"My idea was to retire as soon as possible from the Foreign Service and just crochet," Karen recounted. "But as the time for retirement grew nearer, I realized I might quickly grow bored just staying home to crochet, and I knew I'd miss contact with people. So, I signed up for the CYCA's Certified Instructor Program at the 1997 CGOA conference in Chicago, and I've been teaching part-time ever since."

She started out teaching crochet to coworkers at the State Department during her lunch hour. She held classes two days a week, and they were free to anyone who wanted to sign up.

"I'm sure I learned more than the students," Karen said. "The classes taught me which lessons worked and which didn't. I learned which techniques require the most attention as well as how to deal with different learning styles and levels of motivation. Over time, I developed a class structure that takes students from a beginner level to an intermediate level of crochet."

Karen retired in July of 1999 and formed her own business, KDK Crochet, just 3 months later. She now teaches several days each week at different shops—for a fee. How much she earns and how her fees are determined vary from one shop to another.

"One yarn shop lets me fix the fee, and they take 25 percent. Another shop takes 20%, but has urged me to raise the class fee. The large fabric shop where I'll soon be teaching pays by the hour."

Students are flocking to Karen's classes. "The response to my classes could be overwhelming if I didn't set some limits," she said. "But it's so exciting!"

Like many others who crochet for profit, Karen has found multiple ways to create income, not only by teaching, but also with sample making and doing restoration work for yarn shops in her hometown. She has also ventured into design work, and several of her designs have been published in *Quick & Easy Crochet* magazine. She also serves as the president of the Crochet Guild of America, which takes 3 to 4 hours of her time daily.

Regional and National Teaching

To ferret out local and regional teaching opportunities, you'll need to become a good detective. These teaching opportunities are rarely openly advertised. Local crochet guilds sometimes hire well-known teachers or those who have specialized skills. If you are interested in seeking such opportunities, send out query letters to local guilds and include a brochure about yourself and the talents you have to offer.

Regional teaching opportunities are usually offered to teachers by yarn companies or publishers who participate in regional trade shows. Generally companies approach teachers they know, but sometimes they consider other teachers, too. So you may wish to query and submit brochures to publishers or yarn companies that are specifically seeking teachers.

Kathie Power Johnson of Sarasota, Florida, has increased her teaching income by reaching out beyond the local level. She lands these regional and national teaching engagements through word-of-mouth referrals and by approaching organizations that sponsor seminars. She also sends out brochures describing her workshops to guilds and other groups.

Kathie is willing to travel to far-flung parts of the country to conduct her workshops, and her workshop clients typically pay all her travel expenses. She offers a minimum 1-day workshop and a 2-day workshop, but charges slightly less per day for the 2-day course to encourage groups to hire her for 2 days.

For national guild conferences and events, she pays her own travel expenses, which are offset by the teaching fees she receives.

Kathie teaches at: "Stitches" seminars and camps around the country; CGOA "Chainlink" conferences; Knitting Guild of America's national convention and regional seminars; as well as at local guild retreats and workshops.

Kathie once taught as often as three or four classes a week for local shops and groups in addition to her heavy design and writing schedule.

"It was draining and affected both my performance and enthusiasm," Kathie said. "I changed my schedule, so that I now teach at about six national conferences and do several regional workshops annually. This gives me time to develop new classes and to pursue other aspects of my career."

A full-time knitting and crocheting professional, Kathie spends approximately 25% of her time designing, 25% writing, and 50% teaching. Her ability to diversify and natural desire to develop her talents provide a strong foundation that keeps her business profitable, challenging, and enjoyable.

"To maintain my enthusiasm, I need to continually learn and take my craft in new and different directions. A class might lead to a design and then to an article. I find this makes the most effective and profitable use of my time."

You'll see Kathie's beautiful needlework and articles in some of the following magazines: *Knitters, Family Circle Easy Knitting and Crochet, Fashion Knitting, Knit 'n Style, Knitting Digest, Crochet Digest, Crochet Fantasy, Vogue,* and *Crafts.* She also is currently writing a knitting book.

Writing

If you are a professional designer or teacher, you're likely to develop new and different crochet techniques that might interest

What a Writer Needs to Know

■ How to write query letters that "hook" editors

■ How to interview, research, and check facts

■ How to write like a pro

■ Which publications publish or might publish crochet-related articles

■ Editorial focus and needs of potential publishers of your articles

■ Writers' guidelines of target publications

■ Editorial calendars of target publications

other crocheters. You might be able to profit from writing articles about those techniques for national needlework magazines.

The demand for written articles is much less than the need for designs. As you have probably already noticed, some needlework magazines rarely include articles and others include only two or three, while all craft publications feature several designs in each issue. However, if you have good writing skills and can deliver what specific editors need, you'll be glad to know the pay is quite good. Contributing magazine articles often pays better than designing, considering the number of hours it takes to write an article compared with the time required to create a design and make a model.

In order to write articles about crochet for national magazines, you not only need expertise in crochet, you also need good research, writing, and editing skills. Unless you've had training and experience in professional writing, you may be unfamiliar with all the rules of grammar and punctuation as well as with composition techniques and journalism standards. If you want to create articles for national magazines, you might consider taking a writing or journalism course at your local community college to bring your writing and editing skills up to snuff.

Getting Started

Freelance crochet writers, like designers, need to obtain current writers' guidelines and editorial calendars for magazines that might be interested in publishing their articles on crochet. Don't just collect guidelines and calendars for those publications you wish to write for; also study the editorial content of competing or even seemingly unrelated publications, such as women's, arts, cultural, and spiritual magazines (crochet is relaxing), to help give you fresh, marketable article ideas.

Unless you have considerable experience writing in a particular magazine's genre and have plenty of clips (published writing samples) to prove it, no editors are likely to hire you to write for their publications. So, phoning or writing to request article assignments or a column is usually a waste of your time, and theirs. Some freelance writers produce the article first and then try to sell it. Experienced pros know that the most effective strategy is to query first and write later—after an editor expresses direct interest in a specific article proposal. Even then, you will probably have to write "on speculation," in which case the editor agrees only to *consider* your proposed article, with no contractual obligation to actually publish it until it is finished, submitted, and *accepted* for publication. This is all protocol in the freelance writing arena, but it can seem risky and daunting to newcomers.

Kathie Power Johnson, who trained as a writer, markets her writing by approaching editors with specific article ideas. She sometimes suggests an article to accompany one of her designs. She usually tries to sell a series of articles in order to establish herself with a particular publication. Having already gained a reputation as a writer with several needlework magazines, editors for whom she has written in the past now solicit articles from her.

To begin, however, as with freelance design marketing, you'll need to send query letters to editors, identifying the topic and summarizing the scope of the article you are proposing to write for that particular publication. Cite both your crochet and writing credentials. Include one or two clips of your published writing and, if you think it will help sell your idea, a photo of one of your completed designs or projects. Always include a self-addressed, stamped envelope, and always print the query on letterhead or high-quality 8½ × 11-inch paper. Some editors won't even read queries that are handwritten or on notepaper. Also, make sure to address your letter to the current editor. Editors tend to move from position to position like gypsies, but they'll favor queries addressed to them rather than to their predecessors.

> ### Handy Hint
> Queries that sell usually are typed on a single sheet of white business-size paper and include a sample lead paragraph for the proposed article that "hooks" the editor by clearly and compellingly conveying a unique angle on an interesting crochet topic or technique.

If you're serious about writing, you'll find one of the annual writer's guides a valuable resource. Updated and published yearly, these are directories of consumer and trade magazines, book publishers, and script buyers and include a vital information on editorial needs, submission guidelines, contact information, Web sites, pay rates, and rights.

Remember, the way to reduce your rejection rate is to fill an editorial need, and to do this you must know what the editor has planned for the future. Original, informative, and entertaining articles that fit a particular publisher's editorial focus are always in demand.

Terms and Conditions

When an editor is interested in an article you've proposed in a query letter, she or another editorial staff member will usually contact you to invite you to submit an article of a specified word-length, by a specified deadline, on a speculative basis. If you're an experienced writer or already have a relationship with the magazine, the

JOY'S STORY

Joy Prescott designed her first baby blanket for her newborn son. "I was always looking for ways to make extra money, and I discovered that crocheting was something I liked to do," Joy recalled. "When I sent the baby blanket pattern I'd designed for my new son to *Crochet World*, and they bought it, I was hooked and began designing more patterns."

Joy, who resides in Redmond, Washington, markets her designs to publishers, enters pattern contests, and once sold crocheted items on a seasonal basis and took special orders. She has also found that craft bazaars are a good way to sell design models that are returned after publication. Although she enjoyed the artistic challenge of creating special order and designer items, the profit margin didn't usually justify the time and effort spent.

"I made the best profits on small items I could mass produce, such as Christmas ornaments and novelty or gift items with easy patterns and minimal finish work," she explained. "I'd get a system going, so I could whip up several pieces in the evenings while watching television."

According to Joy, where you live makes a difference in what you can sell and how you sell it. When she lived in Alaska, she found people sought out and valued handmade gifts, because there were so few such items available in local shops. Crocheted items were especially rare. Conversely,

editor might assign the piece to you and send you a contract detailing all the terms and conditions. Sometimes, assignments are given with a "gentlewoman's" agreement, usually verbal, with no formal contract. As a word of advice: get it in writing, if at all possible.

As with design work, contracts are sent out when an article is accepted for publication in a national magazine. The contract states the rights the magazine is buying, the fee offered, the terms of payment, and other pertinent details, such as article length (number of words)

while living in Colorado, the only items she was able to sell were doilies, and at a low profit margin, because they are so intricate.

"Believe it or not, I used my crochet skills to get my first technical job in the spring of 1996," Joy said. "I had just graduated from college with an English degree a few months earlier when one of my professors recommended me for a technical writing position. Not having any professional writing samples, I took a few papers I'd written in school and several of my published crochet patterns to the job interview."

Her ability to clearly and logically describe the technical procedures involved in crocheting a particular item using the specified "code" of written crochet instructions demonstrated a skill that could be transferred to technical writing. Joy got the job, and, for the present time, she can rely on her lucrative position as a technical writer as a means of financial support and reserve her crochet for pure pleasure.

and any illustration requirements. In some cases, the contract is simply a letter from the editor specifying terms and conditions.

Some magazines pay flat fees for articles of a specified number of words. For example, if the length of an article is 300 to 900 words, you are paid a specific dollar amount of, say $50 or $300. Other magazines pay per word. Some magazines pay "only in copies," which means you get one or a few issues of the magazines in lieu of money for your article.

Pattern Editing

It is difficult to clearly differentiate the role of an editor from that of a pattern tester, because the duties of these two positions often overlap, yet each has very different responsibilities.

Noreen Havens, who edits instructions, including the ones in this book, offered these definitions and distinctions: "As I see it, the *pattern editor's* job is to ensure the integrity of the pattern as it is written, making sure all the "T"s are crossed and "I"s are dotted. She checks each pattern for readability and accuracy, making sure it is "doable." This involves careful proofreading, essentially, as well as a small amount of sampling the pattern to get the feel of the stitches.

"The *pattern tester*, on the other hand, normally works all the various stitches and patterns in a design and gives the whole pattern a thorough test run. Of course, they also proof and correct spacing, typing, and spelling errors in the written instructions, and they don't necessarily produce a finished item, though they often do. In the process of physically working through the pattern with hook and thread or yarn, the tester may (and often does) find sections in the pattern that need tweaking.

"So, both roles serve a similar end result, but each approaches the process from a different focus."

Noreen's editing clients sometimes come to her via CGOA, while others contact her through personal referrals. Those who contact her are often designers or self-publishers, but fiber artists also depend upon her editing skills. She sets a minimum rate and then charges by the hour.

The process for getting started as a pattern editor—as well as the fees, contractual terms, and payment methods that apply to pattern editing—are similar to those for pattern testing and stitching. These opportunities are seldom openly advertised. These freelance jobs must be sought after by querying, but sometimes are discovered via word of mouth.

What a Pattern Editor Needs to Know

- Writing and editing standards
- Standards and accepted variations in crochet instruction styles
- Standards and accepted variations in crochet instruction formats
- How to edit technical descriptions for clarity and accuracy

Deborah Levy Hamburg didn't set out to establish a full-time, salaried needlework career: She just wanted to learn how to crochet. At the time, she and her husband lived in an isolated valley with no television. Deborah was bored, pregnant, and after seeing her sister crochet, decided to make a baby blanket.

It started simply enough: with purple variegated thread and a crochet hook. Using the stitches her sister taught her, she made lots of little squares and then crocheted tiny ecru flowers to embellish them. By the time the baby was born, the blanket was finished. Then Deborah's life changed forever. Her son, Christian, was born with a rare and serious metabolic disease that required a strict diet, medications, complicated treatments, and Deborah's constant vigilance to administer to his needs. At age 15, Christian lost his life to the horrific disorder, and Deborah entered a long, hard grieving period. While mourning the loss of her son, Deborah was invited to meet a friend, Donna Robertson, at a trade show. At the time Donna was the product development coordinator for Annie's Attic in Big Sandy, Texas. All the brochures and free samples called out to Deborah, and the wonderful displays inspired her. All the places and events Donna visited as part of her job sounded like fun. Half-heartedly, Deborah said if an opening ever became available at Annie's Attic, she'd be interested.

To her surprise Donna phoned to offer her a position as her assistant a few short weeks later. The Hamburgs packed up and moved to Texas. Before long, Deborah was in charge of the design department and immersed herself in overseeing catalogs, magazines, pattern clubs, and other projects. She began coming up with her own designs. Tentatively, she submitted a crochet sweater pattern and was thrilled when it was accepted and published by Annie's Attic.

Today Deborah works for the corporation that owns Annie's Attic, The Needlecraft Shop, and The House of White Birches. Her many duties include acquiring crochet designs for both Annie's Attic and The Needlecraft Shop. The company produces needlework leaflets, books, catalogs, and various club publications as well as such popular crochet magazines as *Annie's Favorite Crochet, Annie's Crochet to Go!,* The Needlecraft Shop's *Crochet Home & Holiday,* and *Hooked on Crochet*—all with Deborah's expert help, of course.

Deborah often travels to trade shows to keep current on market trends, to promote her company's products and services, and sometimes to teach crochet or other techniques.

Deborah continues to design, and her distinctive work now includes exquisite Victorian embellishment designs, published by Annie's Attic.

A dedicated CGOA member and crocheter, Deborah serves on the board as the industry liaison chairperson and gives countless hours toward promoting public awareness about CGOA.

Crochet Career Specialties

Now that we've covered the ways in which most crocheters earn money with their crochet talents, let's examine a few less common ways to capitalize on your crochet expertise.

Public Relations Consulting

Candi Jensen learned how to crochet at age eight from her baby-sitter.

"I was quite a handful as a child, and my sitter taught me crochet to keep me quiet," Candi remembered. "I am forever grateful."

Candi's exciting, demanding, and unusual career as a public relations media consultant evolved from her love of crochet. "I had been working in politics in San Francisco and was burned out, so I went to work in a yarn store, Straw into Gold. Soon I was applying what I had learned about promoting political campaigns into promoting yarn. The timing was right, because Straw into Gold was introducing a wholesale line of yarns, and I helped them successfully launch it."

Based in Oakland, California, Candi currently provides public relations services to several clients. Her only needlework client is Solutia, Inc. "I promote the use of their fiber in five spinners yarns," Candi explains. "I help get the yarns featured in magazines and on television to promote crocheting and knitting."

Designing for Niche Markets

In 1976 Linda Driscoll's daughters received a dollhouse from their grandparents. It was void of dolls, furniture, and decorations. At the time, miniatures was a new hobby that was rapidly catching on throughout the country. To spruce up the little home, Linda got out needlepoint yarn and crocheted a matching granny afghan, rug, and pillow. In her quest for dolls to inhabit the little abode, she visited Gloria, who had repaired Linda's dolls when she was a child.

When Linda showed her friend the wee afghan, Gloria asked whether she could make a smaller afghan. "Sure! No problem!" Linda blurted out without thinking. Not knowing of a thinner thread, she asked her mother, who suggested tatting thread. She used it to make another mini-afghan and took it to Gloria, who again inquired, "Can you make it smaller?"

For 2 weeks Linda wracked her brain trying to think of a smaller thread. Then it suddenly dawned on her she could use sewing thread! It was the perfect size, and her mom, a couturier and seamstress, had oodles of the stuff in 100% cotton and in every imaginable color.

Linda worked up another teensy afghan and took it to Gloria. After appreciatively inspecting the dainty little throw, Gloria referred Linda to the owner of a miniature store she was sure would buy everything Linda could make. What began as a game of "Can you top this?" thus launched a rapidly flourishing crochet miniatures business: Nouvelle Vision.

Linda quickly expanded her business to include a wide range of collector miniatures—textiles, beaded and crocheted purses, afghans, pillows, doilies—and to clients all over the United States and even overseas. Now known as the creator of the smallest crochet in the world, Linda's miniatures have been featured in California stores for more than 20 years and can be found in museums and private collections in such far-flung places as the Puppenhaus Museum in Switzerland.

As Linda launched and then continued to grow her business, she kept remembering some sage advice she had received from an unexpected source when she was 14 years old. At that time, Linda and her mother had a booth at a craft fair where Jimmy Durante was performing. After his show, Linda ran to Durante's car so she could meet him, and she asked him for some career advice.

Mr. Durante said: "Honey, I'll give you some advice for a lifetime. Find the void and fill it. Learn something new every day, and don't step on any toes on the way, 'cause you'll meet the same people on the way back down."

Linda's done her best to follow Durante's advice ever since!

In the beginning, Linda went to miniature shops with color copies of her work and took orders. From the onset, she has used only the finest natural fibers and materials, and the unique and fine quality of her work quickly earned her the status of *artisan*. She works with 200/2 Egyptian cotton thread and a size 22/24 hook, which is actually a size 14 Boye steel crochet hook filed down by a jeweler. Her miniature crochet pieces are worked to a scale of 1 inch to 1 foot, to give you an idea of how truly tiny they are, and she can also crochet as small as ¼ inch to 12-inch scale.

During the early years of Linda's career, shop owners were so fearful of losing their top artisans to competition, having the artist's techniques copied, or their items mass-produced in Taiwan, that they often kept the artisan's identity a closely guarded secret. Shop owners sometimes invented stories about their artisans to ensure no one would steal their exclusive rights to the crafter's work. So when questions were asked about Linda, people were told she was a Samoan who worked on an isolated island in a grass hut!

In 1990, Nouvelle Vision became Uniqueness and is now a three-generation family business. Linda's mother, Margaret Dailey, a renowned (now retired) designer of custom wedding/formal wear, makes samples and crochets life-size items, such as pot holders, crosses, afghans, and quilts. Linda's daughter, Lottie Burr, began making clothes for the renaissance fair in Northern California a few years ago. In addition to designing unique custom jewelry featuring water-cultured pearls and gemstones, Lottie also crochets hats, halter tops, and shawls. All the Daileys eschew mass production and make only one-of-a-kind designs.

"We custom design anything with crochet, sewing, embroidery, beading, painting, or drawing—to any scale, any size, for miniatures, dolls, or people!" Linda proudly said.

Approximately 75% of the orders Uniqueness receives is through mail-order, and they expect to increase that percentage with secure online ordering from their Web site. All three women continue to participate in craft shows, and they plan to advertise in national magazines.

Running a family enterprise means that each one takes care of different business aspects: Lottie collects receipts and purchases supplies; Margaret keeps the books; and Linda administers the Uniqueness Web site. All three women continue to design and produce their artful creations, and Linda is a crochet restoration expert. She also gives lectures, writes, and teaches classes.

Linda currently works an average of 10 to 12 hours daily, but doesn't seem to mind.

"I crochet by feel, so I can watch television or hold a conversation," Linda said. "Besides, I love what I do so much, it doesn't really feel like work."

For Linda, crochet is a joy that satisfies and energizes her at the same time.

Creating Kits, Patterns, and Books

One day, after 25 years of painting, Lydia Borin suddenly put away all her oil brushes and immersed herself in the world of beads and fibers. She started making beaded earrings that her husband marketed for her in New Mexico, and a whole new life and career began to unfold. Soon crocheting became an extension of her bead and fiber work, and before she knew it, Lydia became known as the Beadwrangler.

Three years ago, Lydia, who now resides in Tampa, Florida, saw some lovely little beaded bags, which she later described to a crocheter friend. To her delight, her friend crocheted a similar little fiber bag—in less than 30 minutes—and gave it to her, suggesting she add her beads to it. Lydia was instantaneously hooked!

"I quickly discovered that I enjoyed making patterns other people could re-create more than I did creating unique artworks for galleries," Lydia recounted. "Three published how-to books, two books in progress, several online kits, and a huge inventory of beads and fiber later, it is more than I had ever dreamed."

The positive feedback from customers affirms for Lydia that her many hours spent creating and testing patterns are worthwhile. Today, her bead crochet kits and her book, *Beadwrangler's Hands-on Crochet with Beads and Fiber* are her bestsellers.

With her admittedly renegade spirit, Lydia finds that crochet allows her spirit to soar as she creates contemporary items with a touch of the past. When she designs a new kit, her ever-increasing cache of admirers are overjoyed to dive into another of her innovative creations. You won't see any "grandma crochet" from this imaginative, multi-talented designer!

"That little hook has been a true gift. I'd feel deprived if I didn't hold that hook in my hand every day." Lydia said. "Even on days when I design on the computer, I still pull out my hook to experiment with new designs and to work up sample pieces for kits."

Lydia markets her kits, books, and supplies on her Web site, which contains more than a thousand pages of free information, tips, storytelling, and projects. Her books are also carried by all major distributors, including Barnes and Noble, Borders, Amazon.com, Lark, Lacis, Helby Import, Unicorn, and Royal publications, as well as neighborhood bookstores and bead stores. Her catalog continues to grow in size as her kits and designs continue to evolve.

Lydia's guests often ask to go through her "idea box," where she keeps samples and creations-in-progress. They love trying to guess what the cacophony of fabrics and beads are going to be. When her visitors finally run out of guesses, Lydia tells them: "It isn't anything yet, but someday it may be a part of something." No doubt, something extraordinary.

Some of Lydia Borin's best ideas come from little crochet parts and pieces that she saves in her special *idea box*. Lydia also keeps brainbooks—5½ × 8½-inch artist sketchbooks—where she records design ideas and notes wherever she might be. "I never leave home without a brainbook, because I never know when inspiration is likely to strike."

Self-Publishing Crochet Patterns

During her early thirties, Marian Nelson taught herself to crochet from crochet designs featured in new magazines at the time, such as *Ladies Home Journal, Needle and Craft,* and *American Home Crafts.* The more she crocheted, the more interested she became in the patterns and techniques of crocheting and knitting. She built up an extensive library of both crafts and began to explore different ethnic styles and techniques.

> ### Handy Hint
>
> Don't let your creative ideas get away! Capture them in an idea box or brainbook!

"My primary interest is in designing my own creations, which are usually too complicated for publication. I particularly enjoy the detailed mathematical calculations and charting," Marian said.

She soon found herself helping others to understand patterns, sometimes translating them into simpler instructions or creating easy-to-follow charts. While continuing to assist others, Marian joined TKGA (The Knitting Guild of America) and CGOA and began teaching mini-classes in both needle arts. She considered going on the road as a teacher or to sell her designs, but decided to take a different fork in the road and began offering editing and charting services. Her services range from one-page editing and number checking to full-pattern writing for a designer's article.

Like many professional crocheters, Marian teaches classes, often at the request of yarn shops or guilds, to diversify her income.

"Talking with yarn shop owners helps me find out what they need in the way of classes or patterns. And if a shop owner is so inclined, I'm willing to create designs for a unique pattern line under the store's name," she explained.

With a background in publishing and layout, it seemed natural for Marian to also publish her own pattern line, Pattern Write Designs. As sole proprietor, she wholesales her patterns to a distributor, who charges a commission to then sell her patterns to yarn shops throughout the western states.

Marion was instrumental in starting a CGOA chapter in her area, Borrego Springs, California, and currently serves as the chapter development chair for CGOA.

Self-Publishing Crochet Books

Then there's the Australian Rebel, Jenny King, whose brilliant career as a designer and crochet book publisher began when she was trying to think of something to crochet for the men in the family. She hit upon the idea of making stadium blankets, called *footy* rugs in Australia, in colors to match the various team colors for Australian football teams—not to be confused with American football. Australians have several types of "foot" ball: rugby, rugby league, Aussie rules AFL, and soccer.

Australian AFL fans are fanatical about their teams and dress themselves, their babies, and even their dogs in team colors. After being rejected as a designer for 2 years, Jenny came up with footy rug designs with stripes done in proportion to the various football teams' sweaters—and was off and running toward a victorious goal of her own!

"I knew I couldn't design, make, and sell the blankets. They were too time consuming, and I knew I'd never make any money going that direction," Jenny explained. "So, I thought the only way to go was to sell my brain power."

Jenny decided to combine her designs into a book, *The Footy Rug*, and to self-publish with the help of a local printer who is a member of her football club. The first print run of 1,000 books sold out in a mere three weeks' time! She then published another 4,000 copies, and they quickly sold.

While promoting her footy rug book, people kept asking Jenny for Tartan rugs. So she "worked like a demon" and got anyone who could crochet to help her, and in amazingly short order published her second book *The Tartan Rug Book,* in an initial printing of 2,000 copies. Again, the demand was so great she had to reprint another 2,000 copies *five* times and has sold every copy.

"I couldn't do what I do without a strong band of crocheters who work with me, testing my patterns and working up models in a crisis. They feel like a part of my team."

Jenny continued, reflecting, "I was like a terrier dog. I sunk my teeth in and just wouldn't let go."

She knew she had good ideas and just stuck to it. For example, one distributor she hoped would buy two thousand copies of her first book only took fifty copies at first, saying, "No one buys crochet patterns, because no one crochets."

"Today that man is my best customer and has bought $10,000 worth of my books—not bad considering he didn't think my books or ideas had a snowflake's chance in hell."

Her third book, *The Footy Rug II,* which featured afghans, scarves, and beanie hats, promptly sold 4,000 copies. Jenny carefully watches over her publishing and printing costs and is careful not to reprint a book until after she recoups her initial printing costs. A crochet clothing pattern book, *Summer Collection,* followed next. Then came *Some'R Hot Bikinis,* which quickly became immensely popular.

When she first saw crochet beadwork in 1998, she says, "I went dotty! I'd never worked with thread or beads before. Everyone who saw my beaded crochet bags wanted a pattern, so I decided I'd better do another book, and I published *Heirloom Beaded Bags* in October 1999."

"I have more ideas for books or patterns than I have time to physically make. I have to allow time for my family, to fill orders, and somehow hold the business together."

For the past 3 years, she has published two books a year. As a self-publisher, Jenny's the one taking all the risks, doing all the work, and making all the decisions about what she creates.

"It's been like a magical carpet ride that started with one idea and it keeps taking me to mysterious destinations. I never know what new idea is waiting around the corner."

Mass-Producing Crochet Jewelry

After earning her Ph.D. in experimental psychology, A.T. Grant worked at the University of California, Los Angeles, Brain Research Institute, where she became a research specialist and studied the origins of creativity in the brain. During that time, she often stayed in Hopi Indian villages, combining the study of southwestern jewelry and crafts with cross-cultural brain research. There, she discovered how the Hopi express deep spirituality through visual, nonverbal modes. Her Hopi experience continues to influence A.T.'s jewelry designs today.

Like others in this chapter, A.T. experienced a creative breakthrough that totally changed the course of her life. In the spring of 1985 she bought a pale pink jumpsuit to wear while running focus groups. Thinking her new outfit needed a long, funky necklace, she found one she liked at Bullock's department store, but was unwilling to pay the tag price of $125.

On the flight back to New York, she kept thinking about how she might design a necklace out of the Plexiglas pieces she'd found at her favorite neighborhood store. How could she connect them so they would still move? Then she thought about her grandmother's beautiful crocheted tablecloths and her own less ambitious crocheted doilies. Soon after, she added a couple of vacation days to a weekend and used the time to formulate a technique for hooking plastics or beads together that she calls Hooked on Plastics.

Hooked on Plastics became a side business, and her jewelry was more than favorably received. A fashionable Madison Avenue boutique proudly featured a window display of her work, the Esprit company pursued her in the hopes of featuring her jewelry in their catalog, and a well-known agent sought to represent her work. Knowing she could not make enough pieces by herself to meet the demand, A.T. began investigating production possibilities. She discovered that crocheting machines do not exist, making it impossible to automate the crocheting process. Offshore production in Asia or India sounded most unappealing, as did the sweatshop concept. Ultimately, A.T. was forced to close down Hooked on Plastics, because she couldn't do that and her "important" full-time career as a vice president for a large New York City research firm.

When she hit the million-mile mark on her airline travel, A.T. came to the overwhelming realization that she had become an "air person," every bit as homeless as any street person. The only difference being she had good food and hotel accommodations.

"My father traveled when I was young, and I didn't like it one bit. There I was doing the same thing to my own young daughter. That recognition gave me a jolt!

"I quit my job and didn't fly anywhere for a year and a half," she continued. "I did a lot of yoga, trying to reground myself. That's when I returned to crochet."

During several trips to Jamaica, she discovered that little-hook crochet is one of the indigenous craft skills of the island—and a way to resolve her earlier production issue. Picking up her hook, she headed to Negril, ready to start Crochet Jamaica. She started by working with Jampro, a government agency that helps foreigners interested in doing business in Jamaica, in part by sponsoring programs that allow tax breaks and duty-free importing of supplies to be manufactured into finished products for export only. But she soon ran into the difficult, if not impossible, government hurdles. In Kingston, they wouldn't allow her to register her company without a work permit; across town, other authorities refused to give her a work permit until the company was registered.

"Some joked that I married a Jamaican to get a work permit," she laughed.

A.T., her daughter, and her new husband, Glendon, settled in Dallas, Texas, while she waited for the U.S. Immigration and Naturalization Service and Jamaica to approve her application for wholesale production. After interminable months and frustrating experiences, she finally received the go-ahead from U.S. officials. Now, A.T. can resume her wrestling match with the Jamaican bureaucracy to move forward with Crochet Jamaica. Meanwhile, A.T. has several crochet books in the works, and fans flock to her national CGOA conference classes, which center around her Jamaican flavor of crochet. Her entertaining and fun classes even feature native music and a slide show! She is developing Jamaican vacation packages that feature Caribbean/Chinese cooking, yoga, water fitness, and of course, crocheting.

I'm keeping my eyes and ears open, because I expect to be reading and hearing about the success of Crochet Jamaica in the near future!

Marketing Your Crochet Business

Advertising and Publicity

▼▼

TO GROW YOUR CROCHET BUSINESS, you need to budget both time and money for marketing. You should plan to devote at least 10% of your work time to promoting your products, services, and yourself. In the beginning, you may need to invest more time, if not more money, in marketing. Like all successful freelancers, you'll also need to continue marketing throughout your crochet career.

Don't expect to see immediate results from your advertising and publicity efforts. It generally takes at least 3 months before you notice a measurable increase in responses and sales. Also, when it comes to marketing, more usually *is* better—that is, the more people you reach with your marketing "message" and the more frequently you reach them, the more likely you are to get more responses and more sales. When it comes to marketing, you must be patient, consistent, and persistent.

So, what are advertising and publicity, and why do you need them? To answer that, let's begin by looking at what each of these activities can and cannot do for you.

Advertising can:

- Help build an image
- Create credibility
- Attract potential customers
- Provide leads, responses, and inquiries

Advertising cannot:

- Force people to contact you
- By itself sell all your products and/or services
- Guarantee business
- Create a relationship with a customer

Publicity can:

- Help establish you as an expert in your field
- Boost your credibility
- Create an emotional bond with readers
- Tell the inside story
- Set you apart from your competitors
- Generate more publicity
- Increase your response rate

Publicity cannot:

- Always be controlled
- Tell the whole story
- Directly solicit sales
- Guarantee anything

Advertising

Unless you are content to market exclusively through word-of-mouth referrals or to folks who happen to cross your path—you must advertise the crochet products and expertise you offer. How and where you advertise depends on whether your "target" market is local, regional, national, or global. Of course, your markets could include any combination or all of these.

If you sell at craft fairs, bazaars, and the like, postcards or newsletters often work well to draw customers to an event.

As soon as you begin to sell your crochet projects, you should keep a running list of customers' names and addresses—your mailing list. If you are brand new to selling and want to do a mailing to potential customers, you may be able to buy a mailing list from another crafter.

You cannot "market" crochet products, talent, services, or expertise! You market benefits and solutions! People buy for one reason only: to fulfill a need or a desire, or to solve a problem—or a combination of these three motivators. If you want to increase your crochet business and achieve financial success, you must advertise not only *what* you're selling—that is, your products and services—but also the features, benefits, and solutions they offer.

Advertising in the *right* magazines, newsletters, or other publications may prove to be profitable for you. Like any kind of advertising, an ad is considered successful based on your response rate and number of orders received. First-time advertisers often have unrealistic expectations about typical response rates. For example, the experts say a 5% response rate is typical for direct mail. So, if you send out direct mailers to two hundred people on your mailing list, you can expect ten people to respond.

On the other hand, advertising in the local media, such as the Yellow Pages, won't help you one iota if you wish to sell only designs and articles to national magazines and yarn companies.

Be sure you understand who your target market is before going to the expense of placing advertising in the print media. For example, if you are selling *crochet patterns for dolls,* a small inexpensive classified ad in a crochet magazine is likely to bring you orders from other crocheters. But if you place a similar ad for *crocheted dolls* in a crochet magazine, you're not likely to receive a high response rate, because the readers are crocheters themselves. Your target market is more likely to be those who collect dolls—readers of a doll magazine.

If you have crochet services to offer, your target market is completely different than your target market for crochet items. The average crocheter is not interested in whether you are a designer, editor, teacher, or pattern tester. Those who have crochet services to offer should contact their potential clients directly by sending out query letters as discussed earlier.

For the record: "New" doesn't sell anything when it comes to any kind of business. The fact that a crochet service or product is "new" holds no meaning to potential clients *unless* they understand how it will satisfy (or exceed) their individual needs and wants. Let's say you are just starting out as a freelance editor, and you're looking for clients. That you are new to the field means nothing to your customers if they don't perceive a need for your service and don't understand the value and benefits it offers them.

Say It Again and Again

Repetition is critical to effective advertising. Your customers and clients won't know what you can do for them unless you tell them and *keep on* telling them. Every day, new potential customers arrive on the scene. People relocate, develop new interests, revive abandoned hobbies, change lifestyles, mature, and develop new and different wants and needs. What if you add to or change your crochet repertoire? If you don't constantly get the word out to the evolving market, how are they going to know they need what you have to offer?

Let's say, for example, that you place a single classified ad for your Southwestern style household textiles—afghans, blankets, placemats, toaster covers—in one issue of one magazine. Four months later, the same magazine runs a great feature article on Southwestern decor. Six months later, Southwestern style is suddenly "the rage," and all the home and fashion media are covering the trend. How likely is it that potential customers and clients are going to remember your one little ad, if they ever saw it at all?

Cooperative Advertising

A good way to reduce your advertising costs while increasing your exposure in the marketplace is *cooperative (co-op) advertising.* Co-op advertising simply means combining your advertising efforts with those of other crafters or even with shops or suppliers.

For example, you and a few fellow exhibitors at an upcoming crafts fair could create a flyer or newspaper ad that not only announces the event but also promotes the products and expertise of each crafter. Another promotional tool that works well is the use of cooperative coupons. You could give your customers a coupon worth 10% off yarn purchased at a specific shop, while the yarn shop gives each of its customers a coupon worth 10% off your next class or made-to-order garments—which just happen to be displayed in the same shop.

The coupon doesn't have to include a discount. You could just exchange promotional postcards with a business that in some way complements yours; then you each hand out the other's postcards to your respective customers. Let's say you sell original designs of Victorian crochet items, and you partner up with a Victorian gift shop. You just slip the gift shop's postcard in with your mail orders, and the shop hands out your postcards to its patrons or keeps a stack of your postcards near the register or, better yet, near a display of models of your designs.

Publicity

Getting publicity simply means getting "coverage" in the media— newspapers, magazines, radio, the Internet, television, newsletters, bulletins, and such—about you, your work, and your participation in crochet-related events and activities. Publicity is necessary for three primary reasons:

1. **To build name recognition within your market**

2. **To establish you as an expert in your chosen field**

3. **To publicize specific events, activities, products, and services**

When you are seeking publicity, remember that an article written *about* you carries the most weight with potential customers, because it implies the publication's endorsement of you and your business and is, therefore, more believable to readers. Editors want new and interesting stories to offer to readers, but all stories must be "newsworthy."

A newsworthy article is one that focuses on any topic that interests other people or that gives a common topic a unique "spin" that appeals to other people—particularly the readers of a specific publication. Let's say you've just added lovely Victorian Christmas stockings to your line of hand-crocheted Christmas stockings. That you added a new item to your line in itself is not newsworthy. By the same token, having a crafts bazaar or a discount sale of your products is not generally compelling enough to warrant an article, whether written by or about you, in any newspaper, newsletter, Web site, or magazine. Of course, sending a press release about such an event could result in the editor posting a notice of the event as a calendar or bulletin listing.

However, you can turn a sale or almost any subject into a newsworthy topic for an article. For example, if you donate 10% of sales receipts for your Christmas stockings over, say, the 4-day Thanksgiving weekend (incidentally, the busiest shopping time of the year) to your local high school basketball team, that is news of interest to your community. Perhaps you can arrange to have a famous or local celebrity appear to kick off the event (charity or otherwise) at which your stockings will be sold: celebrity appearances are usually newsworthy.

You can create a newsworthy event and somehow link it to your crochet work. For example, you can hold a drive for yarn donations and then use the yarn to crochet mittens and hats for the underprivileged. You might choose to honor a local citizen, perhaps an author, builder, or teacher, or you could host a birthday party for the community's oldest citizen and gift that person with your newest crochet design, an afghan. If the article mentions that this new afghan pattern is available in local yarn shops, sales of your pattern are likely to skyrocket in your hometown. All of these deeds are noteworthy to your community.

If you're still stuck for ideas, consider partnering with a local corporation for a worthy cause. Don't be afraid to approach companies with your charitable ideas; most budget funds for charitable donations for tax purposes. Let's say you make arrangements for a corporation to donate a computer, software, or other product to a local elementary school. It will cost you nothing but your time and effort, and being associated with such benevolent, newsworthy projects creates goodwill for you! When you write your press release announcing that you have organized such a community charitable event, do it in a way that can be tied to your business. For example, if you offer crocheting classes for children, then your interest in children, their education, and their needs could be the basis for seeking computer or software programs for local schools.

If you don't speak for yourself and your business, others will do it for you. Are you willing to settle for what they have to say about you?

Let's face it—people talk, whether it's about you, your business, or someone else. Publicity alone is not enough to establish name recognition. If you don't advertise as well as seek publicity, people may not understand what you have to offer or why what you have to offer is valuable. The more times people see your ad, the more it enhances their perception of your business. When you advertise on a regular basis, it tells readers that your business is solid, reliable, and can be depended upon. Advertising is a venue in which you have the freedom to state your case about how and why what you have to offer is unique, fulfills needs, and solves problems.

One of the best ways to increase your earnings and career opportunities is to attain name recognition. How do you become a recognizable "name" within your market? By garnering positive attention that establishes you as a reputable, talented, and experienced expert in your chosen field. One of the best ways to gain that kind of recognition is by getting wide and complimentary coverage in national magazines, newsletters, and other venues. Try to get published as often and in as many appropriate publications as possible—either by writing and submitting press releases and articles to the media, or by inviting or enticing the media to write about you. Approach both the standard print publications as well as the newer online publications.

Online Publicity Opportunities

You can make a name for yourself simply by going online. Check out various crochet sites and browse through the various message boards for postings from people who need help. You'll find tons of them on every board. When you post an answer, don't make your message sound like an ad; keep it simple, friendly, and helpful. Say something like, "Hi, my name is Darla. I'm hoping I can answer your question about how to make an Irish rose, because I frequently use those same roses in my design work." Then, provide the needed information in a clear and direct way. If you can refer them to a helpful book or magazine, do so; all the better if the book or article is yours. You can then add something like, "My pillow design was

Lydia: Working the Publicity Chain

Remember Lydia Borin from chapter 8? Her how-to projects and related articles are often featured in national magazines, such as Beadwork, and other fiber-related publications. These articles, along with the advertisements she places in the magazines, help to acquaint people with her company, her work, and her expertise.

Lydia publicizes her business in many other ways as well. In spite of a dizzying schedule, Lydia and her husband are vendors at every annual CGOA Chain Link conference. When time permits, they also set up their booth at other national shows as well as at some local bead shows. She speaks at local libraries and organizations to educate the community about beads and fibers. She frequently teaches at crochet-related events.

There is also a Beadwrangler's Web site, which is often referred to as the best bead and fiber Web site on the Internet. Lydia and her husband are constantly adding links to other Web sites—and, of course, those Web sites also provide links to the Beadwrangler's site.

Is all the time, energy, and money invested in marketing worth it on the bottom line?

"Definitely!" Lydia says.

The articles Lydia writes and the articles written about her continue to enhance her reputation and name recognition—and bring in new customers. Her speaking engagements and show participation bring in new customers and keep her abreast of customer needs, providing valuable market research she can use to develop future kits and books. Besides, she just plain loves making new friends and sharing ideas.

"I do what I love most of the day, every day," Lydia said. "And I get paid too!"

featured in this month's issue of so and so magazine, perhaps you saw it."

You might also e-mail a webmaster and offer to host a chat room or to serve as an expert designer, writer, or whatever for a crochet Web site. Perhaps the webmaster might be thrilled to accept your proposal to contribute crochet tips and hints on a regular basis or, if you have the time, to provide one free article per month. The more recognizable your name becomes to potential customers, the more likely you are to generate more income.

If you have Internet access and a computer, there are lots of Web sites that provide free advertising. Why not take advantage of these opportunities to let others know about your crochet items or patterns? Some sites allow 30 days free advertising and then charge for ongoing advertising. Just type "free ads" into a multi-search engine and you'll find hundreds of possibilities. If you are new to the Internet, and are unfamiliar with cyberspace etiquette, please remember—message boards are *not* the place to post ads of any kind.

Organizing Your Marketing Efforts

When you run a home-based business, it's easy to promise yourself that you're going to set aside time to promote your business and to then let that promise go when you get busy filling orders, creating designs, or writing articles. The time just slips away, and months pass before you realize you haven't put forth any marketing efforts. Then you feel guilty and try to justify how you've spent the last few months.

I've found that the easiest way to handle marketing, deadlines, and those little chores we never seem to allot enough time for is to write them down on a large desktop calendar. You can buy one at any office supply store for about $3. Plan at least 3 to 6 months in advance, so you can really stay on top of your business. Pencil in deadlines that can be changed if necessary and ink in those deadlines that are absolute.

When your publicity/marketing efforts become part of your weekly routine, they become habit and seem less like work. Marketing then is just something you know must be done, and you do it like you do the grocery shopping and weekly errands. You'll be amazed at what you can achieve in a year's time by committing scheduled time to your marketing efforts.

Calendar Notes and Scheduling

Make sure to schedule time on your business calendar for each of your crochet activities, which might include any or all of the following:

- Advertising
- Charting
- Editing
- Finish work
- Mathematical calculations

- Publicity
- Scheduling
- Sizing
- Swatching and sketching
- Writing

You should also try to plan out your advertising and publicity efforts for a full year. First, establish your marketing goals for the year ahead. Then, plan out what, when, where, and how you want to promote in order to achieve those goals. Develop a mailing list of media contacts and advertising sources, and keep it current. Make sure to mark off time on your calendar for these activities along with any corresponding deadlines.

If you only write 250 words per month, in 2 months' time you'll have written a 500-word article. If you continue to write at the same rate, by year's end you'll have written six articles.

Let's say you send out just two press releases a month to your list of print media. If your list contains five contacts, by year's end you will have sent out more than one hundred! Marketing becomes manageable when you do it in small increments.

Plan to put on two to four publicity events per year. Tie something about yourself or your business to a holiday or commemorative event. Make this event noteworthy by offering to gift a favorite charity, local Boy Scout troop, Cancer Society, or other organization with a percentage of your sales over a specified period of time. The

Example of One-Year Marketing Goals

■ Write six articles.

■ Send one hundred press releases to the print media.

■ Schedule two to four publicity-generating events.

■ Send 24 press releases to broadcast media (radio and television).

■ Obtain free online listings.

■ Join at least one association.

■ Barter for advertising.

more you contribute to your own community and its needs, the more credibility you receive from that community!

Buy, rent, or create your own list of broadcast media—television and radio stations—that do interviews. Send out two press releases per month, and at year's end you will have contacted 24 broadcast media. Talk show hosts are always looking for guests who are articulate about their fields of expertise.

If you have an online service, fire up your search engines to locate online directories, publications (called *e-zines*), and promotional Web sites that might be willing to give you a free listing.

Join at least one association. Depending on the association of your choice, you are sure to benefit from various discounted services. Most associations send out a directory of members and informative newsletters, providing you with contacts and resources.

Barter for advertising with the print media. Many periodicals will print a display ad for you if you agree to provide them with articles, a regular column, book reviews, or other editorial needs in exchange. Though you may not have considered newsletters as a likely source, I'm here to tell you that most newsletter editors/publishers welcome bartering and are often eager to help support newcomers and to get fresh articles and ideas for their readers.

Creative Promotional Ideas

Here are some more things you can do to increase name recognition for yourself or your crochet business:

- Establish yourself as an expert in your field.

- Offer something to readers or listeners: tip sheet, report, or brochure—free with an SASE or for a minimal amount under $5. This is a good way to create or add to your mailing list.

- Use tip sheets as handouts at meetings and workshops. People tend to hang onto them because of the information they contain, while they usually toss brochures and pamphlets. Use tip sheets as you use business cards: Give them to everyone you meet. Tuck them into your mailings too.

- Send press releases to those segments of the media that are often overlooked: trade journals, college newspapers, in-house publications, and associations.

- Try sending to some media who are open to receiving two-paragraph press releases via fax or e-mail. Test your response rate. Some radio stations, in particular, like faxed press releases, while others do not want their fax machines or e-mail plugged with unsolicited messages.

- Write letters to editors.

- Submit ideas, tips, and hints to regular or syndicated columnists in magazines or newspapers.

- Offer to write a column for newspapers, local papers, and journals.

- Create your own newsletter to use as a marketing tool.

- Volunteer to speak to groups, associations, clubs, schools, and other organizations.

- Write articles for publication in exchange for a byline and a blurb stating where and how to contact you.

- Seek out freelance reporters or writers to write articles about you and your business.

- Self-syndicate by writing a regular column and offer it to a variety of publications.

- Don't overlook submitting articles to electronic publications. Fire up your search engine and check them out.

- Check out free ad space on the Internet.

- Reprint unsolicited letters or thank-you notes as testimonials in your promotional materials. When you have enough, arrange the best ones into a collage.

- Make a collage of your published articles to include with promotional materials.

- Keep a box of thank-you notes on hand at all times. Always send a thank-you note for every media mention. Courtesy makes editors take notice and remember you.

- Reply to invitations to comment on editorials aired on local radio or television stations.

- Volunteer to serve as an expert for the media.

How Satisfied Customers Promote a Business

Remember Jenny King, the "Australian Rebel" you met in chapter 8? In the beginning, Jenny and her mother called on craft shops to promote her books. Then a craft magazine published an article about her, and the free publicity began to work its magic. The country newspaper then ran a half-page write-up about her with a great photo, thanks to a loyal follower who contacted the editor.

"I do a lot of mail-order business through word of mouth," Jenny said. "The networking that goes on between crocheters is better than any system Amway could organize! My phone number is on the back of every one of my books, and people freely share it with one another."

At Christmas and each time she launches a new crochet book, Jenny writes a newsletter to all her customers, having discovered that many of her customers live alone and love to receive her newsletters. Many take the time to write back, even if they don't place an order.

"Some people buy whatever I publish just because they've begun to feel like they are a part of my family," Jenny said. "I have four distributors, but my readers take their own copies of my books into shops, and the shopkeepers phone me to place their book orders. Would you believe that a lot of my free press has been orchestrated by my customers?"

- Try an editor in a different department if you don't get a response to a press release you sent to one editor. Lifestyle editors, for example, are open to a wide variety of topics.

- Get listed in the community news section of your local newspaper when you participate in something noteworthy or take a trip that is connected to your work.

By working a consistent, persistent marketing plan, you *can* be your own best publicist! Make an effort to do something in the way of marketing and publicity each and every week, and you'll be on your way.

Marketing successfully means you must combine both advertising and publicity to come up with a winning plan to sell your crochet products and services. When you budget your time, money, and effort, you can increase your name recognition, establish credibility, build your image, and increase your profit margin.

A Mini-Course in Crafts-Business Basics

by Barbara Brabec

▼▼▼

THIS SECTION OF THE BOOK will familiarize you with important areas of legal and financial concern and enable you to ask the right questions if and when it is necessary to consult with an attorney, accountant, or other business adviser. Although the tax and legal information included here has been carefully researched by the author and is accurate to the best of her knowledge, it is not the business of either the author or publisher to render professional services in the area of business law, taxes, or accounting. Readers should therefore use their own good judgment in determining when the services of a lawyer or other professional would be appropriate to their needs.

Information presented applies specifically to businesses in the United States. However, because many U.S. and Canadian laws are similar, Canadian readers can certainly use the following information as a start-up business plan and guide to questions they need to ask their own local, provincial, or federal authorities.

223

Contents

7. Insurance Tips

Homeowner's or Renter's Insurance
Liability Insurance
Insurance on Crafts Merchandise
Auto Insurance

8. Important Regulations Affecting Artists and Craftspeople

Consumer Safety Laws
Labels Required by Law
The Bedding and Upholstered Furniture Law
FTC Rule for Mail-Order Sellers

9. Protecting Your Intellectual Property

Perspective on Patents
What a Trademark Protects
What Copyrights Protect
Copyright Registration Tips
Respecting the Copyrights of Others
Using Commercial Patterns and Designs

10. To Keep Growing, Keep Learning

Motivational Tips

A "Things to Do" Checklist with Related Resources

- Business Start-Up Checklist
- Government Agencies
- Craft and Home-Business Organizations
- Recommended Crafts-Business Periodicals
- Other Services and Suppliers
- Recommended Business Books
- Helpful Library Directories

1. Starting Right

In preceding chapters of this book, you learned the techniques of a particular art or craft and realized its potential for profit. You learned what kinds of products are likely to sell, how to price them, and how and where you might sell them.

Now that you've seen how much fun a crafts business can be (and how profitable it might be if you were to get serious about selling what you make!) you need to learn about some of the "nitty-gritty stuff" that goes hand in hand with even the smallest business based at home. It's easy to start selling what you make and it's satisfying when you earn enough money to make your hobby self-supporting. Many crafters go this far and no further, which is fine. But even a hobby seller must be concerned about taxes and local, state, and federal laws. And if your goal is to build a part- or full-time business at home, you must pay even greater attention to the topics discussed in this section of the book.

Everyone loves to make money . . . but actually starting a business frightens some people because they don't understand what's involved. It's easy to come up with excuses for why we don't do certain things in life; close inspection of those excuses usually boils down to fear of the unknown. We get the shivers when we step out of our comfort zone and try something we've never done before. The simple solution to this problem lies in having the right information at the right time. As someone once said, "Knowledge is the antidote to fear."

The quickest and surest way to dispel fear is to inform yourself about the topics that frighten you. With knowledge comes a sense of power, and that power enables you to move. Whether your goal is merely to earn extra income from your craft hobby or launch a genuine home-based business, reading the following information will help you get started on the right legal foot, avoid financial pitfalls, and move forward with confidence.

When you're ready to learn more about art or crafts marketing or the operation of a home-based crafts business, a visit to your library or bookstore will turn up many interesting titles. In addition to the special resources listed by this book's author, you will find my list of recommended business books, organizations, periodicals, and other helpful resources later in this chapter. This information is arranged in a checklist you can use as a plan to get your business up and running.

Before you read my Mini-Course in Crafts-Business Basics, be assured that I understand where you're coming from because I was once there myself.

For a while I sold my craft work, and this experience led me to write my first book, *Creative Cash*. Now, 20 years later, this crafts-business classic ("my baby") has reached its sixth edition. Few of those who are totally involved in a crafts business today started out with a business in mind. Like me, most began as hobbyists looking for something interesting to do in their spare time, and one thing naturally led to another. I never imagined those many years ago

Social Security Taxes

When your crafts-business earnings are more than $400 (net), you must file a Self-Employment Tax form (Schedule SE) and pay into your personal Social Security account. This could be quite beneficial for individuals who have some previous work experience but have been out of the workplace for a while. Your re-entry into the business world as a self-employed worker, and the additional contributions to your Social Security account, could result in increased benefits on retirement.

Because so many senior citizens are starting home-based businesses these days, it should be noted that there is a limit on the amount seniors age 62 to 65 can earn before losing some Social Security benefits. This dollar limit increases every year, however, and once you are past the age of 65, you can earn any amount of income and still receive full benefits. Contact your nearest Social Security office for details.

when I got serious about my craft hobby that I was putting myself on the road to a full-time career as a crafts writer, publisher, author, and speaker. Because I and thousands of others have progressed from hobbyists to professionals, I won't be at all surprised if someday you, too, have a similar adventure.

2. Taxes and Record Keeping

"Ambition in America is still rewarded . . . with high taxes," the comics quip. Don't you long for the good old days when Uncle Sam lived within his income and without most of yours?

Seriously, taxes are one of the first things you must be concerned about as a new business owner, no matter how small your endeavor. This section offers a brief overview of your tax responsibilities as a sole proprietor.

Is Your Activity a "Hobby" or a "Business"?

Whether you are selling what you make only to get the cost of your supplies back or actually trying to build a profitable business, you need to understand the legal difference between a profitable hobby and a business, and how each is related to your annual tax return.

The IRS defines a hobby as "an activity engaged in primarily for pleasure, not for profit." Making a profit from a hobby does not automatically place you "in business" in the eyes of the Internal Revenue Service, but the activity will be *presumed* to have been engaged in for profit if it results in a profit in at least 3 out of 5 years. Or, to put it another way, a "hobby business" automatically becomes a "real business" in the eyes of the IRS at the point where you can state that you are (1) trying to make a profit, (2) making regular business transactions, and (3) have made a profit 3 out of 5 years.

As you know, all income must be reported on your annual tax return. How it's reported, however, has everything to do with the amount of taxes you must pay on this income. If hobby income is less than $400, it must be entered on the 1040 tax form, with taxes payable accordingly. If the amount is greater than this, you must file a Schedule C form with your 1040 tax form. This is to your advantage, however, because taxes are due only on your *net profit*. Because you can deduct expenses up to the amount of your hobby income, there may be little or no tax at all on your hobby income.

Self-Employment Taxes

Whereas a hobby cannot show a loss on a Schedule C form, a business can. Business owners must pay not only state and federal income taxes on their profits, but self-employment taxes as well. (See sidebar, Social Security Taxes, on page 227.) Because self-employed people pay Social Security taxes at twice the level of regular, salaried workers, you should strive to lower your annual gross profit figure on the Schedule C form through every legal means possible. One way to do this is through careful record keeping of all expenses related to the operation of your business. To quote IRS publications, expenses are deductible if they are "ordinary, necessary, and somehow connected with the operation and potential profit of your business." In addition to being able to deduct all expenses related to the making and selling of their products, business owners can also depreciate the cost of tools and equipment, deduct the overhead costs of operating a home-based office or studio (called the Home Office Deduction), and hire their spouse or children.

> *Avoid this pitfall:* Many new businesses that end up with a nice net profit on their first year's Schedule C tax form find themselves in financial trouble when tax time rolls around because they did not make estimated quarterly tax payments throughout the year. Aside from the penalties for underpayment of taxes, it's

a terrible blow to suddenly realize that you've spent all your business profits and now have no money left for taxes. Be sure to discuss this matter with a tax advisor or accountant when you begin your business.

Given the complexity of our tax laws and the fact that they are changing all the time, a detailed discussion of all the tax deductions currently available to small-business owners cannot be included in a book of this nature. Learning about tax deductions, however, is as easy as reading a book such as *Small Time Operator* by Bernard Kamoroff (my favorite tax and accounting guide), visiting the IRS Web site, or consulting your regular tax adviser.

You can also get answers to specific tax questions 24 hours a day by calling the National Association of Enrolled Agents (NAEA). Enrolled agents (EAs) are licensed by the Treasury Department to represent taxpayers before the IRS. Their rates for doing tax returns are often less than those you would pay for an accountant or CPA.

Keeping Tax Records

Once you're in business, you must keep accurate records of all income and expenses, but the IRS does not require any special kind of bookkeeping system. Its primary concern is that you use a system that clearly and accurately shows true income and expenses. For the sole proprietor, a simple system consisting of a checkbook, a cash receipts journal, a cash disbursements ledger, and a petty cash fund is quite adequate. Post expenses and income regularly to avoid year-end pile-up and panic.

If you plan to keep manual records, check your local office supply store or catalogs for the *Dome* series of record-keeping books, or use the handy ledger sheets and worksheets included in *Small Time Operator*. (This classic tax and accounting guide by CPA Bernard Kamoroff includes details on how to keep good records and prepare financial reports.) If you have a computer, there are a number of accounting software programs available, such as Intuit Quicken, MYOB (Mind Your Own Business) Accounting, and Intuit Quick-

An important concept to remember is that even the smallest business is entitled to deduct expenses related to its business, and the same tax-saving strategies used by "the big guys" can be used by small-business owners. Your business may be small now or still in the dreaming stage, but it could be larger next year and surprisingly profitable a few years from now. Therefore, it is in your best interest to always prepare for growth, profit, and taxes by learning all you can about the tax laws and deductions applicable to your business. (See also sidebar, Keeping Tax Records.)

Sales Tax Is Serious Business

If you live in a state that has a sales tax (all but five states do), and sell products directly to consumers, you are required by law to register with your state's Department of Revenue (Sales Tax division) for a resale tax number. The fee for this in most states ranges from $5 to $25, with some states requiring a bond or deposit of up to $150.

Books, the latter of which is one of the most popular and best bookkeeping systems for small businesses. The great advantage of computerized accounting is that financial statements can be created at the press of a key after accounting entries have been made.

Regardless of which system you use, always get a receipt for everything and file receipts in a monthly envelope. If you don't want to establish a petty cash fund, spindle all of your cash receipts, tally them at month's end, and reimburse your personal outlay of cash with a check written on your business account. On your checkbook stub, document the individual purchases covered by this check.

At year's end, bundle your monthly tax receipt envelopes and file them for future reference, if needed. Because the IRS can audit a return for up to 3 years after a tax return has been filed, all accounting and tax records should be kept at least this long, but 6 years is better. Personally, I believe you should keep all your tax returns, journals, and ledgers throughout the life of your business.

Depending on where you live, this tax number may also be called a Retailer's Occupation Tax Registration Number, resale license, or use tax permit. Also, depending on where you live, the place you must call to obtain this number will have different names. In California, for example, you would contact the State Board of Equalization; in Texas, it's called the State Comptroller's Office. Within your state's revenue department, the tax division may have a name such as sales and use tax division or department of taxation and finance. Generally speaking, if you check your telephone book under "Government," and look for whatever listing comes closest to "Revenue," you can find the right office.

If your state has no sales tax, you will still need a reseller's permit or tax exemption certificate to buy supplies and materials at wholesale prices from manufacturers, wholesalers, or distributors. Note that this tax number is only for supplies and materials used to make your products, not for things purchased at the retail level or for general office supplies.

Once registered with the state, you will begin to collect and remit sales and use tax (monthly, quarterly, or annually, as determined by your state) on all *taxable sales*. This does not mean *all* of your gross income. Different states tax different things. Some states put a sales tax on certain services, but generally you will never have to pay sales tax on income from articles sold to magazines, on teaching or consulting fees, or subscription income (if you happen to publish a newsletter). In addition, sales taxes are not applicable to:

- **Items sold on consignment through a charitable organization, shop, or other retail outlet, including craft malls and rent-a-space shops (because the party who sells directly to the consumer is the one who must collect and pay sales tax).**

- **Products you wholesale to others who will be reselling them to consumers. (Be sure to get their tax-exemption ID number for your own files, however, in case you are ever questioned as to why you did not collect taxes on those sales.)**

As you sell throughout the year, your record-keeping system must be set up so you can tell which income is taxable and which is tax-exempt for reporting on your sales tax return.

Collecting Sales Tax at Craft Shows

States are getting very aggressive about collecting sales tax, and agents are showing up everywhere these days, especially at the larger craft fairs, festivals, and small-business conferences. As I was writing this chapter, a posting on the Internet stated that in New Jersey the sales tax department is routinely contacting show promoters about a month before the show date to get the names and addresses of exhibitors. It is expected that other states will soon be following suit. For this reason, you should always take your resale or tax collection certificate with you to shows.

Although you must always collect sales tax at a show when you sell in a state that has a sales tax, how and when the tax is paid to the state can vary. When selling at shows in other states, you may find that the show promoter has obtained an umbrella sales tax certificate, in which case vendors would be asked to give management a check for sales tax at the end of the show for turning over to a tax agent. Or you may have to obtain a temporary sales tax certificate for a show, as advised by the show promoter. Some sellers who regularly do shows in two or three states say it's easier to get a tax ID number from each state and file an annual return instead of doing taxes on a show-by-show basis. (See sidebar, Including Tax in the Retail Price, on page 234.)

Collecting Sales Tax at a Holiday Boutique

If you're involved in a holiday boutique where several sellers are offering goods to the public, each individual seller will be responsible for collecting and remitting his or her own sales tax. (This means someone has to keep very good records during the sale so each seller receives a record of the sale and the amount of tax on that sale.) A reader who regularly has home boutiques told me that in her community she must also post a sign at her "cash station" stating that sales tax is being collected on all sales, just as craft fair sellers must do in some states. Again, it's important that you get complete details from your own state about its sales tax policies.

> ***Avoid this pitfall:*** Individuals who are selling "just for the fun of it" may think they don't have to collect sales taxes, but this is not true. As an official in my state's Department of Revenue told me, "Everyone who sells anything to consumers must collect sales tax. If you hold yourself out as a seller of merchandise, then you're subject to tax, even if you sell only a couple of times a year." The financial penalties for violating this state law can be severe. In Illinois, for example, lawbreakers are subject to a penalty of 20% over and above any normal tax obligation, and could receive for each offense (meaning each return not filed)

Including Tax in the Retail Price

Is it okay to incorporate the amount of sales tax into the retail price of items being sold directly to consumers? I don't know for sure because each state's sales tax law is different.

Crafters like to use round-figure prices at fairs because this encourages cash sales and eliminates the need for taking coins to make change. Some crafters tell their customers that sales tax has been included in their rounded-off prices, but you should not do this until you check with your state. In some states, this is illegal; in others, you may find that you are required to inform your customers, by means of a sign, that sales tax has been included in your price. You may also have to print this information on customer receipts as well.

If you make such a statement and collect taxes on cash sales, be sure to report those cash sales as taxable income and remit the tax money to the state accordingly. Failure

from 1 to 6 months in prison and a fine of $5,000. As you can see, the collection of sales tax is serious business.

Collecting Tax on Internet Sales

Anything you sell that is taxable in your state is also taxable on the Internet. This is simply another method of selling, like craft fairs or mail-order sales. You don't have to break out Internet sales separately; simply include them in your total taxable sales.

3. The Legal Forms of Business

Every business must take one of four legal forms:

Sole Proprietorship
Partnership
LLC (Limited Liability Company)
Corporation

to do this would be a violation of the law, and it's easy to get caught these days when sales tax agents are showing up at craft fairs across the country.

Even if rounding off the price and including the tax within that figure turns out to be legal in your state, it will definitely complicate your bookkeeping. For example, if you normally sell an item for $5 or some other round figure, you must have a firm retail price on which to calculate sales tax to begin with. Adding tax to a round figure makes it uneven. Then you must either raise or lower the price, and if you lower it, what you're really doing is paying the sales tax for your customer out of your profits. This is no way to do business.

I suggest that you set your retail prices based on the pricing formulas given in this book, calculate the sales tax accordingly, and give your customers change if they pay in cash. You will be perceived as a professional when you operate this way, whereas crafters who insist always on "cash only" sales are sending signals to buyers that they don't intend to report this income to tax authorities.

As a hobby seller, you automatically become a sole proprietor when you start selling what you make. Although most professional crafters remain sole proprietors throughout the life of their business, some do form craft partnerships or corporations when their business begins to generate serious money, or if it happens to involve other members of their family. You don't need a lawyer to start a sole proprietorship, but it would be folly to enter into a partnership, LLC or corporation, without legal guidance. Here is a brief look at the main advantages and disadvantages of each type of legal business structure.

Sole Proprietorship

No legal formalities are involved in starting or ending a sole proprietorship. You're your own boss here, and the business starts when you say it does and ends automatically when you stop running it. As discussed earlier, income is reported annually on a Schedule C form and taxed at the personal level. The sole proprietor is fully liable for all business debts and actions. In the event of a lawsuit, personal assets are not protected.

Partnership

There are two kinds of partnerships: general and limited.

A *general partnership* is easy to start, with no federal requirements involved. Income is taxed at the personal level and the partnership ends as soon as either partner withdraws from the business. Liability is unlimited. The most financially dangerous thing about a partnership is that the debts incurred by one partner must be assumed by all other partners. Before signing a partnership agreement, make sure the tax obligations of your partner are current.

In a *limited partnership*, the business is run by general partners and financed by silent (limited) partners who have no liability beyond an investment of money in the business. This kind of partnership is more complicated to establish, has special tax withholding regulations, and requires the filing of a legal contract with the state.

> ***Avoid this pitfall:*** Partnerships between friends often end the friendship when disagreements over business policies occur. Don't form a partnership with anyone without planning in advance how the partnership will eventually be dissolved, and spell out all the details in a written agreement. What will happen if either partner dies, wants out of the business, or wants to buy out the other partner? Also ask your attorney about the advisability of having partnership insurance, to protect against the complications that would arise if one of the partners becomes ill, incapacitated, or dies. For additional perspective on the pros and cons of partnerships, read the book *The Perils of Partners*.

The Limited Legal Protection of a Corporation

Business novices often think that by incorporating their business they can protect their personal assets in the event of a lawsuit. This is true if you have employees who do something wrong and cause your business to be sued. As the business owner, however, if you personally do something wrong and are sued as a result, you might in some cases be held legally responsible, and the "corporation door" will offer no legal protection for your personal assets.

Or, as CPA Bernard Kamoroff explains in *Small Time Operator,* "A corporation will not shield you from personal liability that you normally should be responsible for, such as not having car insurance or acting with gross negligence. If you plan to incorporate solely or primarily with the intention of limiting your legal liability, I suggest you find out first exactly how limited the liability really is for your particular venture. Hire a knowledgeable lawyer to give you a written opinion." (See section 7, Insurance Tips.)

LLC (Limited Liability Company)

This legal form of business reportedly combines the best attributes of other small-business forms while offering a better tax advantage than a limited partnership. It also affords personal liability protection similar to that of a corporation. To date, few craft businesses appear to be using this business form.

Corporation

A corporation is the most complicated and expensive legal form of business and not recommended for any business whose earnings are less than $25,000 a year. If and when your business reaches this point, you should study some books on this topic to fully understand the pros and cons of a corporation. Also consult an accountant or attorney for guidance on the type of corporation you should select—a "C" (general corporation) or an "S" (subchapter S corporation). One book that offers good perspective on this topic is *INC Yourself—How to Profit by Setting Up Your Own Corporation.*

The main disadvantage of incorporation for the small-business owner is that profits are taxed twice: first as corporate income and again when they are distributed to the owner-shareholders as dividends. For this reason, many small businesses elect to incorporate as subchapter S corporations, which allows profits to be taxed at owners' regular individual rates. (See sidebar, The Limited Legal Protection of a Corporation, on page 237.)

4. Local and State Laws and Regulations

This section will acquaint you with laws and regulations that affect the average art or crafts business based at home. If you've unknowingly broken one of these laws, don't panic. It may not be as bad as you think. It is often possible to get back on the straight and narrow merely by filling out a required form or by paying a small fee of some kind. What's important is that you take steps now to comply with the laws that pertain to your particular business. Often, the fear of being caught when you're breaking a law is much worse than doing whatever needs to be done to set the matter straight. In the end, it's usually what you don't know that is most likely to cause legal or financial problems, so never hesitate to ask questions about things you don't understand.

Even when you think you know the answers, it can pay to "act dumb." It is said that Napoleon used to attend meetings and pretend to know nothing about a topic, asking many probing questions. By feigning ignorance, he was able to draw valuable information and insight out of everyone around him. This strategy is often used by today's small-business owners, too.

Business Name Registration

If you're a sole proprietor doing business under any name other than your own full name, you are required by law to register it on both the local and state level. In this case, you are said to be using an "assumed," "fictitious," or "trade" name. Registration enables authorities to connect an assumed name to an individual who can be held responsible for the actions of a business. If you're doing business under your own name, such as Kay Jones, you don't have to register your business name on either the local or state level. If your name is part of a longer name, however (for example, Kay Jones Designs), you should check to see if your county or state requires registration.

Local Registration

To register your name, contact your city or county clerk, who will explain what you need to do to officially register your business on

Picking a Good Business Name

If you haven't done it already, think up a great name for your new business. You want something that will be memorable—catchy, but not too cute. Many crafters select a simple name that is attached to their first name, such as "Mary's Quilts" or "Tom's Woodcrafts." This is fine for a hobby business, but if your goal is to build a full-time business at home, you may wish to choose a more professional-sounding name that omits your personal name. If a name sounds like a hobby business, you may have difficulty getting wholesale suppliers to take you seriously. A more professional name may also enable you to get higher prices for your products. For example, the above names might be changed to "Quilted Treasures" or "Wooden Wonders."

Don't print business cards or stationery until you find out if someone else is already using the name you've chosen. To find out if the name has already been registered, you

the local level. At the same time, ask if you need any special municipal or county licenses or permits to operate within the law. (See the next section, Licenses and Permits.) This office can also tell you how and where to write to register your name at the state level. If you've been operating under an assumed name for a while and are worried because you didn't register the name earlier, just register it now, as if the business were new.

Registration involves filling out a simple form and paying a small fee, usually around $10 to $25. At the time you register, you will get details about a classified ad you must run in a general-circulation newspaper in your county. This will notify the public at large that you are now operating a business under an assumed name. (If you don't want your neighbors to know what you're doing, simply run the ad in a newspaper somewhere else in the county.) After publication of this ad, you will receive a Fictitious Name Statement that you must send to the county clerk, who in turn will file it with your registration form to make your business completely legit-

can perform a trademark search through a search company or hire an attorney who specializes in trademark law to conduct the search for you. And if you are planning to eventually set up a Web site, you might want to do a search to see if that domain name is still available on the Internet. Go to www.networksolutions.com to do this search. Business names have to be registered on the Internet, too, and they can be "parked" for a fee until you're ready to design your Web site.

It's great if your business name and Web site name can be the same, but this is not always possible. A crafter told me recently she had to come up with 25 names before she found a domain name that hadn't already been taken. (Web entrepreneurs are grabbing every good name they can find. Imagine my surprise when I did a search and found that two different individuals had set up Web sites using the titles of my two best-known books, *Creative Cash* and *Homemade Money*.)

imate. This name statement or certificate may also be referred to as your DBA ("doing business as") form. In some areas, you cannot open a business checking account if you don't have this form to show your bank.

> ***Avoid this pitfall:*** Failure to register your business name may result in your losing it—after you've spent a considerable amount of money on business cards, stationery, advertising, and so on. If someone sees your name, likes it, and finds on checking that it hasn't been registered, they can simply register the name and force you to stop using it.

State Registration

Once you've registered locally, contact your secretary of state to register your business name with the state. This will prevent its use by a corporate entity. At the same time, find out if you must obtain any kind of state license. Generally, home-based crafts businesses will not need a license from the state, but there are always exceptions. An artist who built an open-to-the-public art studio on his property reported that the fine in his state for operating this kind of business without a license was $50 a day. In short, it always pays to ask questions to make sure you're operating legally and safely.

Federal Registration

The only way to protect a name on the federal level is with a trademark, discussed in section 9.

Licenses and Permits

A "license" is a certificate granted by a municipal or county agency that gives you permission to engage in a business occupation. A "permit" is similar, except that it is granted by local authorities. Until recently, few crafts businesses had to have a license or permit of any kind, but a growing number of communities now have new laws on their books that require home-based business owners to obtain a "home occupation permit." Annual fees for such permits may range from $15 to $200 a year. For details about the law in your particular community or county, call your city or county clerk (depending on whether you live within or outside city limits).

Use of Personal Phone for Business

Although every business writer stresses the importance of having a business telephone number, craftspeople generally ignore this advice and do business on their home telephone. Although it's okay to use a home phone to make outgoing business calls, you cannot advertise a home telephone number as your business phone number without being in violation of local telephone regulations. That means you cannot legally put your home telephone number on a business card or business stationery or advertise it on your Web site.

That said, let me also state that most craftspeople totally ignore this law and do it anyway. (I don't know what the penalty for breaking this law is in your state; you'll have to call your telephone company for that information and decide if this is something you want to do.) Some phone companies might give you a slap on the wrist and tell you to stop, while others might start charging you business line telephone rates if they discover you are advertising your personal phone number.

The primary reason to have a separate phone line for your business is that it enables you to freely advertise your telephone number to solicit new business and invite credit card sales, custom order inquiries, and the like. Further, you can deduct 100% of the costs of a business telephone line on your Schedule C tax form, while deductions for the business use of a home phone are severely limited. (Discuss this with your accountant.)

If you plan to connect to the Internet or install a fax machine, you will definitely need a second line to handle the load, but most crafters simply add an additional personal line instead of a business line. Once on the Internet, you may have even less need for a business phone than before because you can simply invite contact from buyers by advertising your e-mail address. (Always include your e-mail and Internet addresses on your business cards and stationery.)

If your primary selling methods are going to be consignment shops, craft fairs, or craft malls, a business phone number would be necessary only if you are inviting orders by phone. If you present a holiday boutique or open house once or twice a year, there should be no problem with putting your home phone number on promotional fliers because you are, in fact, inviting people to your home and not your business (similar to running a classified ad for a garage sale).

If and when you decide a separate line for your business is necessary, you may find it is not as costly as you think. Telephone companies today are very aware of the number of people who are working at home, and they have come up with a variety of affordable packages and second-line options, any one of which might be perfect for your crafts-business needs. Give your telephone company a call and see what's available.

Zoning Regulations

Before you start any kind of home-based business, check your home's zoning regulations. You can find a copy at your library or at city hall. Find out what zone you're in and then read the information under "Home Occupations." Be sure to read the fine print and note the penalty for violating a zoning ordinance. In most cases, someone who is caught violating zoning laws will be asked to cease and desist and a penalty is incurred only if this order is ignored. In other cases, however, willful violation could incur a hefty fine.

Zoning laws differ from one community to another, with some of them being terribly outdated (actually written back in horse-and-buggy days). In some communities, zoning officials simply "look the other way" where zoning violations are concerned because it's easier to do this than change the law. In other places, however, zoning regulations have recently been revised in light of the growing number of individuals working at home, and these changes have not always been to the benefit of home-based workers or self-employed individuals. Often there are restrictions as to (1) the amount of space in one's home a business may occupy (impossible to enforce, in my opinion), (2) the number of people (customers, students) who can come to your home each day, (3) the use of non-family employees, and so on. If you find you cannot advertise your home as a place of business, this problem can be easily solved by renting a PO box or using a commercial mailbox service as your business address.

Although I'm not suggesting that you violate your zoning law, I will tell you that many individuals who have found zoning to be a problem do ignore this law, particularly when they have a quiet business that is unlikely to create problems in their community.

Zoning officials don't go around checking for people who are violating the law; rather, they tend to act on complaints they have received about a certain activity that is creating problems for others. Thus, the best way to avoid zoning problems is to keep a low profile by not broadcasting your home-based business to neighbors. More important, never annoy them with activities that emit fumes or odors, create parking problems, or make noise of any kind.

Although neighbors may grudgingly put up with a noisy hobby activity (such as sawing in the garage), they are not likely to tolerate the same noise or disturbance if they know it's related to a home-based business. Likewise, they won't mind if you have a garage sale every year, but if people are coming to your home every year to buy from your home shop, open house, home parties, or holiday boutiques, you could be asking for trouble if the zoning laws don't favor this kind of activity.

> *Avoid this pitfall:* If you're planning to hold a holiday boutique or home party, check with zoning officials first. (If they don't know what a holiday boutique is, tell them it's a temporary sales event, like a garage sale.) Generally, the main concerns will be that you do not post illegal signs, tie up traffic, or otherwise annoy your neighbors. In some areas, however, zoning regulations strictly prohibit (1) traffic into one's home for any commercial reason; (2) the exchange of money in a home for business reasons; or (3) the transfer of merchandise within the home (affecting party plan sellers, in particular). Some sellers have found the solution to all three of these problems as simple as letting people place orders for merchandise that will be delivered later, with payment collected at time of delivery.

5. General Business and Financial Information

This section offers introductory guidelines on essential business basics for beginners. Once your business is up and running, however, you need to read other crafts-business books to get detailed information on the following topics and many others related to the successful growth and development of a home-based art or crafts business.

Making a Simple Business Plan

As baseball star Yogi Berra once said, "If you don't know where you are going, you might not get there." That's why you need a plan.

Like a road map, a business plan helps you get from here to there. It doesn't have to be fancy, but it does have to be in written form. A good business plan will save you time and money while helping you stay focused and on track to meet your goals. The kind of business plan a craftsperson makes will naturally be less complicated than the business plan of a major manufacturing company, but the elements are basically the same and should include:

- *History*—how and why you started your business
- *Business description*—what you do, what products you make, why they are special
- *Management information*—your business background or experience and the legal form your business will take
- *Manufacturing and production*—how and where products will be produced and who will make them; how and where supplies and materials will be obtained, and their estimated costs; labor costs (yours or other helpers); and overhead costs involved in the making of products
- *Financial plan*—estimated sales and expense figures for 1 year
- *Market research findings*—a description of your market (fairs, shops, mail order, Internet, and so on), your customers, and your competition
- *Marketing plan*—how you are going to sell your products and the anticipated cost of your marketing (commissions, advertising, craft fair displays, and so on)

If this all seems a bit much for a small crafts business, start managing your time by using a daily calendar/planner and start a

Get a Safety Deposit Box

The longer you are in business, the more important it will be to safeguard your most valuable business records. When you work at home, there is always the possibility of fire or damage from some natural disaster, be it a tornado, earthquake, hurricane, or flood. You will worry less if you keep your most valuable business papers, records, computer disks, and so forth off-premises, along with other items that would be difficult or impossible to replace. Some particulars I have always kept in my business safety deposit box include master software disks and computer back-up disks; original copies of my designs and patterns, business contracts, copyrights, insurance policies, and a photographic record of all items insured on our homeowner's policy. Remember: Insurance is worthless if you cannot prove what you owned in the first place.

notebook you can fill with your creative and marketing ideas, plans, and business goals. In it, write a simple mission statement that answers the following questions:

- What is my primary mission or goal in starting a business?
- What is my financial goal for this year?
- What am I going to do to get the sales I need this year to meet my financial goal?

The most important thing is that you start putting your dreams, goals, and business plans on paper so you can review them regularly. It's always easier to see where you're going if you know where you've been.

When You Need an Attorney

Many business beginners think they have to hire a lawyer the minute they start a business, but that would be a terrible waste of money if you're just starting a simple art or crafts business at home, operating as a sole proprietor. Sure, a lawyer will be delighted to hold your hand and give you the same advice I'm giving you here (while charging you $150 an hour or more for his or her time). With this book in hand, you can easily take care of all the "legal details" of a small-business start-up. The day may come, however, when you do need legal counsel, such as when you:

Form a Partnership or Corporation

As stated earlier, an attorney's guidance is necessary in the formation of a partnership. Although many people have incorporated without a lawyer using a good how-to book on the topic, I wouldn't recommend doing this because there are so many details involved, not to mention different types of corporate entities.

Defend an Infringement of a Copyright or Trademark

You don't need an attorney to get a simple copyright, but if someone infringes on one of your copyrights, you will probably need legal help to stop the infringer from profiting from your creativity. You can file your own trademark application (if you are exceedingly careful about following instructions), but it would be difficult to protect your trademark without legal help if someone tries to steal it. In both cases, you would need an attorney who specializes in copyright, patent, and trademark law. (If you ever need a good attorney who understands the plight of artists and crafters, contact me by e-mail at barbara@crafter.com and I'll refer you to the attorney who has been helpful to me in protecting my common-law trademark to *Homemade Money*, my home-business classic. The sixth edition of this book includes the details of my trademark infringement story.)

Negotiate a Contract

Many craft hobbyists of my acquaintance have gone on to write books and sell their original designs to manufacturers, suddenly finding themselves with a contract in hand that contains a lot of confusing legal jargon. When hiring an attorney to check any kind of contract, make sure he or she has experience in the particular field involved. For example, a lawyer specializing in real estate isn't going to know a thing about the inner workings of a book publishing company and how the omission or inclusion of a particular clause or phrase might impact the author's royalties or make it difficult to get publishing rights back when the book goes out of print. Although I have no experience in the licensing industry, I presume the same thing holds true here. What I do know for sure is that the problem with most contracts is not so much what's *in* them, as what *isn't*. Thus you need to be sure the attorney you hire for specialized contract work has done this kind of work for other clients.

Hire Independent Contractors

If you ever grow your business to the point where you need to hire workers and are wondering whether you have to hire employees or can use independent contractors instead, I suggest you seek counsel from an attorney who specializes in labor law. This topic is very complex and beyond the scope of this beginner's guide, but I do want you to know that the IRS has been on a campaign for the past several years to abolish independent contractors altogether. Many small businesses have suffered great financial loss in back taxes and penalties because they followed the advice of an accountant or regular attorney who didn't fully understand the technicalities of this matter.

If and when you do need a lawyer for general business purposes, ask friends for a reference; and check with your bank, too, because it will probably know most of the attorneys with private practices in your area. Note that membership in some small-business organizations will also give you access to affordable prepaid legal services. If you ever need serious legal help but have no funds to pay for it, contact the Volunteer Lawyers for the Arts.

Why You Need a Business Checking Account

Many business beginners use their personal checking account to conduct the transactions of their business, *but you must not do this* because the IRS does not allow commingling of business and personal income. If you are operating as a business, reporting income on a Schedule C form and taking deductions accordingly, the lack of a separate checking account for your business would surely result in an IRS ruling that your endeavor was a hobby and not a business. That, in turn, would cost you all the deductions previously taken on earlier tax returns and you'd end up with a very large tax bill. Don't you agree that the cost of a separate checking account is a small price to pay to protect all your tax deductions?

You do not necessarily need one of the more expensive business checking accounts; just a *separate account* through which you run all business income and expenditures. Your business name does not have to be on these checks so long as only your name (not your spouse's) is listed as account holder. You can save money on your checking account by first calling several banks and savings and loan institutions and comparing the charges they set for imprinted checks, deposits, checks written, bounced checks, and other services. Before you open your account, be sure to ask if the bank can set you up to take credit cards (merchant account) at some point in the future.

> *Avoid this pitfall:* Some banks charge extra for each out-of-state check that is deposited, an expense that is prohibitively expensive for active mail-order businesses. For that reason, I have always maintained a business checking account in a savings and loan association, which has no service charges of any kind (except for bad checks). S&Ls also pay interest on the amount in a checking account, whereas a bank may not. The main disadvantage of doing your business checking through an S&L is that they do not offer credit card services or give business loans. At the

point where I found I needed the latter two services for my publishing business, I had to open a second account with a local bank.

Accepting Credit Cards

Most of us today take credit cards for granted and expect to be able to use them for most everything we buy. It's nice to be able to offer credit card services to your craft fair customers, but it is costly and thus not recommended for beginning craft sellers. If you get into selling at craft fairs on a regular basis, however, at some point you may find you are losing sales because you don't have "merchant status" (the ability to accept credit cards as payment).

Some craftspeople have reported a considerable jump in sales once they started taking credit cards. That's because some people who buy with plastic may buy two or three items instead of one, or may be willing to pay a higher price for something if they can charge it. Thus, the higher your prices, the more likely you are to lose sales if you can't accept credit cards. As one jewelry maker told me, "I always seem to get the customers who have run out of cash and left their checkbook at home. But even when they have a check, I feel uncomfortable taking a check for $100 or more."

This section discusses the various routes you can travel to get merchant status. You will have to do considerable research to find out which method is best for you. All will be costly, and you must have sufficient sales, or the expectation of increased sales, to consider taking credit cards in the first place. Understand, too, that taking credit cards in person (called face-to-face transactions where you have the card in front of you) is different from accepting credit cards by phone, by mail, or through a Web site (called non–face-to-face transactions). Each method of selling is treated differently by bankcard providers.

Avoid this pitfall: If you are relatively new at selling, and uncertain about whether you will be taking credit cards for a long time, do not sign a leasing arrangement for credit card processing equipment. Instead, leave yourself an escape route by opting for a rental agreement you can get out of with a month's notice, such as that offered by some banks and organizations discussed below.

Merchant Status from Your Bank

When you're ready to accept credit cards, start with the bank where you have your business checking account. Where you bank, and where you live, has everything to do with whether you can get merchant status from your bank. Home-business owners in small towns often have less trouble than do those in large cities. One crafter told me Bank of America gave her merchant status with no problem, but some banks simply refuse to deal with anyone who doesn't operate out of a storefront. Most banks now insist that credit card sales be transmitted electronically, but a few still offer manual printers and allow merchants to send in their sales slips by mail. You will be given details about this at the time you apply for merchant status. All banks will require proof that you have a going business and will want to see your financial statements.

Merchant Status through a Crafts Organization

If you are refused by your bank because your business is home based or just too new, getting bankcard services through a crafts or home-business organization is the next best way to go. Because such organizations have a large membership, they have some negotiating power with the credit card companies and often get special deals for their members. As a member of such an organization, the chances are about 95% that you will automatically be accepted into its bankcard program, even if you are a brand-new business owner.

One organization I can recommend to beginning sellers is the National Craft Association. Managing Director Barbara Arena tells me that 60% of all new NCA members now take the

MasterCard/VISA services offered by her organization. "Crafters who are unsure about whether they want to take credit cards over a long period of time have the option of renting equipment," says Barbara. "This enables them to get out of the program with a month's notice. NCA members can operate on a software basis through their personal computer (taking their laptop computer to shows and calling in sales on their cell phone) or use a swipe machine. Under NCA's program, crafters can also accept credit card sales on their Internet site."

For more information from NCA and other organizations offering merchant services, see Craft and Home-Business Organizations on page 296.

Merchant Status from Credit Card Companies

If you've been in business for a while, you may find you can get merchant status directly from American Express or Novus Services, Inc., the umbrella company that handles the Discover, Bravo, and Private Issue credit cards. American Express says that in some cases it can grant merchant status immediately on receipt of some key information given on the phone. As for Novus, many crafters have told me how easy it was to get merchant status from this company. Novus says it needs only your Social Security number and information to check your credit rating. If Novus accepts you, it can also get you set up to take VISA and MasterCard as well, if you meet the special acceptance qualifications of these two credit card companies. (Usually, they require you to be in business for at least 2 years.)

Merchant Status from an Independent Service Organization Provider (ISO)

ISOs act as agents for banks that authorize credit cards, promoting their services by direct mail, through magazine advertising, telemarketing, and on the Internet. Most of these bankcard providers are operating under a network marketing program (one agent representing one agent representing another, and so on). They are everywhere on the Internet, sending unsolicited e-mail messages to Web site owners. In addition to offering the merchant account service itself, many are also trying to get other Web site owners to promote the same service in exchange for some kind of referral fee. I do not recommend that you get merchant status through an ISO because I've heard too many horror stories about them. If you want to explore this option on the Internet, however, use your browser's search button and type "credit cards + merchant" to get a list of such sellers.

In general, ISOs may offer a low discount rate but will sock it to you with inflated equipment costs, a high application fee, and extra fees for installation, programming, and site inspection. You will also have to sign an unbreakable 3- or 4-year lease for the electronic equipment.

> ***Avoid this pitfall:*** Some people on the Internet may offer to process your credit card sales through their individual merchant account, but this is illegal as it violates credit card company rules. And if you were to offer to do this for someone else, your account would be terminated. In short, if you do not ship the goods, you can't process the sale.

As you can see, you must really do your homework where bankcard services are concerned. In checking out the services offered by any of the providers noted here, ask plenty of questions. Make up a chart that lets you compare what each one charges for application and service fees, monthly charges, equipment costs, software, discount rates, and transaction fees.

Transaction fees can range from $0.20 to $0.80 per ticket, with discount rates running anywhere from 1.67 to 5%. Higher rates are usually attached to non–face-to-face credit card transactions, paper transaction systems, or a low volume of sales. Any rate higher than

5% should be a danger signal because you could be dealing with an unscrupulous seller or some kind of illegal third-party processing program.

I'm told that a good credit card processor today may cost around $800, yet some card service providers are charging two or three times that amount in their leasing arrangements. I once got a quote from a major ISO and found it would have cost me $40 a month to lease the terminal—$1,920 over a period of 4 years—or I could buy it for just $1,000. In checking with my bank, I learned I could get the same equipment and the software to run it for just $350!

In summary, if you're a nervous beginner, the safest way to break into taking credit cards is to work with a bank or organization that offers equipment on a month-by-month rental arrangement. Once you've had some experience in taking credit card payments, you can review your situation and decide whether you want to move into a leasing arrangement or buy equipment outright.

6. Minimizing the Financial Risks of Selling

This book contains a good chapter on how and where to sell your crafts, but I thought it would be helpful for you to have added perspective on the business management end of selling through various outlets, and some things you can do to protect yourself from financial loss and legal hassles.

You must accept the fact that all businesses occasionally suffer financial losses of one kind or another. That's simply the nature of business. Selling automatically carries a certain degree of risk in that we can never be absolutely sure that we're going to be paid for anything until we actually have payment in hand. Checks may bounce, wholesale buyers may refuse to pay their invoices, and consignment shops can close unexpectedly without returning merchandise to crafters. In the past few years, a surprising number of craft mall owners have stolen out of town in the middle of the night, taking with them all the money due their vendors, and sometimes the vendors' merchandise as well. (This topic is beyond the scope of this book, but if you'd like more information on it, see my *Creative Cash* book and back issues of my *Craftsbiz Chat* newsletter on the Internet at www.crafter.com/brabec.)

Now, I don't want you to feel uneasy about selling or be suspicious of every buyer who comes your way, because that would take all the fun out of selling. But I *do* want you to know that bad things sometimes happen to good craftspeople who have not done their homework (by reading this book, you are doing *your* homework). If you will follow the cautionary guidelines discussed in this section, you can avoid some common selling pitfalls and minimize your financial risk to the point where it will be negligible.

Selling to Consignment Shops

Never consign more merchandise to one shop than you can afford to lose, and do not send new items to a shop until you see that payments are being made regularly according to your written consignment agreement. It should cover the topics of:

- Insurance (see Insurance Tips, section 7)
- Pricing (make sure the shop cannot raise or lower your retail price without your permission)
- Sales commission (40% is standard; don't work with shop owners who ask for more than this. It makes more sense to wholesale products at 50% and get payment in 30 days)
- Payment dates
- Display of merchandise

- Return of unsold merchandise (some shops have a clause stating that if unsold merchandise is not claimed within 30 to 60 days after a notice has been sent, the shop can dispose of it any way it wishes)

Above all, make sure your agreement includes the name and phone number of the shop's owner (not just the manager). If a shop fails and you decide to take legal action, you want to be sure your lawyer can track down the owner. (See sidebar, State Consignment Laws, below.)

Selling to Craft Malls

Shortly after the craft mall concept was introduced to the crafts community in 1988 by Rufus Coomer, entrepreneurs who understood the profit potential of such a business began to open malls all over the country. But there were no guidebooks and everyone was flying by the seat of his or her pants, making up operating rules along the way. Many mall owners, inexperienced in retailing, have

State Consignment Laws

Technically, consigned goods remain the property of the seller until they are sold. When a shop goes out of business, however, consigned merchandise may be seized by creditors in spite of what your consignment agreement may state. You may have some legal protection here, however, if you live in a state that has a consignment law designed to protect artists and craftspeople in such instances. I believe such laws exist in the states of CA, CO, CT, IL, IA, KY, MA, NH, NM, NY, OR, TX, WA, and WI. Call your secretary of state to confirm this or, if your state isn't listed here, ask whether this law is now on the books. Be sure to get full details about the kind of protection afforded by this law because some states have different definitions for what constitutes "art" or "crafts."

since gone out of business, often leaving crafters holding the bag. The risks of selling through such well-known chain stores as Coomer's or American Craft Malls are minimal, and many independently owned malls have also established excellent reputations in the industry. What you need to be especially concerned about here are new malls opened by individuals who have no track record in this industry.

I'm not telling you *not* to set up a booth in a new mall in your area—it might prove to be a terrific outlet for you—but I am cautioning you to keep a sharp eye on the mall and how it's being operated. Warning signs of a mall in trouble include:

- **Less than 75% occupancy**
- **Little or no ongoing advertising**
- **Not many shoppers**
- **Crafters pulling out (usually a sign of too few sales)**
- **Poor accounting of sales**
- **Late payments**

If a mall is in trouble, it stands to reason that the logical time for it to close is right after the biggest selling season of the year, namely Christmas. Interestingly, this is when most of the shady mall owners have stolen out of town with crafters' Christmas sales in their pockets. As stated in my *Creative Cash* book:

> If it's nearing Christmastime, and you're getting uncomfortable vibes about the financial condition of a mall you're in, it might be smart to remove the bulk of your merchandise— especially expensive items—just before it closes for the holidays. You can always restock after the first of the year if everything looks rosy.

Avoiding Bad Checks

At a craft fair or other event where you're selling directly to the public, if the buyer doesn't have cash and you don't accept credit cards, your only option is to accept a check. Few crafters have bad check problems for sales held in the home (holiday boutique, open house, party plan, and such), but bad checks at craft fairs are always possible. Here are several things you can do to avoid accepting a bad check:

- Always ask to see a driver's license and look carefully at the picture on it. Write the license number on the check.

- If the sale is for a large amount, you can ask to see a credit card for added identification, but writing down the number will do no good because you cannot legally cover a bad check with a customer's credit card. (The customer has a legal right to refuse to let you copy the number as well.)

- Look closely at the check itself. Is there a name and address printed on it? If not, ask the customer to write in this information by hand, along with his or her phone number.

- Look at the sides of the check. If at least one side is not perforated, it could be a phony check.

- Look at the check number in the upper right-hand corner. Most banks who issue personalized checks begin the numbering system with 101 when a customer reorders new checks. The Small Business Administration says to be more cautious with low sequence numbers because there seems to be a higher number of these checks that are returned.

- Check the routing number in the lower left-hand corner and note the ink. If it looks shiny, wet your finger and see if the ink rubs off. That's a sure sign of a phony check because good checks are printed with magnetic ink that does not reflect light.

Collecting on a Bad Check

No matter how careful you are, sooner or later, you will get stuck with a bad check. It may bounce for one of three reasons:

1. Nonsufficient funds (NSF)
2. Account closed
3. No account (evidence of fraud)

I've accepted tens of thousands of checks from mail-order buyers through the years and have rarely had a bad check I couldn't collect with a simple phone call asking the party to honor his or her obligation to me. People often move and close out accounts before all checks have cleared, or they add or subtract wrong, causing their account to be overdrawn. Typically, they are embarrassed to have caused a problem like this.

When the problem is more difficult than this, your bank can help. Check to learn its policy regarding bounced checks. Some automatically put checks through a second time. If a check bounces at this point, you may ask the bank to collect the check for you. The check needs to be substantial, however, because the bank fee may be $15 or more if they are successful in collecting the money.

If you have accepted a check for a substantial amount of money and believe there is evidence of fraud, you may wish to do one of the following:

- Notify your district attorney's office
- Contact your sheriff or police department (because it is a crime to write a bad check)
- Try to collect through small claims court

For more detailed information on all of these topics, see *The Crafts Business Answer Book*.

7. Insurance Tips

As soon as you start even the smallest business at home, you need to give special attention to insurance. This section offers an introductory overview of insurance concerns of primary interest to crafts-business owners.

Homeowner's or Renter's Insurance

Anything in the home being used to generate income is considered to be business-related and thus exempt from coverage on a personal policy. Thus your homeowner's or renter's insurance policy will not cover business equipment, office furniture, supplies, or inventory of finished goods unless you obtain a special rider. Such riders, called a "Business Pursuits Endorsement" by some companies, are inexpensive and offer considerable protection. Your insurance agent will be happy to give you details.

As your business grows and you have an ever-larger inventory of supplies, materials, tools, and finished merchandise, you may find it necessary to buy a special in-home business policy that offers broader protection. Such policies may be purchased directly from insurance companies or through craft and home-business organizations that offer special insurance programs to their members.

Avoid this pitfall: If you have an expensive computer system, costly tools, equipment, or office furnishings, the coverage

Insuring Your Art or Crafts Collection

The replacement cost insurance you may have on your personal household possessions does not extend to "fine art," which includes such things as paintings, antiques, pictures, tapestries, statuary, and other articles that cannot be replaced with new articles. If you have a large collection of art, crafts, memorabilia, or collector's items, and its value is more than $1,500, you may wish to have your collection appraised so it can be protected with a separate all-risk endorsement to your homeowner's policy called a "fine arts floater."

afforded by a simple business rider to your homeowner's policy may be insufficient for your needs. Although you may have replacement-value insurance on all your personal possessions, anything used for business purposes would be exempt from such coverage. In other words, the value of everything covered by the rider would be figured on a depreciable basis instead of what it would cost to replace it. (See also sidebar, Insuring Your Art or Crafts Collection, on page 261.)

Liability Insurance

There are two kinds of liability insurance. *Product* liability insurance protects you against lawsuits by consumers who have been injured while using one of your products. *Personal* liability insurance protects you against claims made by individuals who have suffered bodily injury while on your premises (either your home or the place where you are doing business, such as in your booth at a craft fair).

Your homeowner's or renter's insurance policy will include some personal liability protection, but if someone were to suffer bodily injury while on your premises for *business* reasons, that coverage might not apply. Your need for personal liability insurance will be greater if you plan to regularly present home parties, holiday boutiques, or open house sales in your home where many people might be coming and going throughout the year. If you sell at craft fairs, you would also be liable for damages if someone were to fall and be injured in your booth or if something in your booth falls and injures another person. For this reason, some craft fair promoters now require all vendors to have personal liability insurance.

As for product liability insurance, whether you need it depends largely on the type of products you make for sale, how careful you are to make sure those products are safe, and how and where you sell them. Examples of some crafts that have caused injury to consumers and resulted in court claims in the past are stuffed toys with wire or pins that children have swallowed; items made of yarn or fiber that burned rapidly; handmade furniture that collapsed when someone put an ordinary amount of weight on it; jewelry with sharp points or other features that cut the wearer, and so on. Clearly, the best way to avoid injury to consumers is to make certain your products have no health hazards and are safe to use. (See discussion of consumer safety laws in section 8.)

Few artists and craftspeople who sell on a part-time basis feel they can afford product liability insurance, but many full-time craft professionals, particularly those who sell their work wholesale, find it a necessary expense. In fact, many wholesale buyers refuse to buy from suppliers that do not carry product liability insurance.

I believe the least expensive way to obtain both personal and product liability insurance is with one of the comprehensive in-home or crafts-business policies offered by a crafts- or home-business organization. Such policies generally offer $1 million of both personal and product liability coverage. (See A "Things to Do" Checklist with Related Resources on page 290 and the Resources section for some organizations you can contact for more information. Also check with your insurance agent about the benefits of an umbrella policy for extra liability insurance.)

Insurance on Crafts Merchandise

As a seller of art or crafts merchandise, you are responsible for insuring your own products against loss. If you plan to sell at craft fairs, in craft malls, rent-a-space shops, or consignment shops, you may want to buy an insurance policy that protects your merchandise both at home or away. Note that while craft shops and malls generally have fire insurance covering the building and its fixtures, this coverage cannot be extended to merchandise offered for sale because it is not the property of the shop owner. (Exception: Shops and malls in shopping centers are mandated by law to buy fire insurance on their contents whether they own the merchandise or not.)

This kind of insurance is usually part of the home- or crafts-business insurance policies mentioned earlier.

Auto Insurance

Be sure to talk to the agent who handles your car insurance and explain that you may occasionally use your car for business purposes. Normally, a policy issued for a car that's used only for pleasure or driving to and from work may not provide complete coverage for an accident that occurs during business use of the car, particularly if the insured is to blame for the accident. For example, if you were delivering a load of crafts to a shop or on your way to a craft fair and had an accident, would your business destination and the "commercial merchandise" in your car negate your coverage in any way? Where insurance is concerned, the more questions you ask, the better you'll feel about the policies you have.

8. Important Regulations Affecting Artists and Craftspeople

Government agencies have a number of regulations that artists and craftspeople must know about. Generally, they relate to consumer safety, the labeling of certain products, and trade practices. Following are regulations of primary interest to readers of books in Prima's FOR FUN & PROFIT series. If you find a law or regulation related to your particular art or craft interest, be sure to request additional information from the government agency named there.

Consumer Safety Laws

All product sellers must pay attention to the Consumer Product Safety Act, which protects the public against unreasonable risks of injury associated with consumer products. The Consumer Product

Safety Commission (CPSC) is particularly active in the area of toys and consumer goods designed for children. All sellers of handmade products must be doubly careful about the materials they use for children's products because consumer lawsuits are common where products for children are concerned. To avoid this problem, simply comply with the consumer safety laws applicable to your specific art or craft.

Toy Safety Concerns

To meet CPSC's guidelines for safety, make sure any toys you make for sale are:

- Too large to be swallowed
- Not apt to break easily or leave jagged edges
- Free of sharp edges or points
- Not put together with easily exposed pins, wires, or nails
- Nontoxic, nonflammable, and nonpoisonous

The Use of Paints, Varnishes, and Other Finishes

Since all paint sold for household use must meet the Consumer Product Safety Act's requirement for minimum amounts of lead, these paints are deemed to be safe for use on products made for children, such as toys and furniture. Always check, however, to make sure the label bears a nontoxic notation. Specialty paints must carry a warning on the label about lead count, but "artist's paints" are curiously exempt from CPSC's lead-in-paint ban and are not required to bear a warning label of any kind. Thus you should *never* use such paints on products intended for use by children unless the label specifically states they are *nontoxic* (lead-free). Acrylics and other water-based paints, of course, are nontoxic and completely safe for use on toys and other products made for children. If you plan to use a finishing coat, make sure it is nontoxic as well.

Fabric Flammability Concerns

The Flammable Fabrics Act is applicable only to those who sell products made of fabric, particularly products for children. It prohibits the movement in interstate commerce of articles of wearing apparel and fabrics that are so highly flammable as to be dangerous when worn by individuals, and for other purposes. Most fabrics comply with this act, but if you plan to sell children's clothes or toys, you may wish to take an extra step to be doubly sure the fabric you are using is safe. This is particularly important if you plan to wholesale your products. What you should do is ask your fabric supplier for a *guarantee of compliance with the Flammability Act.* This guarantee is generally passed along to the buyer by a statement on the invoice that reads "continuing guaranty under the Flammable Fabrics Act." If you do not find such a statement on your invoice, you should ask the fabric manufacturer, wholesaler, or distributor to furnish you with their "statement of compliance" with the flammability standards. The CPSC can also tell you if a particular manufacturer has filed a continuing guarantee under The Flammable Fabrics Act.

Labels Required by Law

The following information applies only to crafters who use textiles, fabrics, fibers, or yarn products to make wearing apparel, decorative accessories, household furnishings, soft toys, or any product made of wool.

Different government agencies require the attachment of certain tags or labels to products sold in the consumer marketplace, whether manufactured in quantity or handmade for limited sale. You don't have to be too concerned about these laws if you sell only at local fairs, church bazaars, and home boutiques. As soon as you get out into the general consumer marketplace, however—doing large craft fairs, selling through consignment shops, craft malls, or wholesaling to shops—it would be wise to comply with all the federal labeling laws. Actually, these laws are quite easy to comply with because the required labels are readily available at inexpensive prices, and you can even make your own if you wish. Here is what the federal government wants you to tell your buyers in a tag or label:

- *What's in a product, and who has made it.* The Textile Fiber Products Identification Act (monitored both by the Bureau of Consumer Protection and the Federal Trade Commission) requires that a special label or hangtag be attached to all textile wearing apparel and household furnishings, with the exception of wall hangings. "Textiles" include products made of any fiber, yarn, or fabric, including garments and decorative accessories, quilts, pillows, placemats, stuffed toys, rugs, and so on. The tag or label must include (1) the name of the manufacturer and (2) the generic names and percentages of all fibers in the product in amounts of 5 percent or more, listed in order of predominance by weight.

- *How to take care of products.* Care Labeling Laws are part of the Textile Fiber Products Identification Act, details about which are available from the FTC. If you make wearing apparel or household furnishings of any kind using textiles, suede, or leather, you must attach a permanent label that explains how to take care of the item. This label must indicate whether the item is to be dry-cleaned or washed. If it is washable, you must indicate whether in hot or cold water, whether bleach may or may not be used, and the temperature at which it may be ironed.

- *Details about products made of wool.* If a product contains wool, the FTC requires additional identification under a separate law known as the Wool Products Labeling Act of 1939. FTC rules require that the labels of all wool or textile products clearly indicate when imported ingredients are used. Thus, the label for a skirt knitted in the United States from wool yarn imported from England would read, "Made in the USA from imported products" or similar wordage.

If the wool yarn was spun in the United States, a product made from that yarn would simply need a tag or label stating it was "Made in the USA" or "Crafted in USA" or some similarly clear terminology.

The Bedding and Upholstered Furniture Law

This is a peculiar state labeling law that affects sellers of items that have a concealed filling. It requires the purchase of a license, and products must have a tag that bears the manufacturer's registry number.

A Proper Copyright Notice

Although a copyright notice is not required by law, you are encouraged to put a copyright notice on every original thing you create. Adding the copyright notice does not obligate you to formally register your copyright, but it does serve to warn others that your work is legally protected and makes it difficult for anyone to claim they have "accidentally stolen" your work. (Those who actually do violate a copyright because they don't understand the law are called "innocent infringers" by the Copyright Office.)

A proper copyright notice includes three things:

1. The word *copyright,* its abbreviation *copr.,* or the copyright symbol, ©.

2. The year of first publication of the work (when it was first shown or sold to the public).

3. The name of the copyright owner. Example: © 2000 by Barbara Brabec. (When the words *All Rights Reserved* are added to the copyright notation, it means that copyright protection has been extended to include all of the Western Hemisphere.)

The copyright notice should be positioned in a place where it can easily be seen. It can be stamped, cast, engraved, painted, printed, wood-burned, or simply written by hand in permanent ink. In the case of fiber crafts, you can attach an inexpensive label with the copyright notice and your business name and logo (or any other information you wish to put on the label).

Bedding laws have long been a thorn in the side of crafters because they make no distinction between the large manufacturing company that makes mattresses and pillows, and the individual craft producer who sells only handmade items. "Concealed filling" items include not just bedding and upholstery, but handmade pillows and quilts. In some states, dolls, teddy bears, and stuffed soft sculpture items are also required to have a tag.

Fortunately, only 29 states now have this law on the books, and even if your state is one of them, the law may be arbitrarily enforced. (One exception is the state of Pennsylvania, which is reportedly sending officials to craft shows to inspect merchandise to see if it is properly labeled.) The only penalty that appears to be connected with a violation of this law in any state is removal of merchandise from store shelves or craft fair exhibits. That being the case, many crafters choose to ignore this law until they are challenged. If you learn you must comply with this law, you will be required to obtain a state license that will cost between $25 and $100, and you will have to order special "bedding stamps" that can be attached to your products. For more information on this complex topic, see *The Crafts Business Answer Book*.

FTC Rule for Mail-Order Sellers

Even the smallest home-based business needs to be familiar with Federal Trade Commission (FTC) rules and regulations. A variety of free booklets are available to business owners on topics related to advertising, mail-order marketing, and product labeling (as discussed earlier). In particular, crafters who sell by mail need to pay attention to the FTC's Thirty-Day Mail-Order Rule, which states that one must ship customer orders within 30 days of receiving payment for the order. This rule is strictly enforced, with severe financial penalties for each violation.

Unless you specifically state in your advertising literature how long delivery will take, customers will expect to receive the product within 30 days after you get their order. If you cannot meet this shipping date, you must notify the customer accordingly, enclosing a postage-paid reply card or envelope, and giving them the option to cancel the order if they wish. Now you know why so many catalog sellers state, "Allow 6 weeks for delivery." This lets them off the hook in case there are unforeseen delays in getting the order delivered.

9. Protecting Your Intellectual Property

"Intellectual property," says Attorney Stephen Elias in his book, *Patent, Copyright & Trademark,* "is a product of the human intellect that has commercial value."

This section offers a brief overview of how to protect your intellectual property through patents and trademarks, with a longer discussion of copyright law, which is of the greatest concern to individuals who sell what they make. Because it is easy to get patents, trademarks, and copyrights mixed up, let me briefly define them for you:

- A *patent* is a grant issued by the government that gives an inventor the right to exclude all others from making, using, or selling an invention within the United States and its territories and possessions.

- A *trademark* is used by a manufacturer or merchant to identify his or her goods and distinguish them from those manufactured or sold by others.

- A *copyright* protects the rights of creators of intellectual property in five main categories (described in this section).

Perspective on Patents

A patent may be granted to anyone who invents or discovers a new and useful process, machine, manufacture or composition of matter, or any new and useful improvement thereof. Any new, original, and ornamental design for an article of manufacture can also be patented. The problem with patents is that they can cost as much as $5,000 or more to obtain, and, once you've got one, they still require periodic maintenance through the U.S. Patent and Trademark Office. To contact this office, you can use the following Web sites: www.uspto.com or www.lcweb.loc.gov.

Ironically, a patent doesn't even give one the right to sell a product. It merely excludes anyone else from making, using, or selling your invention. Many business novices who have gone to the trouble to patent a product end up wasting a lot of time and money because a patent is useless if it isn't backed with the right manufacturing, distribution, and advertising programs. As inventor Jeremy Gorman states in *Homemade Money,* "Ninety-seven percent of the U.S. patents issued never earn enough money to pay the patenting fee. They just go on a plaque on the wall or in a desk drawer to impress the grandchildren 50 years later."

What a Trademark Protects

Trademarks were established to prevent one company from trading on the good name and reputation of another. The primary function of a trademark is to indicate origin, but in some cases it also serves as a guarantee of quality.

You cannot adopt any trademark that is so similar to another that it is likely to confuse buyers, nor can you trademark generic or descriptive names in the public domain. If, however, you come up with a particular word, name, symbol, or device to identify and distinguish your products from others, you may protect that mark by trademark provided another company is not already using a similar mark. Brand names, trade names, slogans, and phrases may also qualify for trademark protection.

Many individual crafters have successfully registered their own trademarks using a how-to book on the topic, but some would say never to try this without the help of a trademark attorney. It depends on how much you love detail and how well you can follow directions. Any mistake on the application form could cause it to be rejected, and you would lose the application fee in the process. If this is something you're interested in, and you have designed a mark you want to protect, you should first do a trademark search to see if someone else is already using it. Trademark searches can be done using library directories, an online computer service (check with your library), through private trademark search firms, or directly on the Internet through the Patent and Trademark Office's online search service (see A "Things to Do" Checklist with Related Resources). All of these searches together could still be inconclusive, however, because many companies have a stash of trademarks in reserve waiting for just the right product. As I understand it,

Selling How-To Projects to Magazines

If you want to sell an article, poem, or how-to project to a magazine, you need not copyright the material first because copyright protection exists from the moment you create that work. Your primary consideration here is whether you will sell "all rights" or only "first rights" to the magazine.

The sale of first rights means you are giving a publication permission to print your article, poem, or how-to project once, for a specific sum of money. After publication, you then have the right to resell that material or profit from it in other ways. Although it is always desirable to sell only "first rights," some magazines do not offer this choice.

If you sell all rights, you will automatically lose ownership of the copyright to your material and you can no longer profit from that work. Professional designers often refuse to work this way because they know they can realize greater profits by publishing their own pattern packets or design leaflets and wholesaling them to shops.

these "nonpublished" trademarks are in a special file that only an attorney or trademark search service could find for you.

Like copyrights, trademarks have their own symbol, which looks like this: ®. This symbol can be used only after the trademark has been formally registered through the U.S. Patent and Trademark Office. Business owners often use the superscript initials: ™ with a mark to indicate they've claimed a logo or some other mark, but this offers no legal protection. While this does not guarantee trademark protection, it does give notice to the public that you are claiming this name as your trademark. However, after you've used a mark for some time, you do gain a certain amount of common-law protection for that mark. I have, in fact, gained common-law protection for the name of my *Homemade Money* book and successfully defended it against use by another individual in my field because this title has become so closely associated with my name in the home-business community.

Whether you ever formally register a trademark or not will have much to do with your long-range business plans, how you feel about protecting your creativity, and what it would do to your business if someone stole your mark and registered it in his or her own name. Once you've designed a trademark you feel is worth protecting, get additional information from the Patent and Trademark Office and read a book or two on the topic to decide whether this is something you wish to pursue. (See A "Things to Do" Checklist with Related Resources.)

What Copyrights Protect

As a serious student of the copyright law, I've pored through the hard-to-interpret copyright manual, read dozens of related articles and books, and discussed this subject at length with designers, writers, teachers, editors, and publishers. I must emphasize, however, that I am no expert on this topic, and the following information does not constitute legal advice. It is merely offered as a general guide to a very complex legal topic you may wish to research further on your own at some point. In a book of this nature, addressed to hobbyists and beginning crafts-business owners, a discussion of copyrights must be limited to three basic topics:

- What copyrights do and do not protect
- How to register a copyright and protect your legal rights
- How to avoid infringing on the rights of other copyright holders

One of the first things you should do now is send for the free booklets offered by the Copyright Office (see A "Things to Do" Checklist with Related Resources). Various free circulars explain copyright basics, the forms involved in registering a copyright, and how to submit a copyright application and register a copyright.

Protecting Your Copyrights

If someone ever copies one of your copyrighted works, and you have registered that work with the Copyright Office, you should defend it as far as you are financially able to do so. If you think you're dealing with an innocent infringer—another crafter, perhaps, who has probably not profited much (if at all) from your work—a strongly worded letter on your business stationery (with a copy to an attorney, if you have one) might do the trick. Simply inform the copyright infringer that you are the legal owner of the work and the only one who has the right to profit from it. Tell the infringer that he or she must immediately cease using your copyrighted work, and ask for a confirmation by return mail.

If you think you have lost some money or incurred other damages, consult with a copyright attorney before contacting the infringer to see how you can best protect your rights and recoup any financial losses you may have suffered. This is particularly important if the infringer appears to be a successful business or corporation. Although you may have no intention of ever going to court on this matter, the copyright infringer won't know that, and one letter from a competent attorney might immediately resolve the matter at very little cost to you.

They also discuss what you cannot copyright. Rather than duplicate all the free information you can get from the Copyright Office with a letter or phone call, I will only briefly touch on these topics and focus instead on addressing some of the particular copyright questions crafters have asked me in the past.

Things You Can Copyright

Some people mistakenly believe that copyright protection extends only to printed works, but that is not true. The purpose of the copyright law is to protect any creator from anyone who would use the creator's work for his or her own profit. Under current copyright law, claims are now registered in seven classes, five of which pertain to crafts:

1. *Serials* (Form SE)—periodicals, newspapers, magazines, bulletins, newsletters, annuals, journals, and proceedings of societies.
2. *Text* (Form TX)—books, directories, and other written works, including the how-to instructions for a crafts project. (You could copyright a letter to your mother if you wanted to— or your best display ad copy, or any other written words that represent income potential.)
3. *Visual Arts* (Form VA)—pictorial, graphic, or sculptural works, including fine, graphic, and applied art; photographs, charts; technical drawings; diagrams; and models. (Also included in this category are "works of artistic craftsmanship insofar as their form but not their mechanical or utilitarian aspects are concerned.")
4. *Performing Arts* (Form PA)—musical works and accompanying words, dramatic works, pantomimes, choreographic works, motion pictures, and other audiovisual works.
5. *Sound Recordings* (Form SR)—musical, spoken, or other sounds, including any audio- or videotapes you might create.

Things You Cannot Copyright

You can't copyright ideas or procedures for doing, making, or building things, but the *expression* of an idea fixed in a tangible medium may be copyrightable—such as a book explaining a new system or technique. Brand names, trade names, slogans, and phrases cannot be copyrighted, either, although they might be entitled to protection under trademark laws.

The design on a craft object can be copyrighted, but only if it can be identified separately from the object itself. Objects themselves (a decorated coffee mug, a box, a tote bag) cannot be copyrighted.

Copyright Registration Tips

First, understand that you do not have to formally copyright anything because copyright protection exists from the moment a work is created, whether you add a copyright notice or not.

So why file at all? The answer is simple: If you don't file the form and pay the fee (currently $30), you'll never be able to take anyone to court for stealing your work. Therefore, in each instance where copyright protection is considered, you need to decide how important your work is to you in terms of dollars and cents, and ask yourself whether you value it enough to pay to protect it. Would you actually be willing to pay court costs to defend your copyright, should someone steal it from you? If you never intend to go to court, there's little use in officially registering a copyright; but because it costs you nothing to add a copyright notice to your work, you are foolish not to do this. (See sidebar, Protecting Your Copyrights, on page 274.)

If you do decide to file a copyright application, contact the Copyright Office and request the appropriate forms. When you file the copyright application form (which is easy to complete), you must include with it two copies of the work. Ordinarily, two actual copies of copyrighted items must be deposited, but certain items are exempt from deposit requirements, including all three-dimensional sculptural works and any works published only as reproduced in or on jewelry, dolls, toys, games, plaques, floor coverings, textile and other fabrics, packaging materials, or any useful article. In these cases, two photographs or drawings of the item are sufficient.

Note that the Copyright Office does not compare deposit copies to determine whether works submitted for registration are similar to any material already copyrighted. It is the sender's responsibility to determine the originality of what's being copyrighted. (See discussion of "original" in the next section, under Respecting the Copyrights of Others.)

Mandatory Deposit Requirements

Although you do not have to officially register a copyright claim, it *is* mandatory to deposit two copies of all "published works" for the collections of the Library of Congress within 3 months after publication. Failure to make the deposit may subject the copyright owner to fines and other monetary liabilities, but it does not affect copyright protection. No special form is required for this mandatory deposit.

Note that the term *published works* pertains not just to the publication of printed matter, but to the public display of any item. Thus you "publish" your originally designed craftwork when you first show it at a craft fair, in a shop, on your Web site, or any other public place.

Respecting the Copyrights of Others

Just as there are several things you must do to protect your "intellectual creations," there are several things you must not do if you wish to avoid legal problems with other copyright holders.

Copyright infringement occurs whenever anyone violates the exclusive rights covered by copyright. If and when a copyright case goes to court, the copyright holder who has been infringed on must

Changing Things

Many crafters have mistakenly been led to believe that they can copy the work of others if they simply change this or that so their creation doesn't look exactly like the one they have copied. But many copyright court cases have hinged on someone taking "a substantial part" of someone else's design and claiming it as their own. If your "original creation" bears even the slightest resemblance to the product you've copied—and you are caught selling it in the commercial marketplace—there could be legal problems.

Crafters often combine the parts of two or three patterns in an attempt to come up with their own original patterns, but often this only compounds the possible copyright problems. Let's imagine you're making a doll. You might take the head from one pattern, the arms and legs from another, and the unique facial features from another. You may think you have developed an original creation (and perhaps an original pattern

prove that his or her work is the original creation and that the two works are so similar that the alleged infringer must have copied it. This is not always an easy matter, for *original* is a difficult word to define. Even the Copyright Office has trouble here, which is why so many cases that go to court end up setting precedents.

In any copyright case, there will be discussions about "substantial similarity," instances where two people actually have created the same thing simultaneously, loss of profits, or damage to one's business or reputation. If you were found guilty of copyright infringement, at the very least you would probably be ordered to pay to the original creator all profits derived from the sale of the copyrighted work to date. You would also have to agree to refund any orders you might receive for the work in the future. In some copyright cases where the original creator has experienced considerable financial loss, penalties for copyright infringement have been as high as $100,000. As you can see, this is not a matter to take lightly.

you might sell), but you haven't. Because the original designer of any of the features you've copied might recognize her work in your "original creation" or published pattern, she could come after you for infringing on "a substantial part" of her design. In this case, all you've done is multiply your possibilities for a legal confrontation with three copyright holders.

"But I can't create my own original designs and patterns!" you moan. Many who have said this in the past were mistaken. With time and practice, most crafters are able to develop products that are original in design, and I believe you can do this, too. Meanwhile, check out Dover Publications' *Pictorial Archive* series of books (see A "Things to Do" Checklist with Related Resources). Here you will find thousands of copyright-free designs and motifs you can use on your craft work or in needlework projects. And don't forget the wealth of design material in museums and old books that have fallen into the public domain. (See sidebar, What's in the Public Domain? on page 282.)

This is a complex topic beyond the scope of this book, but any book on copyright law will provide additional information if you should ever need it. What's important here is that you fully understand the importance of being careful to respect the legal rights of others. As a crafts-business owner, you could possibly infringe on someone else's designs when you (1) quote someone in an article, periodical, or book you've written; (2) photocopy copyrighted materials; or (3) share information on the Internet. Following is a brief discussion of these topics.

1. **Be careful when quoting from a published source.** If you're writing an article or book and wish to quote someone's words from any published source (book, magazine, Internet, and so on), you should always obtain written permission first. Granted, minor quotations from published sources are okay when they fall under the Copyright Office's Fair Use Doctrine, but unless you completely understand this doctrine, you should protect yourself by

obtaining permission before you quote anyone in one of your own written works. It is not necessarily the quantity of the quote, but the value of the quoted material to the copyright owner.

In particular, never *ever* use a published poem in one of your written works without written permission. To the poet, this is a "whole work," much the same as a book is a whole work to an author. Although the use of one or two lines of a poem, or a paragraph from a book may be considered "fair use," many publishers now require written permission even for this short reproduction of a copyrighted work.

2. **Photocopying can be dangerous.** Teachers often photocopy large sections of a book (sometimes whole books) for distribution to their students, but this is a flagrant violation of the copyright law. Some publishers may grant photocopying of part of a work if it is to be used only once as a teaching aid, but written permission must always be obtained first.

   It is also a violation of the copyright law to photocopy patterns for sale or trade because such use denies the creator the profit from a copy that might have been sold.

3. **Don't share copyrighted information on the Internet.** People everywhere are lifting material from *Reader's Digest* and other copyrighted publications and "sharing" them on the Internet through e-mail messages, bulletin boards, and the like. *This is a very dangerous thing to do.* "But I didn't see a copyright notice," you might say, or "It indicated the author was anonymous." What you must remember is that *everything* gains copyright protection the moment it is created, whether a copyright notice is attached to it or not. Many "anonymous" items on the Internet are actually copyrighted poems and articles put there by someone who not only

violated the copyright law but compounded the matter by failing to give credit to the original creator.

If you were to pick up one of those "anonymous" pieces of information and put it in an article or book of your own, the original copyright owner, upon seeing his or her work in your publication, would have good grounds for a lawsuit. Remember, pleading ignorance of the law is never a good excuse.

Clearly there is no financial gain to be realized by violating the rights of a copyright holder when it means that any day you might be contacted by a lawyer and threatened with a lawsuit. As stated in my *Crafts Business Answer Book & Resource Guide:*

> The best way to avoid copyright infringement problems is to follow the "Golden Rule" proposed by a United States Supreme Court justice: "Take not from others to such an extent and in such a manner that you would be resentful if they so took from you."

Using Commercial Patterns and Designs

Beginning crafters who lack design skills commonly make products for sale using commercial patterns, designs in books, or how-to instructions for projects found in magazines. The problem here is that all of these things are published for the general consumer market and offered for *personal use* only. Because they are all protected by copyright, that means only the copyright holder has the right to profit from their use.

That said, let me ease your mind by saying that the sale of products made from copyrighted patterns, designs, and magazine how-to projects is probably not going to cause any problems *as long as sales are limited, and they yield a profit only to you, the crafter.* That means no sales through shops of any kind where a sales commission or profit is received by a third party, and absolutely no wholesaling of such products.

It's not that designers and publishers are concerned about your sale of a few craft or needlework items to friends and local buyers; what they are fighting to protect with the legality of copyrights is their right to sell their own designs or finished products in the commercial marketplace. You may find that some patterns, designs, or projects state "no mass-production." You are not mass-producing if you make a dozen handcrafted items for sale at a craft fair or holiday boutique, but you would definitely be considered a mass-producer if you made dozens, or hundreds, for sale in shops.

Consignment sales fall into a kind of gray area that requires some commonsense judgment on your part. This is neither wholesaling nor selling direct to consumers. One publisher might con-

What's in the Public Domain?

For all works created after January 1, 1978, the copyright lasts for the life of the author or creator plus 50 years after his or her death. For works created before 1978, there are different terms, which you can obtain from any book in your library on copyright law.

Once material falls into the public domain, it can never be copyrighted again. As a general rule, anything with a copyright date more than 75 years ago is probably in the public domain, but you can never be sure without doing a thorough search. Some characters in old books—such as Beatrix Potter's *Peter Rabbit*—are now protected under the trademark law as business logos. For more information on this, ask the Copyright Office to send you its circular, "How to Investigate the Copyright Status of a Work."

Early American craft and needlework patterns of all kind are in the public domain because they were created before the copyright law was a reality. Such old patterns may

sider such sales a violation of a copyright while another might not. Whenever specific guidelines for the use of a pattern, design, or how-to project are not given, the only way to know for sure if you are operating on safe legal ground is to write to the publisher and get written permission on where you can sell reproductions of the item in question.

Now let's take a closer look at the individual types of patterns, designs, and how-to projects you might consider using once you enter the crafts marketplace.

Craft, Toy, and Garment Patterns

Today, the consumer has access to thousands of sewing patterns plus toy, craft, needlework, and woodworking patterns of every kind and description found in books, magazines, and design or project leaflets. Whether you can use such patterns for commercial use

show up in books and magazines that are copyrighted, but the copyright in this case extends only to the book or magazine itself and the way in which a pattern has been presented to readers, along with the way in which the how-to-make instructions have been written. The actual patterns themselves cannot be copyrighted by anyone at this point.

Quilts offer an interesting example. If a contemporary quilt designer takes a traditional quilt pattern and does something unusual with it in terms of material or colors, this new creation would qualify for a copyright, with the protection being given to the quilt as a work of art, not to the traditional pattern itself, which is still in the public domain. Thus you could take that same traditional quilt pattern and do something else with it for publication, but you could not publish the contemporary designer's copyrighted version of that same pattern.

depends largely on who has published the pattern and owns the copyright, and what the copyright holder's policy happens to be for how buyers may use those patterns.

To avoid copyright problems when using patterns of any kind, the first thing you need to do is look for some kind of notice on the pattern packet or publication containing the pattern. In checking some patterns, I found that those sold by *Woman's Day* state specifically that reproductions of the designs may not be sold, bartered, or traded. *Good Housekeeping,* on the other hand, gives permission to use their patterns for "income-producing activities." When in doubt, ask!

Whereas the general rule for selling reproductions made from commercial patterns is "no wholesaling and no sales to shops," items made from the average garment pattern (such as an apron, vest, shirt, or simple dress) purchased in the local fabric store *may* be an exception. My research suggests that selling such items in your local consignment shop or craft mall isn't likely to be much of a problem because the sewing pattern companies aren't on the lookout for copyright violators the way individual craft designers and major corporations are. (And most people who sew end up changing those patterns and using different decorations to such a degree that pattern companies might not recognize those patterns even if they were looking for them.)

On the other hand, commercial garment patterns that have been designed by name designers should never be used without permission. In most cases, you would have to obtain a licensing agreement for the commercial use of such patterns.

> *Avoid this pitfall:* In addition to problems in using copyrighted patterns, anyone who uses fabric to make a product for the marketplace has yet another concern: designer *fabrics.* Always look at the selvage of a patterned fabric. If you see a copyright notice with a designer's name and the phrase "for individual consumption only" (or similar wordage), *do not use this fabric to make any item for sale without first obtaining written permission from the fabric manu-*

facturer. In many instances, designer fabrics can be used commercially only when a license has been obtained for this purpose.

Be especially careful about selling reproductions of toys and dolls made from commercial patterns or design books. Many are likely to be for popular copyrighted characters being sold in the commercial marketplace. In such cases, the pattern company will have a special licensing arrangement with the toy or doll manufacturer to sell the pattern, and reproductions for sale by individual crafters will be strictly prohibited.

Take a Raggedy Ann doll, for example. The fact that you've purchased a pattern to make such a doll does not give you the right to sell a finished likeness of that doll any more than your purchase of a piece of artwork gives you the right to re-create it for sale in some other form, such as notepaper or calendars. Only the original creator has such rights. You have simply purchased the *physical property* for private use.

> **Avoid this pitfall:** Don't *ever* make and sell *any* replica in any material of a famous copyrighted character anywhere, such as the Walt Disney or Warner Brothers characters, Snoopy, or the Sesame Street gang. It's true that a lot of crafters are doing this, but they are inviting serious legal trouble if they ever get caught. Disney is particularly aggressive in defending its copyrights.

How-To Projects in Magazines and Books

Each magazine and book publisher has its own policy about the use of its art, craft, or needlework projects. How those projects may be used depends on who owns the copyright to the published projects. In some instances, craft and needlework designers sell their original designs outright to publishers of books, leaflets, or magazines. Other designers authorize only a one-time use of their projects, which gives them the right to republish or sell their designs to another market or license them to a manufacturer. If guidelines about selling finished

Online Help

Today, one of the best ways to network and learn about business is to get on the Internet. The many online resources included in A "Things to Do" Checklist in the next section will give you a jump start and lead to many exciting discoveries.

For continuing help and advice from Barbara Brabec, be sure to visit her Web sites at www.BarbaraBrabec.com and www.IdeaForest.com. Here you will find a wealth of information to help you profit from your crafts, including newsletters, feature articles, special tips, and recommended books.

products do not appear somewhere in the magazine or on the copyright page of a book, you should always write and get permission to make such items for sale. In your letter, explain how many items you would like to make, and where you plan to sell them, as that could make a big difference in the reply you receive.

In case you missed the special note on the copyright page of this book, you *can* make and sell all of the projects featured in this and any other book in Prima's FOR FUN & PROFIT series.

As a columnist for *Crafts Magazine,* I can also tell you that its readers have the right to use its patterns and projects for money-making purposes, but only to the extent that sales are limited to places where the crafter is the only one who profits from their use. That means selling directly to individuals, with no sales in shops of any kind where a third party would also realize some profit from a sale. Actually, this is a good rule-of-thumb guideline to use if you plan to sell only a few items of any project or pattern published in any magazine, book, or leaflet.

In summary, products that aren't original in design will sell, but their market is limited, and they will never be able to command the kind of prices that original-design items enjoy. Generally speaking, the more original the product line, the greater one's chances for building a profitable crafts business.

As your business grows, questions about copyrights will arise, and you will have to do a little research to get the answers you need. Your library should have several books on this topic and there is a wealth of information on the Internet. (Just use your search button and type "copyright information.") If you have a technical copyright question, remember that you can always call the Copyright Office and speak to someone who can answer it and send you additional information. Note, however, that regulations prohibit the Copyright Office from giving legal advice or opinions concerning the rights of persons in connection with cases of alleged copyright infringement.

10. To Keep Growing, Keep Learning

Everything we do, every action we take, affects our life in one way or another. Reading a book is a simple act, indeed, but trust me when I say that your reading of this particular book *could ultimately change your life.* I know this to be true because thousands of men and women have written to me over the years to tell me how their lives changed after they read one or another of my books and decided to start a crafts business. My life has changed, too, as a result of reading books by other authors.

Many years ago, the purchase of a book titled *You Can Whittle and Carve* unleashed a flood of creativity in me that has yet to cease. That simple book helped me to discover unknown craft talents, which in turn led me to start my first crafts business at home. That experience prepared me for the message I would find a decade later in the book *On Writing Well* by William Zinsser. This author changed my life by giving me the courage to try my hand at writing professionally. Dozens of books later, I had learned a lot about the art and craft of writing well and making a living in the process.

Now you know why I believe reading should be given top priority in your life. Generally speaking, the more serious you become about anything you're interested in, the more reading you will need to do. This will take time, but the benefits will be enormous. If a crafts business is your current passion, this book contains all you need to know to get started. To keep growing, read some of the wonderful books recommended in the Resources. (If you don't find the books you need in your local library, ask your librarian to obtain them for you through the inter-library loan program.) Join one or more of the organizations recommended. Subscribe to a few periodicals or magazines, and "grow your business" through networking with others who share your interests.

Motivational Tips

As you start your new business or expand a moneymaking hobby already begun, consider the following suggestions:

- *Start an "Achievement Log."* Day by day, our small achievements may seem insignificant, but viewed in total after several weeks or months, they give us important perspective. Reread your achievement log periodically in the future, especially on days when you feel down in the dumps. Make entries at least once a week, noting such things as new customers or accounts acquired, publicity you've gotten, a new product you've designed, the brochure or catalog you've just completed, positive feedback received from others, new friendships, and financial gains.

- *Live your dream.* The mind is a curious thing—it can be trained to think success is possible or to think that success is only for other people. Most of our fears never come true, so allowing our minds to dwell on what may or may not happen cripples us, preventing us from moving ahead, from having confidence, and from living out our dreams. Instead of "facing fear," focus on the result you want. This may automatically eliminate the fear.

- *Think positively.* As Murphy has proven time and again, what can go wrong will, and usually at the worst possible moment. It matters little whether the thing that has gone wrong was caused by circumstances beyond our control or by a mistake in judgment. What does matter is how we deal with the problem at hand. A positive attitude and the ability to remain flexible at all times are two of the most important ingredients for success in any endeavor.

- *Don't be afraid to fail.* We often learn more from failure than from success. When you make a mistake, chalk it up to experience and consider it a good lesson well learned. The more you learn, the more self-confident you will become.

- *Temper your "dreams of riches" with thoughts of reality.* Remember that "success" can also mean being in control of your own life, making new friends, or discovering a new world of possibilities.

Until now you may have lacked the courage to get your craft ideas off the ground, but now that you've seen how other people have accomplished their goals, I hope you feel more confident and adventurous and are ready to capitalize on your creativity. By following the good advice in this book, you can stop dreaming about all the things you want to do and start making plans to do them!

I'm not trying to make home-business owners out of everyone who reads this book, but my goal is definitely to give you a shove in that direction if you're teetering on the edge, wanting something more than just a profitable hobby. It's wonderful to have a satisfying hobby, and even better to have one that pays for itself; but the nicest thing of all is a real home business that lets you fully utilize your creative talents and abilities while also adding to the family income.

"The things I want to know are in books," Abraham Lincoln once said. "My best friend is the person who'll get me a book I ain't read." You now hold in your hands a book that has taught you many things you wanted to know. To make it a *life-changing book,* all you have to do is act on the information you've been given.

I wish you a joyful journey and a potful of profits!

A "Things to Do" Checklist with Related Resources

INSTRUCTIONS: Read through this entire section, noting the different things you need to do to get your crafts business "up and running." Use the checklist as a plan, checking off each task as it is completed and obtaining any recommended resources. Where indicated, note the date action was taken so you have a reminder about any follow-up action that should be taken.

Business Start-Up Checklist

☐ Call city hall or county clerk

    ☐ to register fictitious business name

    ☐ to see if you need a business license or permit

    ☐ to check on local zoning laws
       (info also available in your library)

    *Follow up:*_____

☐ Call state capitol

    ☐ secretary of state: to register your business name;
       ask about a license

    ☐ Department of Revenue: to apply for sales tax number

    *Follow up:*_____

☐ Call your local telephone company about

    ☐ cost of a separate phone line for business

    ☐ cost of an additional personal line for Internet access

☐ any special options for home-based businesses

*Follow up:*_____

☐ Call your insurance agent(s) to discuss

    ☐ business rider on house insurance
       (or need for separate in-home insurance policy)
    ☐ benefits of an umbrella policy for extra liability insurance
    ☐ using your car for business
       (how this may affect your insurance)

*Follow up:*_____

☐ Call several banks or S&Ls in your area to

    ☐ compare cost of a business checking account
    ☐ get price of a safety deposit box for valuable business records

*Follow up:*_____

☐ Visit office and computer supply stores to check on

    ☐ manual bookkeeping systems, such as the
       Dome Simplified Monthly
    ☐ accounting software
    ☐ standard invoices and other helpful business forms

*Follow up:*_____

☐ Call National Association of Enrolled Agents at (800) 424-4339

    ☐ to get a referral to a tax professional in your area
    ☐ to get answers to any tax questions you may have (no charge)

*Follow up:*_____

☐ Contact government agencies for information relative to your business.

(See Government Agencies checklist.)

☐ Request free brochures from organizations

(See Craft and Home-Business Organizations.)

☐ Obtain sample issues or subscribe to selected publications.

(See Recommended Crafts-Business Periodicals.)

☐ Obtain other information of possible help to your business.

(See Other Services and Suppliers.)

☐ Get acquainted with the business information available to you in your library.

(See list of Recommended Business Books and Helpful Library Directories.)

Government Agencies

☐ Consumer Product Safety Commission (CPSC), Washington, DC 20207. (800) 638-2772. Information Services: (301) 504-0000. Web site: www.cpsc.gov. (Includes a "Talk to Us" e-mail address where you can get answers to specific questions.) If you make toys or other products for children, garments (especially children's wear), or use any kind of paint, varnish, lacquer, or shellac on your products, obtain the following free booklets:

☐ *The Consumer Product Safety Act of 1972*
☐ *The Flammable Fabrics Act*

Date Contacted:_____Information Received:_____

*Follow up:*_____

☐ Copyright Office, Register of Copyrights, Library of Congress, Washington, DC 20559. To hear recorded messages on the Copyright Office's automated message system (general information, registration procedures, copyright search info, and so on), call (202) 707-3000. You can also get the same information online at www.loc.gov/copyright.

To get free copyright forms, a complete list of all publications available, or to speak personally to someone who will answer your special questions, call (202) 797-9100. In particular, ask for:

☐ Circular R1, *The Nuts and Bolts of Copyright*

☐ Circular R2 (a list of publications available)

Date Contacted:_____Information Received:_____

*Follow up:*_____

☐ Department of Labor. If you should ever hire an employee or independent contractor, contact your local Labor Department, Wage & Hour Division, for guidance on what you must do to be completely legal. (Check your phone book under "U.S. Government.")

Date Contacted:_____Information Received:_____

*Follow up:*_____

☐ Federal Trade Commission (FTC), 6th Street and Pennsylvania Avenue, NW, Washington, DC 20580. Web site: www.ftc.gov. Request any of the following booklets relative to your craft or business:

☐ *Textile Fiber Products Identification Act*

☐ *Wool Products Labeling Act of 1939*

☐ *Care Labeling of Textile Wearing Apparel*

☐ *The Hand Knitting Yarn Industry* (booklet)

☐ *Truth-in-Advertising Rules*

☐ *Thirty-Day Mail-Order Rule*

Date Contacted:_____Information Received:_____

Follow up: _____

☐ Internal Revenue Service (IRS). Check the Internet at www.irs.gov to read the following information online or call your local IRS office or (800) 829-1040 to get the following booklets and other free tax information:

☐ *Tax Guide for Small Business—#334*

☐ *Business Use of Your Home—#587*

☐ *Tax Information for Direct Sellers*

Date Contacted:_____Information Received:_____

*Follow up:*_____

☐ Patent and Trademark Office (PTO), Washington, DC 20231. Web site: www.uspto.gov.

For patent and trademark information 24 hours a day, call (800) 786-9199 (in northern Virginia, call (703) 308-9000) to hear various messages about patents and trademarks or to order the following booklets:

☐ *Basic Facts about Patents*
☐ *Basic Facts about Trademarks*

To search the PTO's online database of all registered trademarks, go to www.uspto.gov/tmdb/index.html.

Date Contacted:_____Information Received:_____

*Follow up:*_____

☐ Social Security Hotline. (800) 772-1213. By calling this number, you can hear automated messages, order information booklets, or speak directly to someone who can answer specific questions.

Date Contacted:_____Information Received:_____

*Follow up:*_____

☐ U.S. Small Business Administration (SBA). (800) U-ASK-SBA. Call this number to hear a variety of prerecorded messages on starting and financing a business. Weekdays, you can speak personally to an SBA adviser to get answers to specific questions and request such free business publications as:

☐ *Starting Your Business* —#CO-0028
☐ *Resource Directory for Small Business Management*—#CO-0042
   (a list of low-cost publications available from the SBA)

The SBA's mission is to help people get into business and stay there. One-on-one counseling, training, and workshops are available through 950 small-business development centers across the country. Help is also available from local district offices of the SBA in the form of free business counseling and training from SCORE volunteers. The SBA office in Washington has a special Women's Business Enterprise section that provides free information on loans, tax deductions, and other financial matters. District offices offer special training programs in management, marketing, and accounting.

A wealth of business information is also available online at www.sba.gov and www.business.gov (the U.S. Business Adviser site). To learn whether there is an SBA office near you, look under U.S. Government in your telephone directory, or call the SBA's toll-free number.

Date Contacted:_____Information Received:_____

*Follow up:*_____

☐ SCORE (Service Corps of Retired Executives). (800) 634-0245. There are more than 12,400 SCORE members who volunteer their time and expertise to small-business owners. Many crafts businesses have received valuable in-depth counseling and training simply by calling the organization and asking how to connect with a SCORE volunteer in their area.

In addition, the organization offers e-mail counseling via the Internet at www.score.org. You simply enter the specific expertise required and retrieve a list of e-mail counselors who represent the best match by industry and topic. Questions can then be sent by e-mail to the counselor of your choice for response.

Date Contacted:_____Information Received:_____

*Follow up:*_____

Craft and Home-Business Organizations

In addition to the regular benefits of membership in an organization related to your art or craft (fellowship, networking, educational conferences or workshops, marketing opportunities, and so on), membership may also bring special business services, such as insurance programs, merchant card services, and discounts on supplies and materials. Each of the following organizations will send you membership information on request.

☐ The American Association of Home-Based Businesses, PO Box 10023, Rockville, MD 20849. (800) 447-9710. Web site: www.aahbb.org. This organization has chapters throughout the country. Members have access to merchant card services, discounted business products and services, prepaid legal services, and more.

Date Contacted:_____Information Received:_____
*Follow up:*_____

☐ American Crafts Council, 72 Spring Street, New York, NY 10012. (800)-724-0859. Web site: www.craftcouncil.org. Membership in this organization will give you access to a property and casualty insurance policy that will cost between $250 and $500 a year, depending on your city, state, and the value of items being insured in your art or crafts studio. The policy includes insurance for a craftsperson's work in the studio, in transit, or at a show; $1 million coverage for bodily injury and property damage in studio or away; and $1 million worth of product liability insurance. This policy is from American Phoenix Corporation; staff members will answer your specific questions when you call (800) 274-6364, ext. 337.

Date Contacted:_____Information Received:_____
*Follow up:*_____

☐ Arts & Crafts Business Solutions, 2804 Bishop Gate Drive, Raleigh, NC 27613. (800) 873-1192. This company, known in the industry as the Arts Group, offers a bankcard service specifically for and tailored to the needs of the art and crafts marketplace. Several differently priced packages are available, and complete information is available on request.

Date Contacted:_____Information Received:_____

*Follow up:*_____

☐ Home Business Institute, Inc., PO Box 301, White Plains, NY 10605-0301. (888) DIAL-HBI; Fax: (914) 946-6694. Web site: www.hbiweb.com. Membership benefits include insurance programs (medical insurance and in-home business policy that includes some liability insurance); savings on telephone services, office supplies, and merchant account enrollment; and free advertising services.

Date Contacted:_____Information Received:_____

*Follow up:*_____

☐ National Craft Association (NCA), 1945 E. Ridge Road, Suite 5178, Rochester, NY 14622-2647. (800) 715-9594. Web site: www.craftassoc.com. Members of NCA have access to a comprehensive package of services, including merchant account services; discounts on business services and products; a prepaid legal program; a check-guarantee merchant program; checks by fax, phone, or e-mail; and insurance programs. Of special interest to this book's readers is the "Crafters Business Insurance" policy (through RLI Insurance Co.) that includes coverage for business property; art/craft merchandise or inventory at home, in transit, or at a show; theft away from premises; up to $1 million in both personal and product liability insurance; loss of business income; and more. Members have the option to select the exact benefits they need. Premiums range from $150 to $300, depending on location, value of average inventory, and the risks associated with one's art or craft.

Date Contacted:_____Information Received:_____

*Follow up:*_____

Recommended Crafts-Business Periodicals

Membership in an organization generally includes a subscription to a newsletter or magazine that will be helpful to your business. Here are additional craft periodicals you should sample or subscribe to:

☐ *The Crafts Report—The Business Journal for the Crafts Industry,* Box 1992, Wilmington, DE 19899. (800) 777-7098. On the Internet at www.craftsreport.com. A monthly magazine covering all areas of crafts-business management and marketing, including special-interest columns and show listings.

☐ *Craft Supply Magazine—The Industry Journal for the Professional Crafter,* Krause Publications, Inc., 700 E. State Street, Iowa, WI 54990-0001. (800) 258-0929. Web site: www.krause.com. A monthly magazine that includes crafts-business and marketing articles and wholesale supply sources.

☐ *Home Business Report,* 2949 Ash Street, Abbotsford, BC, V2S 4G5 Canada. (604) 857-1788; Fax: (604) 854-3087. Canada's premier home-business magazine, relative to both general and craft-related businesses.

☐ *SAC Newsmonthly,* 414 Avenue B, PO Box 159, Bogalusa, LA 70429-0159. (800) TAKE-SAC; Fax: (504) 732-3744. A monthly national show guide that also includes business articles for professional crafters.

☐ *Sunshine Artist Magazine,* 2600 Temple Drive, Winter Park, FL 32789. (800) 597-2573; Fax: (407) 539-1499. Web site: www. sunshineartist.com. America's premier show and festival guide. Each monthly issue contains business and marketing articles of interest to both artists and craftspeople.

Other Services and Suppliers

Contact any of the following companies that offer information or services of interest to you.

☐ American Express. For merchant account information, call the Merchant Establishment Services Department at (800) 445-AMEX.

Date Contacted:_____Information Received:_____

*Follow up:*_____

☐ Dover Publications, 31 E 2nd Street, Mineola, NY 11501. Your source for thousands of copyright-free designs and motifs you can use in your craftwork or needlecraft projects. Request a free catalog of books in the *Pictorial Archive* series.

Date Contacted:_____Information Received:_____

*Follow up:*_____

☐ Novus Services, Inc. For merchant account information, call (800) 347-6673.

Date Contacted:_____Information Received:_____

*Follow up:*_____

☐ Volunteer Lawyers for the Arts (VLA), 1 E. 53rd Street, New York, NY 10022. Legal hotline: (212) 319-2910. If you ever need an attorney, and cannot afford one, contact this nonprofit organization, which has chapters all over the country. In addition to providing legal aid for performing and visual artists and craftspeople (individually or in groups), the VLA also provides a range of educational services, including issuing publications concerning taxes, accounting, and insurance.

Date Contacted:_____Information Received:_____

*Follow up:*_____

☐ Widby Enterprises USA, 4321 Crestfield Road, Knoxville, TN 37921-3104. (888) 522-2458. Web site: www.widbylabel.com. Standard and custom-designed labels that meet federal labeling requirements.

Date Contacted:_____Information Received:_____

*Follow up:*_____

Recommended Business Books

When you have specific business questions not answered in this beginner's guide, check your library for the following books. Any not on library shelves can be obtained through the library's interlibrary loan program.

☐ *Business and Legal Forms for Crafts* by Tad Crawford (Allworth Press)

☐ *Business Forms and Contracts (in Plain English) for Crafts People* by Leonard D. DuBoff (Interweave Press)

☐ *Crafting as a Business* by Wendy Rosen (Chilton)

☐ *The Crafts Business Answer Book & Resource Guide: Answers to Hundreds of Troublesome Questions about Starting, Marketing & Managing a Homebased Business Efficiently, Legally & Profitably* by Barbara Brabec (M. Evans & Co.)

☐ *Creative Cash: How to Profit from Your Special Artistry, Creativity, Hand Skills, and Related Know-How* by Barbara Brabec (Prima Publishing)

☐ *422 Tax Deductions for Businesses & Self-Employed Individuals* by Bernard Kamoroff (Bell Springs Publishing)

☐ *Homemade Money: How to Select, Start, Manage, Market, and Multiply the Profits of a Business at Home* by Barbara Brabec (Betterway Books)

☐ *How to Register Your Own Trademark with Forms*, 2nd ed., by Mark Warda (Sourcebooks)

☐ *INC Yourself: How to Profit by Setting Up Your Own Corporation*, by Judith H. McQuown (HarperBusiness)

☐ *Make It Profitable! How to make Your Art, Craft, Design, Writing or Publishing Business More Efficient, More Satisfying, and More Profitable* by Barbara Brabec (M. Evans & Co.)

☐ *Patent, Copyright & Trademark: A Desk Reference to Intellectual Property Law* by Stephen Elias (Nolo Press)

☐ *The Perils of Partners* by Irwin Gray (Smith-Johnson Publisher)

☐ *Small Time Operator: How to Start Your Own Business, Keep Your Books, Pay Your Taxes & Stay Out of Trouble* by Bernard Kamoroff (Bell Springs Publishing)

☐ *Trademark: How to Name a Business & Product* by Kate McGrath and Stephen Elias (Nolo Press)

Helpful Library Directories

☐ *Books in Print* and *Guide to Forthcoming Books* (how to find out which books are still in print, and which books will soon be published)

☐ *Encyclopedia of Associations* (useful in locating an organization dedicated to your art or craft)

☐ *National Trade and Professional Associations of the U.S.* (more than 7,000 associations listed alphabetically and geographically)

☐ *The Standard Periodical Directory* (annual guide to U.S. and Canadian periodicals)

☐ *Thomas Register of American Manufacturers* (helpful when you're looking for raw material suppliers or the owners of brand names and trademarks)

☐ *Trademark Register of the U.S.* (contains every trademark currently registered with the U.S. Patent & Trademark Office)

Glossary

The following crochet terms and abbreviations may be found in crochet instructions although all of them may not be mentioned in this book.

Alternate Rows: Every other crochet row.

Asterisk(*): A symbol in crochet instructions used to shorten instructions. Marks beginning of a sequence of stitches to be repeated across a row or as many times as specified.

Base: Foundation chain.

Blocking: Technique used for shaping a crocheted piece.

Bobble: Cluster or group of stitches worked into the same place and pulled together at the top.

Bouclé: Yarns plied at different tensions, held in place by another yarn, forming loops.

Brackets: Used to enclose a sequence.

Cable(s): Twisted stitches that form a ropelike design.

Chain: The base or foundation on which all crochet stitches are formed.

Changing color: Joining in or changing from one yarn color to another.

Cluster (Cl): A fancy crochet stitch.

Contrasting color: Secondary color used in color work or for edging.

Decrease: Working two or more stitches together to shape crochet pieces.

Drape: How fabric hangs.

Drop loop: Remove hook from work.

Dye lot: Numbers or letters on yarn label assigned to all yarn dyed in the same dye batch at the same time.

End off: Also called *fasten off* and *finish off*. Consists of cutting yarn and drawing through last loop(s) on hook.

Established pattern: Continue to work in pattern per instructions.

Fabric: Material produced as you crochet.

Face to face: Placing two pieces together with right sides facing each other.

Fancy stitch(es): Various crochet stitches combined to create distinctive patterns.

Felt(ing): The process of matting wool fibers together by means of heat, moisture, pressure, wear or agitation.

Float: Contrasting color(s) of yarn carried on wrong side of work.

Gauge: Number of stitches and rows crocheted per inch.

Granny square(s): Small, distinctive, patterned square(s) used for many projects such as afghans, pillows, tablecloths, and other household items as well as garments.

Group: Several stitches worked into the same place.

Hook: Crochet hook. A tool used to form crochet stitches.

Increase: Working one or more stitches in the same stitch to shape crochet pieces.

Irish crochet: Distinctive three-dimensional lace crochet developed in Ireland.

Join(ing): Method(s) for connecting crochet stitches or pieces.

Lace: Any open-work pattern, usually made with a combination of yarn overs and decreased or increased stitches.

Loop(s): Created by yarning over (YO) and drawing through loop or loops on hook to form a stitch.

Main color: Primary color used in crochet work.

Maintain pattern: Continue to repeat pattern sequence as instructed.

Marker: Contrasting strand of yarn, safety pin, or other device placed on fabric as it is worked to denote right side of work, beginning of a pattern sequence, or beginning of shaping, etc.

Motif(s): Crochet pieces made in various shapes: round, square, triangular, hexagons, etc. that fit together or that can be joined together.

Multiples: The number of stitches required to crochet a particular pattern stitch.

Note: Procedure or instructions spelled out at the beginning of a set of instructions.

Now and throughout: This phrase usually follows immediately after the turning chain and is shown in parentheses. It means that the instructions contained within the parentheses are only given once and pertain to the turning chain.

Parentheses: Also used to enclose a sequence.

Picots: Usually a chain loop formed into a closed ring. Often used in decorative edgings.

Ply: The number of strands used in making a yarn.

Popcorn (PC): Group of complete stitches, worked into the same place and pulled closely together at the top.

Post stitches: Same as relief stitches, worked around the post of a stitch as specified.

Puff stitch: Cluster or group of stitches worked into the same place to create a soft lump.

Raised/relief stitches: Worked by inserting hook around the post of a stitch as specified.

Repeat (Rep): Number of times stitches or a sequence is to be repeated.

Reverse single crochet (rev sc): Also referred to as "crab stitch," used as a decorative edging, and is created by working stitches in the "wrong" direction to create a cording effect.

Ribbing: Pattern stitches often used at the bottom, top, and edges of a garment.

Right side: Usually the smooth side of work. Instructions generally tell you to mark this side of work.

Rip(ping): Pulling stitches out to eliminate mistakes.

Rounds: Crochet worked in a circular manner.

Row: A series of horizontal stitches.

Schematic: A scale drawing showing specific measurements of all the pieces of a garment.

Slipknot: The first loop placed on a crochet hook to begin a chain.

Slip stitch: Used to shape or contour crochet pieces. Shortest of all crochet stitches.

Spikes: Made by inserting the hook farther down into the fabric than usual to create elongated stitches for textural interest.

Stitch checker: Slotted measuring device used to determine gauge.

Swatch: Small crochet sample worked to establish gauge.

Tapestry or yarn needle: Blunt-nosed needle with a large eye used for sewing or joining crochet pieces together.

Tension: Determined by how the thread or yarn moves through the fingers, the size of hook, and the type of yarn or thread being used. Often used interchangeably with the word "gauge."

Turning chain (tc): The specified number of chains required to turn a row.

Weave in ends: Working in loose ends so they don't unravel or appear unsightly.

Work/crochet even: Continue crocheting in the same manner without making any changes.

Working row: Row on which you are crocheting.

Working yarn: Yarn currently being crocheted.

Wrong side: Usually the irregular, less smooth side of work.

Yarn bobbin: Holds small amount of yarn for color work.

Yarn over: Part of creating every crochet stitch. Yarn is *always* placed over hook from the back to the front of hook.

Resources

▼▼

Recommended Books

Crochet Books

Beadwrangler's Hands-On Bead Stringing by Lydia Borin (Hooty Owl Media, 1997).

Beadwrangler's Hands-On Crochet with Beads & Fibers by Lydia Borin (Hooty Owl Media, 1997).

The Complete Idiot's Guide to Knitting and Crocheting by Gail Diven and Cindy Kitchel (Alpha Books, 1999).

Crochet by Amy Carroll (Ballantine, 1985).

Crochet, History and Technique by Lis Paludan (Interweave Press, 1995).

Crochet with Style by Melissa Leapman (Taunton Press, 2000).

Crocheted Christmas Ornament Covers by Susan Allen (Susan Allen Enterprises, 1253 Nesbitt Drive, Virginia Beach, VA 23456).

Crocheting Fashion Sweaters for Women by Annette Lep (Dover, 1986).

Designing Knitwear by Deborah Newton (Taunton Press, 1998).

Encyclopedia of 300 Crochet Patterns, Stitches and Design ed. by Brenda Parks (Frank Cawood and Associates Publishing, 1995).

50 Heirloom Buttons to Make by Nancy Nehring. (Taunton Press, 1996).

Glorious Crocheted Sweaters ed. by Nola Theiss (Sterling/Lark, 1989).

The Footy Rug by Jenny King (Jenny King, 13 Murray Grey Drive, Kureelpa 4560, Queensland, Australia).

Footy Rug II by Jenny King (Jenny King, 13 Murray Grey Drive, Kureelpa 4560, Queensland, Australia).

Great Crocheted Sweaters in a Weekend by Chris Rankin and Nola Theiss (Sterling/Lark, 1993).

The Harmony Guide to 100's More Crochet Stitches (Lyric Books Ltd., 1992).

The Harmony Guide to Crochet Stitches (Lyric Books Ltd., 1986.)

Heirloom Beaded Bags by Jenny King (Jenny King, 13 Murray Grey Drive, Kureelpa 4560, Queensland, Australia).

A Living Mystery, The International Art and History of Crochet by Annie Louise Potter (A.J. Publishing International, 1990).

In Love with Crochet ed. by Anne Van Wagner Childs (Leisure Arts, 1997).

Medicine Pouch Jewelry by Lydia Borin (Hooty Owl Media, 1997).

150 Favorite Crochet Designs ed. by Mary Carolyn Waldrep. (Dover, 1995).

Some'R Hot Bikinis by Jenny King (Jenny King, 13 Murray Grey Drive, Kureelpa 4560, Queensland, Australia).

Summer Collection by Jenny King (Jenny King, 13 Murray Grey Drive, Kureelpa 4560, Queensland, Australia).

Sweater Design in Plain English by Maggie Righetti (St. Martins Press,1990).

The Tartan Rug Book by Jenny King (Jenny King, 13 Murray Grey Drive, Kureelpa 4560, Queensland, Australia).

300 Crochet Stitches: *Includes Basic Stitches, Lace Patterns, Motifs, Filet, Clusters, Shells, Bobbles, Loops* (Collins & Brown, 1998).

A Treasury of Crocheted Sweaters by (Sedgewood Press, 1985).

Craft Business/ Home Business Books

The Basic Guide to Selling Arts and Crafts by James Dillehay (Warm Snow Publishers, 1995).

Business and Legal Forms for Crafts by Tad Crawford (Watson-Gupthill, 1998).

The Complete Idiot's Guide to Making Money in Freelancing by Janet Bernstel and Christy Heady (MacMillan, 1998).

Crafting as a Business by Anne Childress and Wendy Rosen (Sterling, 1998).

Crafting for Dollars: Turn Your Hobby into Serious Cash by Sylvia Landman (Prima Publishing, 1996).

The Crafts Business Answer Book and Resource Guide by Barbara Brabec (M. Evans, 1998).

Crafts Market Place: Where and How to Sell Your Craft ed. by Argie Manolis (Betterway, 1997).

Creative Cash: How to Profit from Your Special Artistry, Creativity, Hand Skills, and Related Know-How, 6th edition by Barbara Brabec (Prima Publishing, 1998).

Handmade for Profit: Hundreds of Secrets to Success in Selling Arts and Crafts by Barbara Brabec (M. Evans, 1996).

Directory of Home-Based Business Resources by Priscilla Y. Huff (Pilot Books, 1997).

Homemade Money: How to Select, Start, Manage, Market and Multiply the Profits of a Business at Home, revised 5th edition by Barbara Brabec (Betterway, 1997).

How to Show and Sell Your Crafts by Kathryn Caputo (Betterway, 1997).

Make It Profitable! How to Make Your Art, Craft, Design, Writing, or Publishing Business More Efficient, More Satisfying, and More Profitable by Barbara Brabec (Evans, 2000).

Small Business Toolkit—Marketing for the Self-Employed by Martin Edic (Prima Publishing, 1997).

Start and Run a Profitable Craft Business by William G. Hynes (Self Counsel Press, 1996).

How to Start a Home-Based Crafts Business,
2nd edition by Ken Oberrecht
(Globe Pequot Press, 1997).

The Crafter's Guide to Pricing Your Work
by Dan Ramsey (Betterway, 1997).

Cash for Your Crafts by Wendy Rosen
(Krause Publications, 1999).

*Crafting as a Business: Tools and Resources
for Building a Profitable Craft Business*
by Wendy Rosen (The Rosen Group,
1994).

*Create the Job You Love (and Make Plenty
of Money)* by Barbara JohnsonWitcher
(Prima Publishing, 1997).

Recommended Magazines and Newsletters

Crochet Magazines

American Country Afghans
Rita Greenfeder, editor
243 Newton Sparta Rd.
Newton, NJ 07860

Annie's Crochet to Go!
Andy Ashley, editorial director
103 N. Pearl
Big Sandy, TX 75755
Web site: www.anniesattic.com

Annie's Favorite Crochet
Andy Ashley, editorial director
103 N. Pearl
Big Sandy, TX 75755
Web site: www.anniesattic.com

Country Afghans
Barbara Jacksier, editor
1115 Broadway
New York, NY 10010

Creative Stitches
Judith Carter, editor
2 News Plaza
Peoria, IL 61656
E-mail: mcneedle@aol.com

Crochet Digest
Laura Scott, editor
306 East Parr Rd.
Berne, IN 46711
Phone: 800-829-5865

Crochet Fantasy
Karen Manthey, editor.
243 Newton-Sparta Rd.
Newton, NJ 07860
Phone: 800-877-5527

Crochet Home & Holiday
Jennifer McClain, senior editor
23 Old Pecan Rd.
Big Sandy, TX 75755
Web site: www.needlecraftshop.com

Crochet World
Susan Hankins, editor
House of White Birches
P.O. Box 776
Henniker, NJ 03242
Web site: www.whitebirches.com

Crochet with Heart
Carla Bentley, editor
Leisure Arts
P.O. Box 420494
Palm Coast, FL 32142-0404
Phone: 800-276-2438

Decorative Crochet
Valeria Kurita, editor
U.S. Distributor
108 Mill Plain Rd.
Danbury, CT 06810
E-mail: Valkurita@aol.com

Family Circle Easy Knitting & Crochet
Rosemary Drysdale, editor
161 Avenue of the Americas
New York, NY 10013
E-mail: fcknitting@vogueknitting.com

Hooked on Crochet
Jennifer McClain, senior editor
23 Old Pecan Rd.
Big Sandy, TX 75755
Web site: www.needlecraftshop.com

Magic Crochet
U.S. Distributor
108 Mill Plain Rd.
Danbury, CT 06810
Phone: 203-792-7844

Old-Time Crochet
Brenda Wendling, editor
House of White Birches
P.O. Box 776
Henniker, NJ 03242
Phone: 800-829-5865

Quick & Easy Crochet
Valerie Kurita, editor
450 Seventh Ave., Ste. 1701
New York, NY 10123-1799
Phone: 212-244-2351

Arts & Crafts Magazines

Better Homes & Garden Crafts Showcase
Beverly Rivers, editor
Meredith Corp.
P.O. Box 37228
Boone, IA 50037-2228

Crafts 'N Things
Barbara Sunderlage, editor
2400 Devon, Ste. 375
Des Plaines, IL 60018
Phone: 800-444-0441
E-mail: 72567.1006@compuserve.com
Web site: www.craftsnthings.com

Crafts
Miriam Olson, editor
2 Crafts Plaza
Peoria, IL 61656
Phone: 800-727-2387

Craftworks
Jane Gutherie, editor
243 Newton-Sparta Rd.
Newton, NJ 07860
Phone: 800-877-5527

Fiberarts
Ann Batchelder, editor
50 College St.
Asheville, NC 28801
E-mail: fiberarts@larkbooks.com
Web site: www.larkbooks.com/fiberarts

Great American Crafts
Julie Stephani, editor
700 E. State St.
Iola, WI 54990
Web site: www.krause.com/crafts/ga

Leisure Arts, the Magazine
Cathy Hardy, editor
5701 Ranch Dr.
Little Rock, AR 72212
Phone: 800-643-8030

Pack-O-Fun
Billie Ciancio, editor
2400 Devon Ave.
Des Plaines, IL 60018
E-mail: 72567.1006@compuserve.com

Piecework
Deborah Cannarella, editor
Interweave Press
201 East Fourth St.
Loveland, CO 80537

Sew News
Linda Turner Griepentrog, editor
741 Corporate Circle, Ste. A
Golden, CO 80401
E-mail: sewnews@aol.com

Shuttle, Spindle and Dyepot
Sandra Bowles, editor
3327 Duluth Hwy.
Two Executive Concourse, Ste. 201
Duluth, GA 30096
E-mail: 73744.202@compuserve.com
Web site: www.weavespindye.org

Threads
Christine Timmons, editor
P.O. Box 5507
Newtown, CT 06470-5506
Phone: 800-888-8286

Business Magazines

Craft and Needlework Age (CNA)
Karen Ancona, editor in chief
Krause Publications, Inc.
700 East State St.
Iola, WI 54990
Phone: 800-238-0929

Craftrends
Primedia Special Interest Publications
Bill Gardner, editorial director
741 Corporate Circle, Ste. A
Golden, CO 80401
Phone: 800-677-5212
Web site:www.crafttrends.com

The Crafts Report
Beradette Finerty, editor
300 Water St.
Wilmington, DE 19899
Phone: 302-656-2209
Web site: www.craftsreport.com

Industry Contacts

Crochet, Craft, and Business Associations

Association of Crafts & Creative Industries (ACCI)
P.O. Box 3388
Zanesville, OH 43702
Phone: 740-452-4541
Fax: 740-452-2552
E-mail: acci.info@offinger.com
Web site: www.accicrafts.org/index.html
The ACCI is a vertical trade association serving the $10-billion craft and creative industries. Through its trade shows, educational offerings and publications, ACCI has become known as the "leader in creativity," providing innovative opportunities for the exchange of ideas, goods, and services to grow the crafts and creative industries. ACCI has almost 6,000 members in nearly 40 countries. Membership is available to any person actively engaged in the buying, selling, promotion, utilization, or manufacturing of art, craft, hobby, and creative industries merchandise. ACCI's membership represents each segment of the craft industry, including independent and multiple retailers, mail-order companies, professional crafters, manufacturers, wholesalers/distributors, publishers, manufacturing reps, designer/teachers, and consultants.

Hobby Industry Association (HIA)
319 East 54th St., P.O. Box 348
Elmwood Park, NJ 07407
Phone: 201-794-1133
Fax: 201-797-0657
E-mail: brandt@hobby.org
Web site: www.hobby.org
Founded in 1940, HIA is a nonprofit trade association consisting of 4,000 member companies engaged in the manufacturing and merchandising of craft and hobby products.

National Craft Association
1945 E. Ridge Rd., Ste. 5178
Rochester, NY 14622
Phone: 800-715-9594
Fax: 800-318-9410
E-mail: nca@craftassoc.com
Web site: www.craftassoc.com
This association links arts and craft entrepreneurs with resources to help them succeed and thrive in their businesses. Develops and encourages educational programs that help members maximize their potential. Fosters and encourages networking within the arts-and-craft industry.

The National Needlework Association (TNNA)
P.O. Box 3388
Zanesville, OH 43702
Phone: 740-455-6773 or 800-889-8662
Fax: 740-452-2552
E-mail: tnna.info@offinger.com
Web site: www.tnna.org
Established in 1974 and incorporated in 1975, TNNA is a national trade organization comprised of professional designers, manufacturers, publishers, retailers, mail order companies, manufacturer's repre-

sentatives, and wholesalers of upscale needleart products and services, including hand-painted needlepoint canvases; hand-dyed and specialty crochet; knitting yarns; embroidery, needlepoint, and cross-stitch kits; furniture; notions; gifts; books; publications; accessories; tools; and more.

Society of Craft Designers (SCD)
P.O. Box 3388, 1100 H Brandwine Blvd.
Zanesville, OH 43702
Phone: 740-452-4541
Fax: 740-452-2552
E-mail: scd@offinder.com
The SCD provides educational and marketing opportunities to members, and displays designers' work at seminars for editors, publishers, and manufacturers.

Educational Opportunities

Craft Yarn Council of America (CYCA)
P.O. Box 9
Gastonia, NC 28053
Phone: 800-824-7838
Fax: 704-824-7366
E-mail: cycainfo@aol.com
Web site: www.craftyarncouncil.com

The CYCA, formed in 1981 to raise awareness of yarns, is the industry's trade association. Council members provide between 85-90% of the yarn, tools and accessories sold in the United States. The council offers Certified Instructor Programs for crocheting and knitting. CYCA acts as a clearinghouse for the craft-yarn industry, answering consumer inquiries when possible and providing links to consumer knitting and crocheting guilds. CYCA also sponsors community-based programs, such as Warm Up America and Caps for Kids, which keeps us in touch with thousands of knitters and crocheters around the country.

Crochet Guild of America (CGOA)
2502 Lowell Rd.
Gastonia, NC 28054
Phone: 877-852-9190
E-mail: CGOA@crochet.org
Web site: www.crochet.org
This guild promotes the art and skill of crochet. It also preserves historical projects, promotes future crochet designs, and strives towards excellence in all facets of crochet.

Business Suppliers

Advertising and Printing Supplies

ADG Printing
19231 36th Ave. W., Ste. D
Lynnwood, WA 98036
Phone: 800-342-3282
Fax: 425-771-7942
E-mail: info@adgprinting.com

Web site: www.adgprinting.com
Produces only four products: postcards, business cards, flyers, and brochures. Competitive and affordable prices.

American Printing
5324 Hohman Ave.
Hammond, IN 46320
Phone: 888-PRINT40
E-mail: apprint@apprint.com

Web site: www.apprint.com
Free printing quote service; gets free
quotes from printing companies around
the country. Postcards, newsletters,
brochures, mailers, presentation folders,
etc. Free shipping.

Chiappone Mail Enterprises Inc.
P.O. Box 1300
W. Babylon, NY 11704
Phone: 516-884-6309
Fax: 516-884-2411
E-mail: LChiappone@worldnet.att.net
Web site: www.lcme.com
Family enterprise that accommodates
all kinds of printed materials and mailing
lists.

Printing Industry Exchange LLC
P.O. Box 2238
Ashburn, VA 20146
Phone: 703-631-4533
Fax: 703-729-2268
E-mail: info@printindustry.com

Office Supplies

Action Bag & Display
501 N. Edgewood Ave.
Wood Dale, IL 60191
Phone: 800-824-BAGS (2247)
or 630-766-2881
Fax: 800-400-4451 or 630-766-3548
All kinds of bags, merchandising and adver-
tising tools, boxes, ribbon, labels, packaging

Fetpak Inc.
70 Austin Blvd.
Commack, NY 11725
Phone: 800-883-3872
E-mail: fetpak@fetpak.com

Web site: www.fetpak.com
Displays, packing, shipping, labels,
boxes, pricing materials, and more

Office Depot
Phone: 888-GO-DEPOT
Fax: 800-685-5010
Web site: www.officedepot.com
Free delivery

Office Max Online
Web site: www.Officemax.com
Free delivery

Saket
7249 Atoll Ave.
North Hollywood CA 91605
Phone: 818-764-0110
Plastic bags of all sizes. Free
catalog/price list, send SASE

Staples
Web site: www.Staples.com
Free delivery over $5

Craft Show Display Aids

Creative Canopies
4338 Austin Blvd.
Island Park, NY 11558
Phone: 516-431-4127
Web site: www.creativecanopies.com
Canopies and other show supplies

Dealers Supply, Inc.
P. O. Box 717
Matawan, NJ 07747
Phone: 800-524-0576
Fax: 732-591-8571
Web site: www.dlrsupply.com
Display supplies, canopies, table
covers, security materials

Elaine Martin Company
25685 Hillview Ct., Ste. E
Mundelein, IL 60060
Phone: 800-642-1043
E-mail: sales@emartin.com
Web site: www.emartin.com
Indoor booths, display systems, chairs,
tarps, pedestals

Flourish Company
Fax: 501-677-3380
E-mail: info@flourish.com
Web site: www.flourish.com
Art and craft supplies, canopies, flame
resistant fabrics, display panel covers

Supply Source
P.O. Box 554
Springboro, OH 45066
Phone: 937-274-4650
Fax: 937-274-8143
Canopies

Crochet Design Software

Cochenille Design Studio—*Stitch Painter
Gold*, includes crochet palette.
Web site: www.cochenille.com

FrauComp Software—*Pattern Designer,
Crochet for Windows*
Web site: members.aol.com/
FrauComp/index.html

Sand Castle Designs—Filet crochet
Web site: CrochetDesigns.com

Labels and Hangtags

BCI Labels
BCI Corporation,
2608 2nd Ave., Ste. 250
Seattle, WA 98121

Phone: 206-937-2656 or 888-224-9477
Fax: 206-937-2656
E-mail: info@bcizippers.com
Web site: www.bcizippers.com
Custom printed or woven labels and zippers

E & S Creations
P.O. Box 68
Rexburg, ID 83440
Phone: 208-356-6812
Web site: www.cranberryjunction.com
Hang tags, card stock

General Label Mfg.
P.O. Box 640371
Miami FL 33164
Fax: 305-949-2662
E-mail: general50@aol.com
Web site: www.generallabel.com
Care, content, and all kinds of labels

Heirloom Labels
P.O. Box 428
Moorestown, NJ 08057
Phone: 856-722-1618
Fax: 856-722-8905
E-mail: www.heirlooml@aol.com
Web site: members.aol.com/heirlooml

Identify Corporation
P.O. Box 140204
Brooklyn, NY 11214
Phone: 888-60 LABEL
Personal fabric labels, craft and
sewing notions

Name Maker, Inc.
P.O. Box 43821
Atlanta, GA 43821
Phone: 800-241-2890
E-mail: cs@namemaker.com
Web site: www.namemaker.com

Northwest Tag and Label
2435 SE Eleventh Avenue
Portland, OR 97214

Service Notions and Trimmings
256 West 38th St.
New York, NY 10018
Phone: 800-508-7353
Web site: www.hatsny.com
Custom printed and woven labels, and
care labels, small minimums

Sterling Name Tape Co.
P.O. Box 939
Winsted, CT 06098.
Phone: 800-654-5210
Fax: 860-379-0394.
E-mail: postman@sterlingtape.com
Web site: www.sterlingtape.com

Arts & Crafts Shows and Malls

Show List Publications and Web sites

Arts and Crafts Festivals, Inc. (States
of NY and CT only)
P.O. Box 227
Granby, CT 06060
Phone: 860-653-6671 or 800-784-9744
Web site: www.HandMadeinAmerica.com

Arts & Crafts Shows
Web site: www:artandcraftshows.net
Online database of over 2,000 shows and
events

Craft Shows USA
Web site: www.craftshowsusa.com
E-mail: infor@castleberryfairs.com
Web site: www.castleberryfairs.com
Online listing of 2,000 + shows

Country Peddler Shows (States of NE,
OH, and TX.)
American Country Shows
P.O. Box 1129
Fredericksburg, TX 78624
Phone: 800-775-2774

Fax: 830-997-0453
E-mail: peddler@ktc.com

Harvest Festival
601 N. McDowell Blvd.
Petaluma, CA 94954
Phone: 800-321-1213 or 707-778-6300
Fax: 707-763-5346
Web site: www.harvestfestival.com

RoadStar Productions (Texas only)
Web site: www.roadstarproductions.com
Largest online list of craft shows, events,
and concerts in Texas

Sunshine Artist Magazine
2600 Temple Dr.
Winter Park, FL 32789
Phone: 800-804-4607
Web site: www.sunshineartist.com
The largest, most complete listings of shows

Craft Malls (Retail Stores)

American Craft Malls, Inc.
P.O. Box 799
Azle, TX 76098
Phone: 817-221-1099 or 800-335-2544

Fax: 817-221-4556
Web site: www.procrafter.com

Cape Cod Crafters of New England
P.O. Box 428
Mystic, CT 06355
Phone: 800-321-6240
Web site: www.capecodcrafters.com

Coomer's Craft Malls
6012 Reef Point Ln., Ste. F
Ft. Worth, TX 76135
Phone: 817-237-4588
Fax: 817-237-4875
Web site: www.coomers.com

Craftworks
6189 Executive Blvd.
Rockville, MD 20852
Phone: 888-CWORKS7 (888-296-7577)
Web site: www.craftworksonline.com

Homespun Crafter's Mall
Phone: 888-463-7786
Web site: www.homespuncrafters.com

Craft Malls (Online)

Biggest Little Craft Mall—Bookstore,
message board for crochet
www.craftmall.com

Craftables.com—Crafts by and for
Canadians
www.craftables.com

Crafters Gallery—Crafters' resource center
www.crafts4u.com

Crafters Internet—Online mall with
crocheters, bulletin board, chat
www.craftedgifts.com

CraftNetVillage
www.craftnet.org

Crafts Search—Search engine for crafts
www.bella-decor.com/index.htm

Crochet 'N' More—Gift collection
http://www.crochetnmore.com

Debby's Craftmall—Craft links, gift mall
www.craftlinks.com

Get Creative!—Professional crafter's
resource center, arts and crafts shop
www.getcreativeshow.com

Grandma's Shop—Gifts, crafts, art,
paintings, household items, newsletter
www.grandmas-shop.com

Lady MacSnood—Handmade snoods and
bun covers
members.aol.com/srdunham/snood.html

Lims—Handwork fashion
www.lims-inc.com

The Needlearts Mall—Bunka, candlewick,
crewel, hardanger, cross stitch, needlepoint, tatting
www.needlearts.com

Craft/Crochet Suppliers

Crochet Hooks

Brittany
P.O. Box 130
Elk, CA 95432
Phone: 888-488-9669
E-mail: brittany@mcn.org
Web site: www.brittanyneedles.com

Bryspun Flexibles
Bryson Distributing
4065 W. 11th Ave. #39
Eugene, OR 97402
Phone: 541-485-1884

Busy Fingers—Afghan and cro-hooks
Web site: www.busy-fingers.com

Clover Needlecraft, Inc.
1007 E. Dominquez St.
Carson, CA 94702
Phone: 800-233-1703
E-mail: clovercni@earthlink.net

Crystal Palace
3006 San Pablo Ave.
Berkeley, CA 94702
Phone: 510-548-9988
Web site: www.straw.com/cpy

Hooked on You—Wood, bone, and ebony
hooks carved by Niles Clark, plus Win a
Hook contest.
Web site: business.fortunecity.com/
anschutz/131/Hooked_On_You/
Page_1x.html

Shirret—Special needle and crochet
stitches to make fabric strips into rugs.
Web site: www.shirret.com

Skacel
P.O. Box 88110
Seattle, WA 98138
Phone: 800-255-1278
Web site: www.skacelknitting.com

Spool Doodles—Wood spool and hook to
make woven cords.
Web site: www.spooldoodles.com

Susan Bates
Coats & Clark Consumer Services,
P.O. Box 12009, Greenville, SC 29612
Web site: www.coatsandclark.com

Turn of the Century—Handmade wooden
hooks.
Web site: www.turn2001.com/hooks.htm

Yarn Manufacturers

Make sure to contact manufacturers when
asking for color cards or yarn samples, as
most companies charge a fee for these.

Brown Sheep
100662 County Rd. 16
Mitchell, NE 69357
Phone: 800-826-9136
Web site: www.brownsheep.com

Caron International
P.O. Box 222
Washington, NC 27889
Web site: www.caron.com

Coats & Clark
Consumer Services
P.O. Box 12229
Greenville, SC 29612

Phone: (800) 648-1479
Web site: www.coatsandclark.com
Luster Sheen, Red Heart, Southmaid,
Susan Bates

Curl Bros. Textiles Ltd.
21 Kenview Blvd., Unit 27
Brampton, ON L6T 5G7 Canada
E-mail: curl.yarns@curlbros.com
Web site: www.curlbros.com

DMC
Web site: www.dmc-usa.com
Baroque, Cebelia

Fine Fibers
665 Colby St.
Spencerport, NY 14559
Phone: 716-352-5538
E-mail: finefibers@aol.com
Web site: www.finefibers.com
Fleece, roving, woolen yarns from Mohair
goats

King Cole
P.O. Box 66
Limefield Mills, Wood St.
Bingley, West Yorkshire, BD16 2BH
Phone: 44-0-1274 510566
Fax: 44-0-1274 551095
Web site: www.kingcole.co.uk
Yarns from England: St. John's Wools,
King Cole, Hayfield, Sirdar

Kreinik
3106 Timanus Ln., Ste. 101
Baltimore, MD 21244
Phone: 800-537-2166
Fax: (410) 281-2519
E-mail: Kreinik@kreinik.com
Web site: www.kreinik.com
Metallic threads, blending filament

Lion Brand Yarn Company
34 West 15th St.
New York, New York 10011
Phone: 800-258-YARN
E-mail: Lionyarn@aol.com
Web site: www.lionbrand.com
Homespun, Jamie, Jiffy, Wool Ease

Madeira USA
9631 N.E. Colfax
Portland, OR 97220
Phone: 888-MADEIRA (623-3472)
Fax: 503-252-7280
Web site: www.madeirathreads.com
Embroidery threads sewing and
craft supply

Plymouth Yarn Company
E-mail: pyc@plymouthyarn.com
Web site: www.plymouthyarn.com
Applause, Encore, Galway

R & M Yarns
105 Railroad St.
Adairsville, GA 30103
Phone: 800-343-9276
Web site: www.rmyarns.com

Rayon Yarn Corporation
2375 E. Main St, Ste. A-300
Spartanburg, SC 29307
Phone: 864-579-4880
E-mail: info@stevelathan.com
Web site: www.rayonyarn.com

Rowan Yarns
Web site: www.rowanyarns.co.uk
Designer yarns from England, wool,
tweeds, cotton chenille, denim

Silk City Fibers
155 Oxford St.
Patterson, NJ 07522

Phone: 973-942-1100
Fax: 888-899-6736
E-mail: scfwerv@aol.com

Skacel Collection
P.O Box 88110
Seattle, WA 98138
Phone: 800-255-1278
Web site: www.skacelknitting.com
Fashion yarns, hooks, and accessories

Solutia
Web site: www.thesmartyarns.com

Spinrite
P.O. Box 435
Lockport, NY 14094
E-mail: inquire@spinriteyarns.com
Web site: www.spinriteyarns.com

John Wilde & Brother, Inc.
P.O. Box 4662
3737 Main St.
Philadelphia, PA 19127
Phone: 215-482-8800
Fax: 215-482-8210

Internet Resources

Art/Craft Resource Centers

Barbara Brabec's Web sites
www.BarbaraBrabec.com
www.IdeaForest.com

Craft & Hobby Webring
www.zianet.com/mmlhess.craft.html

Craft Site Directory
www.bobbilynn.com/directory.html

Crafter.com—Resources for professional
crafters
www.crafter.com

Craftmark—Links to craft sites
www.craftmark.com

Craftsearch—Searchable database
www.craftsearch.com

I Craft—Hobby Industry Association's
consumer site with tips, projects
www.i-craft.com

Loretta Radeschi—Craft business guides
www.voicenet.com/ ~ radeschi/
Loretta-Radeschi.html

Maria Nerius's Web site
www.procrafter.com/maria.htm

Pennsylvania Arts and Crafts Emporium—
Supplies, resources, catalogs, books,
videos
www.demanddigital.com

The Professional Crafter
www.procrafter.com

Professional Crafter's Mailing List
www.welcome.to/professional-crafters

Crochet Books, Leaflets, and Magazines

Amazon/Crochet Partners—Specialty Amazon store devoted to crochet books
www.bizfocus.com/bookstore/arts/crochet

American School of Needlework (ASN)—Publisher of pattern booklets
www.ASNPub.com

Annie's Attic—Magazines, pattern books, clubs, catalog
www.anniesattic.com

Barnes & Noble—Online bookstore
www.barnesandnoble.com

Books Now—Online bookstore
www.booksnow.com

Borders—Online bookstore
www.borders.com

C&T Publishing—Crochet and other books
www.ctpub.com

Country Yarns—ASN, Leisure Arts, Annie's Attic and Annie Potter leaflets
www.countryyarns.com

Free Shop—Free and trial samples of consumer goods
t5.freeshop.com

Frugal Knitting Haus–Online catalog of crochet leaflets and books
www.frugalhaus.com

GLP International—European craft magazines: Anna, Burda
www.glpnews.com/Crafts.html

Halcyon Yarns—Crochet books
www.halcyonyarn.com

Hamilton Books—Discount bookseller
www.hamiltonbook.com

Hard-to-Find Needlework Books—Bette Feinstein, out-of-print books.
www.needleworkbooks.com

House of White Birches—Publisher of crochet magazines, books, and catalogs
www.whitebirches.com

Internet Magazine Stand—Magazines
www.magazine.netline.com

Krause Publication—Publisher of Great American Crafts magazines, other hobby and craft periodicals, and books
www.krause.com

Lark Books—Publisher of how-to books
www.larkbooks.com

Magazania—Online subscription ordering, including craft and crochet magazines
www.magazania.com

NBAF Magazine Subscriptions
www.nbaf.com/USsubscriptions.html

Needlecraft Shop—Publishers of magazines, patterns, booklets and books
www.needlecraftshop.com/welcome.html

Paradise Publications—Pattern books for fashion dolls
www.paradisedolls.com

Pastime Publications—series of historical pattern books
www.pastimepubs.com

Pauline Turner—Crochet design books, videos, correspondence course
www.crochet.co.uk

Ruth Kern Books—Out-of-print books, search service
www.needlearts.com/ruth_kern_books/welcome2.htm

Te Corp—Close Knit Press patterns for 18-inch dolls and 16-inch stuffed animals
www.tecorp.com

Crochet Pattern Web sites

Abby's Basket—Crochet and knit patterns
www.abbysbasket.com

Across the Board Discounts—Select crafts and hobbies, then crochet
www.atbdiscounts.com

AfriCreations—Afrocentric hat designs
www.africreations.com

Alice's Wonderland—Pom Tree, Loop Crochet Work Station, videos, patterns
www.pom-poms.com

Anybody Can Play—Crochet patterns for 18-inch dolls and more
www.anybodycanplay.com/CROCHET.htm

By the Hook—Custom crochet, patterns, plus message board, tips
www.angelfire.com/biz/bythehook

Clever Creations—Craft patterns
www.clevercreations.com

The Crochet Collection—Patterns with pictures
members.aol.com/SAG55/index.html

Crochet4—Patterns, hooks, free patterns
www.homestead.com/crochet4u

Crochet Partners
www.crochetpartners.org

CrochetGal's Afghan Patterns—Themed: flags, medical, sports, college
members.tripod.com/~CrochetGal

Crochet Memories—Original thread crochet patterns
www.crochetmemories.com

Crochet Treasures—Vintage patterns 1890–1959
www.crochettreasures.com

Crochet Trends & Traditions—Patterns by Carol Alexander and Brenda Stratton
www.crochettrends.com

Darla's Designs—Original designer crochet patterns
www.2ndMile.com

Heirloom Creations—Family name and religious filet crochet patterns
www.yesterdazes.com/heirloom

Herrschners—Internet and mail-order needlwork catalog
www.herrschners.com

Illustrated Patchwork Crochet—Illustrated crochet instructions
members.aol.com/bswebworks/crochet/crochet.htm

Knitted Threads—Custom crochet, crochet stitches, patterns
home.earthlink.net/~kthreads

Lori Jean Karluk's Teddy Bears—Patterns
members.aol.com/hugmybear/crochet.htm

Mad as a Hatter Studio—Contemporary crochet, hat, shawl, art-to-wear patterns and crochet jewelry
members.aol.com/_ht_a/madartmuse/index.html

Maggie's Crochet—Leaflets and kits from Maggie Weldon
www.maggiescrochet.com

Nana's Treasure Chest—Patterns for afghans, animal blankies, tote bags
www.nanastreasurechest.com

New Kits on the Block—Kits for Paradise fashion doll costumes
www.getcreativeshow.com/newkitsontheblock.htm

Once Upon a Pattern—Victorian crochet patterns, pattern translation
www.onceuponapattern.com

Perfect Little Angels—Patterns for thread crochet christening gowns
www.burgoyne.com/pages/sharjon

Sand Castle Designs—Crochet patterns and filet crochet software
www.ghgcorp.com/rmerkel/crochet/index.html

Smart Crochet—Filet crochet patterns, finished crocheted items
www.smartcrochet.com

The Tennessee Hooker—Animal, flag, sports afghans, customized patterns
www.afghans.homestead.com

A World of Crocheted Crafts—Holiday patterns
www.angelfire.com/tx3/CrochetedCrafts

Woven Stitch Crochet—Navajo-Hopi-Sioux-Mogollon patterns
www.zianet.com/mikemosier/index.html

Free Crochet Patterns

Crafts 'n Things—Patterns from *Crafts 'n Things* magazine
www.craftsnthings.com

Crochet Partners' Patterns—More than 100 patterns
www.crochetparners.org/PattMrns

CroShare—Patterns, exchanges
www.homestead.com/croshare

FreePatterns.com—Download .pdf files from Annie's Attic, House of White Birches, the Needlecraft Shop
www.freepatterns.com

Guide to Free Crochet Supplies Home Page
www.ppi-free.com/crochet.htm

Just Plain Fun—Free patterns
www.jpfun.com/patterns

Lee's World Patterns—Patterns from designer Lee Mathewson
www.chebucto.ns.ca/~aj514/pindex.html

Lots of Links—Many links to free patterns
www.esosoft.com/kneadles/linkmat.htm

Soft Memories—Crochet patterns 1921–1958
www.softmemories.com/AntiqueCrochet/index.htm

Yarn Lover's Room—Book on how to convert knit to crochet, knit and crochet patterns
www.knitting-crochet.com

Yarn Retailers

Amazing Yarns—Fashion silks, rayons
www.pw2.netcom.com/~amazing5/
amazingyarns.htm

Black Sheep Spindles—Yarns, spindles,
shuttles, lace bobbins
www.blacksheepspindles.com

Blue Sky Alpacas—Imported Alpaca yarn
www.radparker.com/bluesky

Common Threads—Fiberart store
www.fiberartshop.com

Cotton Clouds—Mail order cotton yarns
www.cottonclouds.com

Craft and Yarn Depot—Acrylic and natural
fibers, DMC threads
www.cryd.com

Discount Yarns—Classic Elite, Prism,
Tahki, Stahl, King Cole, Berroco
www.gotyarn.com

Elann Fibre Co.—Natural fibers from
Canada
www.elann.com

Elegant Stitches—Fashion yarns
members.aol.com/elegantst/index.html

Holy Cow! It's a Yarn Shop!—Mountain
Colors, imported yarns
www.holycowyarn.com

Jane's Wool Studio—Patons yarn, hooks
www.janeswool.com

Knit 'N Kneedle—Hand and cone yarn
members.aol.com/knk1944

Lana & Cotone—Wool, cotton, blends, and
novelty yarns
www.wtp.net/lana-cot/index.html

Mary Maxim
www.MaryMaxim.com

Merribee Needlearts & Crafts—Hooks,
thread, yarn
www.merribee.com

Michaels
www.michaels.com/main/mic-main.html

Northwest Peddlers—Discount yarn, hooks
Web site: www.nwpeddlers.com

Offray Ribbon
www.offray.com

Patternworks Home Page—Yarns listed by
weight, accessories
www. Patternworks.com

Perfect Touch Yarns—Yarn, patterns,
hooks, tools
www.ptyarns.com

R & M Yarns—Buys and sells yarns, odd
lots, over runs, mill ends
www.rmyarns.com

Ritzy Things—Crocheters and knitters
super supply store
www.knittingthings.com

Rochelle Imber's Knit Knit Knit—High
fashion boutique yarns
www.knitknitknit.com/index.html

School Products Co.—Fashion yarns,
supplies, books
www.schoolproducts.com

Snowgoose—Lacemaking, tatting, and bobbin lace supplies
www.catalog.com/lacemkrs/snowgoose

Velona Needlecrafts—Fashion yarns, DMC threads, crochet books
www.velona.com

Wal-Mart
www.wal-mart.com

Webs-America's Yarn Store—Famous name yarns, specials
www.yarn.com

Wellspring Gallery—Threads and notions, crochet history books
www.wellspringgallery.com

Wool Connection—Yarns, accessories
www.woolconnection.com

Wooly Knits—Designer yarn superstore
www.woolyknits.com

Yarn Forward Home Page—Patons, Sirdar
www.yarnfwd.com

Yarn Lady Home Page—Yarn, hooks
www.yarnlady.com

Yarns And—Famous name yarns, knit machines, computer software
www.yarns-and.com

Yarns Plus—Hand-painted and hand-dyed rayon chenille
www.yarnsplus.com

Spinners/Yarn Suppliers

Babe's Fiber Garden—Yarn, spinning wheels, weaving looms
www.smartgate.com/yarnspin

Blackberry Ridge Woolen Mill—Custom spinning
www.blackberry-ridge.com

Halcyon Yarn—Spins their own yarn and carries other handspun brands
www.halcyonyarn.com

The Mannings—Hand-weaving school and supply center
www.themannings.com

Sosusiespins—Susie spins her own wool, cashmere, angora, alpaca, exotic blends
www.sosusiespins.8m.com

The Woolery—Spinning, weaving, yarns, fiber-arts supplies
www.woolery.com

Other Craft Suppliers

Bag Lady—Purse frames
www.baglady.com/SupplyList.htm

Crafts, Etc!—Art supplies, beads, jewelry-making
www.craftsetc.com

Hanky Blanks—Hemstitched hankies and runners that are crochet-ready
www.hankyblanks.com

Hobby Lobby—Craft stores
www.hobbylobby.com

Hugg'ems Collectables—Dolls
members.tripod.com/~huggems2/huggemsx.html

KnitKnack—Judy Grill designs, rhinestone pins, and craft hooks
www.knitknack.com/index.html

LACIS Home Page—Threads for lace-making & tatting, crochet hooks
www.lacis.com

Needleworld—Crochet purse kits
www.needleworld.com

Rag Rug Fiber Supply—Crochet kits to make rag rugs
www.artpiece.com/ragrug

Yarn Shop Locators

To find shops close to you.

ComFind Search—Search: yarn retail or yarn wholesale
www.comfind.com/search/comfind

Wool Works Stores (Emily Way's List)
www.woolworks.org/stores.html

Helpful Information

Crochet Partners List of Resources—Crochet industry contacts
www.crochetpartners.org/resources.htm

How to Crochet with Wire—From Sea Fore
www.seafore.com/index.html

Lee's World Supplier List—Mail order & catalog sources
www.chebucto.ns.ca/~aj514/supplier.html

Crochet Internet Groups

CafeCrochet—Crochet Partners chat room for crocheters
www.crochetpartners.org/cafecrochet

Craft Mall Crochet Message Forum—Find patterns and answers to crochet problems
www.craftmall.com/forums/crochet

CrochetPartners—E-mail listserve, exchanges, patterns
www.crochetparners.org

Crochet Musings—E-mail listserv, exchanges, patterns
www.crochet.rpmdp.com

Crochet Network—E-mail listserv, message board, crochet info, links, suppliers
members.tripod.com/TheCrochetNetwork1

Doll Crochet Parlour—Doll crochet
www.dollcrochet.rpmdp.com

OneList—Search for crochet lists
www.OneList.com

Crochet Web sites of Individuals

Alorna's Keep—Patterns, photos of antique hooks, tatting shuttles, projects
www.geocities.com/Heartland/Hills/7511

Lydia Borin, The Beadwrangler
www.beadwrangler.com

Brenda Stratton's in Stitches—Designer's home on the Web
www.geocities.com/SoHo/Lofts/2777

Carly's Crochet Corner—Basic terms, tips, patterns, mailing list
drwnet.com/crochet

Crochet Cabana—Tutorials for broomstick lace, Tunisian crochet
www.stcharlesparish.com/CrochetCabana

J. Barrett's Craft Pages—Patterns, charity info, design guidelines
members.home.net/jbarrett5/
CRAFT.htm

Jennifer Down Under—Patterns, plus info on Australia
www.crochet.theshoppe.com

Melissa's Crochet Parlor—Patterns, links
members.aol.com/Alyssa5000/
page/CROCHETmel.htm

Nancy's Nanletts—Crocheted birds, bird musings
www.home.sprynet.com/ ~ nrobinson

Priscilla's Crochet—Patterns, message board, links
members.aol.com/lffunt/page.html

Sue's Crochet & Knitting Page—Patterns
personal.nbnet.nb.ca/fnorrad/
crochet.htm

Tina's Crochet Corner—Patterns and photos of Tina's projects
www.castle.net/ ~ tina/crochet.html

Charities

Afghans for Angels—Afghans for parents whose babies have died
www.angelfire.com/ia/afghansforangels/
index.html

AIDS Project Hartford—Crocheted afghans and lap robes
www.townusa.com/aidsprojecthartford

Barb's Caring Touch—Burial gowns and preemie outfits for babies
www.geocities.com/Heartland/Lane/9238

Blankets for Canada Society—Canadian version of Warm Up America!
www.blankets4canada.ca

Caps for Kids—Caps for needy children
www.craftyarncouncil.com/caps.html

Care Wear—Preemie-sized hats, booties, blankets, and burial gowns for hospital neonatal units
www.hood.edu/carewear

Charity Crafts—Information, patterns
www.osmond.net/osnet/family/ccpals/
charity

Charity Message Board
www.insidetheweb.com/messageboard/
mbs.cgi/mb22538

Children in Common—Orphanages in eastern Europe mentioned in chapter 6
Web site: www.yarnheaven.com

Community Angels, Inc.—Crochet/crafts and other help for those in need
members.aol.com/GORLEY/main.html

Granny's Daughters for Charity—Sponsored by Crochet Partners, supporting a variety of charities
www.ttsw.com/CPGDC

Earth Angel Charity Web Ring—Internet charity ring
members.tripod.com/ ~ countrycottage
crafts/charityring.html

Ellie's Angels—Afghans for hospices
www.accessatlanta.com/community/
groups/elliesangels

Hats for the Homeless
www.angelfire.com/ct/barnart

Hugs for Homeless Animals—Afghans for animals in shelters
www.h4ha.org

Littlest Lambs Program—Items for premature babies, such as caps, booties
www.lionshouse.org/little

Meadowlark's Orphanage—Blankets, hats, slippers for orphans in Mexico
www.mexpage.com/page/Chariety1

Newborns in Need—Blankets, clothing for infants in hospitals and shelters
www.newbornsinneed.com
www.newbornsinneed.org

Operation Comfort Pin—Lapel pins
www.angelfire.com/co2/operationcomfortpin

Custom Crocheters, Designers, and Producers

Susan Allen
1253 Nesbitt Dr.
Virginia Beach, VA 23456
E-mail: SusanAll@aol.com
Web site: members.aol.com/susanall/index.htm

Joy E. Bauer
302 E Garfield
P.O. Box 215
Cissna Park, IL 60924
E-mail: jeb1017@winslow.net66.net

Sharon Blosch
8388 Lucania St.
Dublin, CA 94568
Phone: 925-828-6341 (eves)
E-mail: crochet@home.com

Delphia Dennis
12235 SE 56th #294
Bellevue, WA 98006
E-mail: nomeknitter@msn.com

Linda Driscoll, Uniqueness by Dailey
P.O. Box 700
Fairfield, CA 94533
Phone: 707-426-6247
E-mail: Udailey@earthlink.net
Miniatures, beading, restoration

A.T. Grant
3726 Fairfax Ave.
Dallas, TX 75209
Phone: 214-526-2456
E-mail: aaytee@aol.com

Noreen Havens
7430-180th St. SW
Edmonds, WA 98026
Phone: 425-778-1418
E-mail: neeronbh@aol.com
Editing, custom crochet

Jenny King
13 Murry Grey Drive
Kureelpa 4560
Queensland, Australia
E-Mail:footyrug@squirell.com.au

Karen Klemp, KDK Crochet
3608 N. Upland St.
Arlington, VA 22207
Phone: 703-237-2766
E-mail: crochet@yclept.com

Jeanne Leech
PMB #1228, 1020 Green Acres Rd. #4
Eugene, OR 97408
Phone: 206-618-5405
E-mail: hideaway2@juno.com

Marian Nelson
P.O. Box 49000
Borrego Springs, CA 92004
Phone: 760-767-3709
Fax: 760-767-3433
E-mail: marigold@uia.net
Charting, editing, custom crochet

Joy Prescott
8500 148th Ave. NE #F1021
Redmond, WA 98052
Phone: 425-895-5440
E-mail: joy.prescott@gte.net

Janet Rehfeldt, Knitted Threads
83 Weston Dr., Daly City, CA 94015-3048
Phone: 650-757-1862
Web site: www.knittedthreads.com

Arlene Ritzhaupt, Ritzy Things
16132 NE 87th St.
Redmond, WA 98052
Phone: 425-883-2442
E-mail: ritzy@premier1.net

Lester Vaughn
13814 125th Ave. NE
Kirkland, WA 98034
Phone: 425-823-1134

Tarie Dillard Williams, Yarn Heaven
1292 W. Arkansas Lane, Arlington,
TX 76013

Other Crochet Professionals

Becky's By Hand Creations—Infant and
doll afghans, doilies, custom orders, etc.
http://members.aol.com/furbyhome/
creations.htm

Blankets-for-Baby—Crochet-to-order
www.expage.com/page/1Butch

Caitang Jianxing—Woolen handicraft
factory, Chinese crochet, knit, woven
clothing.
www.chaozhou.com/jianxing

Carla's Crochet—Handmade crochet
doilies.
www.craftmark.com/carla/crochet.htm

Christina's Crochet—Handmade crochet
items to order.
http://members.aol.com/cdw122869/
bizcard/

Prestige Plus Crochet Patterns—Crocheted
wild animals of the west.
www.mallwest.com/TradingPost/PPlus/
default.shl

Syndee's Crafts—Dolls and doll supplies.
www.syndee.com/

Things Unlimited—Crafts, crochet,
jewelry and gifts.
www.homestead.com/thingsunlimited/

Victorian Crochet—Victorian purses and
amulet bag book, bead spinner.
www.victoriancrochet.com/

Acknowledgments

Many thanks to Hans and Ingrid Skacel of the Skacel Collection, Inc. for providing the wonderful yarns for all the crochet projects in this books. The Skacels are wholesalers of fine yarns and knitting accessories.

Skacel Collections, Inc.
PO Box 88110
Seattle, WA 98138-2110.
Web site: www.skacelknitting.com
Phone: (253) 854-2710
Fax: (253) 854-2571

Index

About the Author

DARLA SIMS, has been a professional knit/ crochet designer for 20 years. More than 1,000 of her original designs have been published in national magazines and publications. In addition, Darla has written articles on many topics for national magazines, newspapers, and newsletters. She has written several other books and has developed marketing, publicity, and promotional materials for other authors, publishers, and small businesses. Currently Darla is vice president for the national Crochet Guild of America, as well as serving on the CGOA Professional Design Development committee, and the education committee. Darla is a member of the Society of Craft Designers, The Knitting Guild of America, and the National Writers Union.

About the Series Editor

BARBARA BRABEC, one of the world's leading experts on how to turn an art or craft hobby into a profitable home-based business, is the author of six books, including the national bestseller *Creative Cash,* 6th Ed. (Prima). She regularly communicates with thousands of creative people through her Web sites.

To Order Books

...llowing items:

Title	Unit Price	Total
...ft Sewing For Fun & Profit	$ _____	$ _____
Crocheting For Fun & Profit	$ _____	$ _____
Decorative Painting For Fun & Profit	$ _____	$ _____
Holiday Decorations For Fun & Profit	$ _____	$ _____
Knitting For Fun & Profit	$ _____	$ _____
Quilting For Fun & Profit	$ _____	$ _____
Rubberstamping For Fun & Profit	$ _____	$ _____
Soapmaking For Fun & Profit	$ _____	$ _____
Woodworking For Fun & Profit	$ _____	$ _____

Subtotal	$ _____
7.25% Sales Tax (CA only)	$ _____
7% Sales Tax (PA only)	$ _____
5% Sales Tax (IN only)	$ _____
7% G.S.T. Tax (Canada only)	$ _____
Priority Shipping	$ _____
Total Order	$ _____

FREE
Ground Freight in U.S. and Canada

Foreign and all Priority Request orders:
Call Customer Service
for price quote at 916-787-7000

Name _____

Address _____

City _____ State _____ ZIP _____

MC/Visa/American Express# _____ Exp. _____

Check/money order enclosed for $ _____ Payable to Prima Publishing

Daytime telephone _____

Signature _____